THE FATEFUL BATTLE LINE

The Fateful Battle Line

The Great War Journals and Sketches
of Captain Henry Ogle, MC

Edited and introduced by Michael Glover

LEO COOPER

London

First published in 1993 by
LEO COOPER
190 Shaftesbury Avenue, London WC2H 8JL
an imprint of
Pen & Sword Books Ltd
47 Church Street, Barnsley, South Yorkshire S70 2AS

A CIP catalogue record for the book is
available from the British Library

ISBN 0 85052 560 8

Typeset by Yorkshire Web, Barnsley, South Yorkshire

Printed by
Redwood Press
Melksham, Wiltshire

... the fateful battle line
That loops the ghost of Ypres, a name
By sacrifice of youth immortal made.

'Very Lights', *Henry Ogle, 1915*

'Light Music' of the Battle Line:

In 1915 the barbed wire was often hung about with empty tins which it was hoped would act as alarm bells, but they were a nuisance, giving false alarms in a breeze or when a rat climbed to investigate. The Germans actually did tie little iron bells to their wire. I still have one as a souvenir of a 'danger-spot' in Pacaut Wood in 1918, and it has since tinkled more merrily in children's games than ever it did for the Germans.

The sentry whose spell of duty coincided with the beginning of rain would hear innumerable little tinny but musical runs 'Drip, drip, drip, Drop, drop, drop, Drip, drip Drop' as the water discharged from barbed-wire points which happened to be above empty tins. Some filled faster than others, and a gamesome sentry could observe carefully, then back the tin of his choice against all others to fill first, cursing the interfering gust of wind that wasted his precious drips and drops.

A man with an ear for music could find much to interest him in these otherwise doleful surroundings... the quality, timbre or sonority of the drops went through the proper ascending scale until the tin was full, to continue on a flatter and less colourful note, unless the tin overbalanced and provided a cascading sound for variety. With scores of tins within earshot, in varying positions, shapes and sizes, the resulting miniature symphony may be imagined. Gusts of wind provided variation in tempo. Above a certain strength the wind hummed and throbbed forlornly through the forest of wire like ghosts of a thousand little harps, giving a gentle, sad accompaniment, rising even to play a brief and thrilling major part, then dying away to let the tins take up the watery theme.

It seems a pity that these sounds should have gone almost without appreciation or even interest; sooner or later, though, they had to be noticed. Then an unappreciative and, finally exasperated sentry would hurl a clod of clay at a tin with 'Take THAT! and stop your bloody tap, you blasted everlasting, drip dropping, sodding bastard!' But what's a clod of clay on maybe forty miles of dripping British front! With comic disregard both of human feeling and its lack, the symphony would go on.

'Water Music', *Henry Ogle*

CONTENTS

PREFACE

War in its nature is a dangerous and uncomfortable business, and in Britain it has become accepted truth that the fighting on the Western Front between 1914 and 1918 was the supreme example of its unpleasantness. Other nations have other standards by which to judge the nadir of military loathesomeness; the French and the Germans may well feel that even the agony of Verdun did not measure up to the miseries their armies suffered in Russia in 1812 and 1944 respectively, while it is the hell of Gallipoli rather than the ANZAC experience in France and Flanders that is lodged in the national consciousness of Australia and New Zealand. It is impossible to compare the unpleasantness of battles fought in differing climates at different times—and, save that they were conducted on a very much larger scale, who can say that for those engaged the Somme in 1916 or Ypres in the following year were more hideous than Keren, Cassino or Kohima?

Henry Ogle's narrative does not play down the horrors of the Western Front but it goes far to correct the picture of unrelieved ghastliness that so often emerges from accounts of the fighting there. There were quiet sectors and, even at the worst of times, lighter moments. There was comradeship to help in making the unendurable endurable. For two years he served on the Continent in the ranks, and for the last ten months of the war he was a successful officer until his second wound saved him from taking part in the final advance to victory. He recorded his experience with keen insight, an eye for detail, and a serviceable sense of humour. The outstanding feature is the complete lack of bitterness at the loss of four years of his life and the death or maiming of so many of his friends and comrades. Certainly there is no hatred of the German enemy, whom he admired as highly professional fighting men; neither does he indulge in the corrosive bitterness against his senior commanders, as is the fashion in so many memoirs of the time. Like any soldier he complains, but his butts are those who contrived to keep clear of the fighting, especially the 'Base Wallahs' who, to an even greater extent than in the war of 1939-45, made life hideous for those who were forced to spend time in depots and transit camps. Almost as bad were the junior staff officers, not so much because they were incompetent, which was not their own fault, but because, by their attitude and particularly by their dress, they distanced themselves from those who had to do the dirty work of fighting. This is a grouse to be found in all memoirs of the 1914-18 war, except those written by staff officers, and seems to have been abundantly justified. It is

1

to the Army's credit that in the Second German War the gulf between regimental soldiers and the staff was never allowed to develop.

When war broke out in August 1914 Henry Ogle was twenty-five. He had been born in New South Wales, where his father, a compositor and first-generation immigrant, had established a printing business near Sydney. Traumatically, he collapsed and died in front of Henry, who was then aged four. Two years later Henry's mother sent him back to England in a sailing ship to be adopted by his uncle, another Henry Ogle, Congregational Minister of Pickup Bank, Hoddlesden, near Darwen in Lancashire. Uncle Henry had married the daughter of a Sunderland shipyard owner, Alice Mills, but she seems not to have brought money into the marriage since a place was found for young Henry at a school for the sons of 'impoverished clergy'—Silcoats School, Wakefield—where he stayed until the school was destroyed by fire in 1904. By this time he had a love of books, natural history and, above all, painting, in all of which he was supported by his adoptive parents. He completed his schooling at a less congenial establishment, and in 1909 went for teacher training at Chester College, moving on from there to Leamington Spa College of Art where he met and fell in love with a fellow student, Muriel Annie Harper, who lived near Stratford-upon-Avon. It was probably because of her that when the time came to find a job as a teacher of art he took a post in Warwickshire, at Redditch; this was just five months before war came.

The army which Ogle joined in September 1914 was an amateur affair. Britain was having to pay, and for some years continued to have to pay, for her refusal to introduce conscription in peacetime and for her belief, refuted over the centuries, that an army could be improvised when it was needed. While Germany could immediately field 4.3 million trained soldiers and France 3.5 million, the British Army and its immediate reserves amounted to less than half a million, of whom nearly a third were scattered across the world, in India and in colonial garrisons. The reinforcement most nearly available were about a quarter of a million men in the Territorial Force who, if undertrained and under-equipped, were at least organised into units and formations. It had been intended to expand the Regular Army on the basis of the TF but, when the need came, it was decided to rustle up a whole new army of seventy divisions regardless of the fact that there were no arms or equipment to be enlisted, few trained officers or NCOs to train the men, no commanders and no staff officers to administer them. Arms and equipment could, in time, be manufactured, but there was no way of creating generals and staff officers, the more so since the Staff College was closed for the duration, instructors and pupils being sent to posts in the existing divisions, only two of which had more than a skeleton staff before mobilisation. To provide commanders for all the new divisions, to say nothing of those for the corps and armies into which they were grouped, could only be done by scraping the barrel. One New Army division went into action commanded by a man who had retired from the Regulars as a major in 1905. The wonder is not that the British Expeditionary Force did not achieve more in the early years of the war but that it managed to survive at all.

Henry Ogle decided to join the Territorials and, after a sketchy training, went to France with his battalion in March 1915 as a private soldier, rising to corporal during the Battle of the Somme. In 1917 he was commissioned, but he did not see serious action again until the late spring of 1918 when he quickly showed his capabilities and won a Military Cross before being disabled, late in September, by a wound in the hand, which kept him out of battle until the Armistice. He had previously been wounded in 1915, and a piece of metal from this incident stayed in his leg for the rest of his life.

Throughout his service he carried a miniature paint-box, and whenever possible he recorded his impressions of scenery, in battle and out, and of his companions. He was not an artist of the first rank—by his own admission he would have been 'quite incapable of making a living' as a painter—but he was a highly competent draughtsman and brought to his painting the same eye for detail that enlivens his writing. It was his collection of drawings and watercolours, executed on any paper that happened to be available, that formed the basis of this book. As he wrote,

> The first few essays began as explanation of a book of drawings done during the war. These accompanying explanations grew, beginning in 1937-38 when I underwent a long period of illness, and were re-written many times but not in their present form until after 1955.

After demobilisation in 1919 Ogle, who had married Muriel Harper in 1916, went back to teaching, first at schools near Blackburn, and from 1926 at Preston Grammar School where he remained until he retired in 1946. When in 1937 he developed a lung complaint which necessitated a long stay in a sanatorium, Muriel Ogle took over his art classes. Between 1920 and 1930 they had four children, the eldest son being killed in May 1940 at about the time that Henry Ogle joined the Local Defence Volunteers (later Home Guard), in which he became a captain. He continued painting, developed a keen interest in architecture and, after his retirement, took up carving in boxwood, and weaving. He also learned Greek.

After thirteen years of retirement at Woodmancote in Gloucestershire, he developed cancer and in 1963, Muriel Ogle being bedridden, they returned to Preston where, ten weeks after his wife, Henry Ogle died in August 1969, a few days before his eightieth birthday.

3

In their final form, Ogle's memoirs consisted of a hundred and fifty-nine separate essays of varying lengths, which overlapped each other at some points. In editing them I have, apart from omitting duplications and some material of purely family interest, contented myself with arranging the essays to form a continuous narrative. To this I have added such notes as seemed necessary to explain or amplify points that might be obscure. Apart from my introduction to each chapter and these explanatory notes, the text is entirely in Henry Ogle's words though the order of sentences and paragraphs is not always as he left them. On very rare occasions a linking word or phrase has been added to preserve continuity.

Michael Glover
March 1990

INTRODUCTION

In common with thousands of other young civilians, I joined the war as soon as it was possible to do so, and in the nearest army unit. This was determined largely by what my friends were doing at the time. So it was that, more by ordinary circumstances than by exercising much thought, I found myself in a Warwickshire battalion of Territorials rumoured to be sent out possibly in ten weeks' time.[1] That was only a month after the war had begun. Meanwhile the First Hundred Thousand of the New or Kitchener's Army were enrolling and in training. Our training took about six months. On the morning of 22 March 1915 the Royal Warwicks, part of 48th Division TF, landed at Le Havre and on the following day went 'up the line' to the sector between Ypres and Armentières. We settled down to a routine of In and Out of the breastworks, and as the war dragged on through 1915 and our division had taken no part in any serious battle, it became clear to us that we were not regarded as first-class troops. To begin with we were Territorials, and as such we became accustomed to being shifted about to fill gaps in 'cushy places' between those liable to attack by the Germans, or near where ours were to attack. We continued in these minor roles until the Battle of the Somme in which we fought from its bloody beginning to its slimy end. We were lucky to escape the heavy casualties of the New Armies, mainly because of the neglect of our possibilities as attacking troops already seasoned in fifteen months of routine trench warfare. It is no more than a guess of mine that the social background of our very good officers, as non-public-school men, prevented their advancement. Most of the officers I knew in two divisions of Territorials were of the business, professional and works-managerial classes with 'nothing more' than provincial university outlook or perhaps grammar school or even less. But their outlook was wide and their personal knowledge of men of many walks of life far greater than that of the Regular Army officer. Before the middle of the war there were many ex-ranker officers, all of whom lacked the sporting horsemanship and hunt connections at least which had made advancement possible under cavalry generals, both British and French. Few of us 'knew anybody'.

As 'other ranks' we knew nothing of our General Staff beyond what we saw of them, and as that was never in the forefront of the battle, our opinion of them could not be high. Behind the actual trench systems they were to be seen at close quarters only when guards were turned out for inspection. We were apt to express ourselves forcibly and somewhat indiscriminately about all 'brass-hats and red tabs'[2] with more and more rancour as the war went on. We knew that they, like us, had to 'soldier on' to the best of their ability but we questioned that ability in what we considered their role as liaison officers between the fighters and the planners who could order us to useless and certain death through lack of full information. For this tragic state of affairs, I suppose we all, as a nation, were responsible in that in 1914 we left the planning and leadership to professional soldiers who failed to appreciate the extraordinary qualities of the young men who rushed to join the Army.

I

ENGLAND 1914:
YOUR KING AND COUNTRY

Although he wrote that he 'joined the war as soon as it was possible to do so', Harry Ogle actually waited for four weeks before he volunteered. It was on 7 August that the famous poster with the slogan YOUR KING AND COUNTRY NEED YOU appeared with the picture of Lord Kitchener pointing at the viewer. Within a few days the First Hundred Thousand had been enlisted and the number was up to half a million by mid-September.

Kitchener's New Army seems not to have appealed to Ogle and, influenced by his friends, he enlisted in the Territorial Force, only to find it very much the poor relation of the New Army. After the mismanagements of the South African war, Lord Haldane widely reformed the Army so that it would be fit for campaigning on the continent of Europe, and created the Territorial Force of part-time soldiers from the Volunteers and Yeomanry so that it could form the basis for the expansion of the Army in time of war and could, as soon as war broke out, relieve the Regulars of their home defence liabilities. The TF consisted of fourteen infantry divisions and fourteen brigades of cavalry complete with all supporting units, a force half the size that Haldane had originally envisaged but as large as financial constraints would allow. It was recognised that such a force would require six months' full-time training before it would be fit for continental war but at worst it provided a basis for greatly expanding the Army. Kitchener, unfortunately, thought differently and, rightly recognising that it would be a very long war, decided to raise a wholly new army for which no existing organisation existed.

The accepted legend is that Kitchener had no faith in Territorials as he bracketed them in his mind with the Armée Territoriale, the most elderly class of French Reservists of whom he had formed a poor opinion during the Franco-Prussian war forty years earlier. There may be some truth in this but the fact is that the bulk of the Regular Army took a low view of part-time soldiers who were not trained to their own exacting standards. One distinguished regiment 'never accepted [their Territorial battalions], disowning them contemptuously as "dog-shooters".' The Director of Military Operations at the War Office dismissed them as having 'no officers, no transport, no mobility, no compulsion [to go abroad], no discipline, obsolete guns, no horses'. There were some grounds for this scathing list of deficiencies. At the outbreak of war the number of officers, as of other ranks, was about a third below their establishment but this state of affairs was remedied within weeks. Technically there was no obligation to serve abroad but it was open to all members to volunteer for General Service and as soon as 60 per cent of a unit had volunteered the unit could be ordered abroad, the deficiencies being made up with recruits. Five units had volunteered before the outbreak of war and the rest speedily followed suit, transferring those who did not accept the overseas liability to second-line, home defence battalions. It was also true that Territorial discipline differed from that of the Regulars but it was nevertheless a very real force, the compulsion of men already established in civil life who were ready to give up their careers to serve their country.

The other defects noted by the DMO were the fault not of the TF but of the government, which had failed to supply them with horses, transport and modern artillery, and the shortage of all these and other essentials was made worse when Kitchener conjured up his vast New Army. As the Official Historian wrote, 'Instructors, officers and non-commissioned officers were lacking; and though accommodation was gradually provided—first in public buildings and billets, and later on in tents—clothing and equipment were insufficient even for training purposes.' The vast expansion of the Army undertaken in 1914 would, under any circumstances, have thrown an intolerable strain on the recruiting and training machinery, the more so since the Regulars were suffering irreplaceable losses in battle, but it was made infinitely worse by Kitchener's insistence on ignoring the existing framework of the TF. It also had the result that there were, as Sir Douglas Haig pointed out as early as November 1915, three classes of army, 'Territorials, K's and Regular Armies', instead of a single army so that there were inevitable cross-posting problems made worse since each of the three classes of army viewed the other with suspicion.

In the struggle for experienced leaders, instructors and equipment the Territorials inevitably came off worst but the Regulars would have been hard put to hold the line in Flanders without them. Before the end of 1914 six and a half Yeomanry regiments and twenty-three infantry battalions were on the Western Front as were eight Territorial engineer units. On 31 October the London Scottish became the first TF battalion to launch an attack. Meanwhile four complete TF divisions sailed for the Mediterranean or India in 1914 and, from February 1915, Territorial divisions began arriving in France. Undertrained and usually short of their full complement of artillery, they were, as Ogle suggests, mostly deployed in supposedly quiet sectors but, in the long run, it was the enemy who decided which sectors were quiet.

In July 1914 my friend Ted Pullen and I were teaching at Bridge Street Boys' Council School, Redditch, both of us having joined the staff in February of that year. Ted was a Territorial in the Gloucesters of the 48th or South Midland Division and was looking forward with more than the usual interest, in the month of rumours of war,[1] to his annual summer camp. Meanwhile we tramped the pretty Worcestershire and Warwickshire countryside with my little tent nearly every weekend. I also looked forward to a summer camp of a very different kind. I had arranged a camping and sketching holiday on the Roman Wall in Northumberland with my friend Lewis Duckett, a student at the Royal College of Art. Ted and I parted, Lewis and I met, all of us uncertain of the future, for war with Germany seemed probable and was actually declared on 4 August. Ted's South Midland Division was mobilised while at camp and he did not return to school.

Our sketching holiday was eventful. One day we went to Bardon Hill on the South Tyne to buy food and a newspaper and saw fully equipped soldiers boarding a train. We noted their equipment and arms with interest when we learned that they were on the first stage of their journey to France. Towards the end of our trip we made a detour up to the North Tyne by way of the old Roman road. We had passed the reservoirs of the Newcastle and Gateshead Waterworks that day and had pitched camp for the night on the wide verge of the road. We were having a supper of Bovril and raw onion when we heard sudden footsteps as someone dismounted from a bicycle. The tent flaps parted and we saw the head and shoulders of a police sergeant who took a good look at us. We had been reported by Boy Scouts as probable spies intent on poisoning the water supply. The sergeant looked at our sketches, asked a few questions and, though he dismissed the Scouts' idea, advised us to curtail our holiday and go home because of the widespread spy scare. We went to Sunderland, which was Duckett's home and that of my uncle, W. D. Ogle.

On the following day we were silly enough to be on Ryhope beach with our sketchbooks watching a steamer. Artists look at things in a thorough way, standing, squatting and moving to fresh viewpoints. This sort of thing was too much for the detachment of the East Yorkshire Regiment that was guarding the Ryhope shore, and a sergeant with two private soldiers arrested us at the point of two bayonets. 'Follow me,' said the sergeant and began to ascend the Ryhope Dene, we following with bayonets very close to our backs. The Dene seemed to be filled with shouting people and some of the collier women screamed, 'Gi'e the clarty spies a dig wi' the cauld airn!' By the time we reached the East Yorks' Headquarters in a Ryhope pub there was quite a crowd of people in the main street and we were glad to be hustled inside. The two officers and a sergeant-major seemed inclined at first to take a lenient view of our foolishness as the sort of irresponsible behaviour to be expected from artists. Didn't we know that we had contravened the Emergency Regulations which forbade photography and sketching in the vicinity of military works? We had never heard of them and as for military works, we had noted trenches and barbed wire and soldiers only when we had looked behind us for a possible background. Though this pleased them as a compliment to the siting of their trench, it failed to deflect them from the stern path of duty. Finally the sergeant-major came to the rescue with the idea of ringing up our relatives in Sunderland. The NE Railway vouched for Duckett, his father probably at that moment dealing with trains on Newcastle High Level Bridge, for he was a signalman. My uncle, W.D. Ogle, Wholesale Yeast and Egg Merchant, vouched for me. The officers relaxed and began to chuckle, then let themselves go in a jolly good laugh, and all was over.

We both went back to our duties, Duckett to the Royal College of Art and I to the school in Redditch. A wave of fear seemed to have spread over the country and young men not in uniform were presented with white feathers by young women (also not in uniform). Men over forty, thinking themselves safe behind 'important' jobs, urged those to enlist who were too young to have anything to lose but their lives. The elderly and painfully religious couple whose lodger I was were cold to me, loudly praising Ted Pullen who, as the newspapers had it, had gallantly 'placed his young life at the service of the Nation'. My fellow lodger, no less liable to military service than I was, openly asked me why I didn't enlist. I answered nobody, for my own thoughts were forming.

On 3 September I received a telegram from Muriel, then at Leamington School of Art preparatory to studying art at Clapham. It read: FRIENDS JOINING LEAMINGTON TODAY. SHALL UNCLE FETCH YOU IMMEDIATELY.

I answered 'Yes', and Muriel's Uncle George fetched me that afternoon. The friends were Frank Wallsgrove, in business with his father, a master painter, Joe Parsons, an art teacher, and John Rogers, ARIBA, all of Leamington where we had all met and studied at the School of Art during the previous two years. Along with many other friends and acquaintances we joined the 'Pal's Company'[2] of 7th Battalion, Royal Warwickshire Regiment TF, a unit of the South Midland Division[3]; Ted Pullen, being in the Gloucesters, was in the same division. About that time the victorious battle of the Marne was being fought and the Germans were actually in retreat. We 'Pals' were afraid that the war might be over by Christmas. Then a rumour started that we would be in France in ten weeks' time. We knew not the Germans in those days. Our sergeant-major, Jack Morris, when consulted about this, laughed and said, 'It's a long way to Tipperary.'

We trained for a fortnight in Victoria Park, Leamington, under what we imagined were the admiring eyes of relatives and friends—but we probably looked quite unimpressive in our civilian clothes (and later we all looked positively villainous in khaki). Jack Morris ran us round the park, taught us to form fours and to perform simple squad drill. Then we went to Coventry, headquarters of the Seventh (County) Battalion of the Warwicks.

At the drill hall we received regimental numbers, uniform, equipment and, best of all, arms. After being 'fitted' (a euphemism for having clothes thrown at us after a cursory glance) with uniforms, the recruits of C and the other companies took train to Essex to join the old 'Terriers' who were already there. We detrained at Mark's Tey, marched to Tiptree, where we spent the night in a jam factory, and next day arrived at the pleasant little town of Witham. Here we stayed until we left for active service in France on 22 March 1915.

Now we learned by gradual stages that military training takes much longer than ten weeks. There were daily drills, exercises in squads, platoon and company movements, arms drill, care and maintenance of arms, lots of marching and battalion mass evolutions leading up to brigade and divisional manoeuvres. I remember at the end of all that a red-faced general shouting, 'That will *not* do!' There was firing practice on the ranges at Colchester, where we spent a happy week and now that the war had, in the current phrase, become static, a lot of trench digging in the sticky Essex clay. There were alarms at night and appointed lines to man in case of invasion—the Germans were often reported as about to land at Maldon. There were a few military funerals with slow marching and reversing of arms and I for one heard for the first time the sounding of the Last Post and the parting volley. What we only dimly realised at first, though gradually it became clear, was that we were changing from a mere crowd of enthusiastic young men into an organised body of comrades. Jack Morris was right—the day was near when we would be proud not so much of ourselves, as of the Royal Warwicks.

Some companies were quartered in a seed factory but C Company was lucky to be billeted in private houses, to my secret disappointment for to me this was not the Real Thing. Twelve of us in 12 Platoon found a comfortable, noisy home in Darby's Cyclists' Rest in the main street. We slept in beds, fed together at a long trestle table and, unfortunately for Mr and Mrs Darby, had a sitting room. There we yarned, argued, talked shop, smoked and sang, and thought it a jolly old war.

Of the tens of thousands of recruits who enlisted in 1914 many, or most, were so anxious to get to the front that they were almost impatient of training. The new soldiers must have puzzled the old Territorials and the Regulars. Some of our NCOs, exasperated by our everlasting questions, our habits of putting unnecessary frills on the old stuff of Field Training and our strange ways in general, described their new-style charges as 'Intelligent Duds'. In the pubs it was a debatable point whether an Intelligent Dud ranked lower on the military scale than a Plain Dud. An ID was incalculable and might be a positive danger, whereas his plain brother could be relied upon in any situation to be himself and could therefore be provided for. Whereas the old style of recruit had nothing to lose but his life, the new kind, even if he survived, had a great deal to lose. He gave up security, safety, comfort, and sometimes hard-won advancement or seniority in his job. He offered his services for the duration of the war as an amateur or temporary soldier to be taught as quickly as possible enough to make him useful in the emergency which had arisen. He was not only willing but anxious to learn, with confidence in his own ability to tackle the ordinary problems of the soldier's trade and, above all, to accept responsibility when it was offered him.

Had we ever been asked to comment on our uniform we might have had much to say about it, not all of it complimentary but I do not remember anyone grousing seriously about it on active service. We just took it for granted. On route marches of course we passed other troops similarly engaged. Of them we thought and said, 'What a scruffy lot! Like gaolbirds. What coarse, evil-looking faces, pasty and unhealthy too! Brummagem scum!' Later we got to know these same units, the 5th, 6th and 8th Royal Warwicks, and on comparing notes, found that they had thought and said almost the same as us though, as Brummies, they had expressed themselves in picturesque and forcible terms such as we had not yet acquired. It was at last borne in on us that the colour and cut of the 1914 service dress for infantry could make an archbishop, a saint or even a 7th Royal Warwick look like an idiot or a criminal.

The colour was a filthy browny-yellow, designed with complete success to look like mud or dust. It buttoned right up to the neck, where the wide down-turned collar gave no relief or transition from square body-shape to round head-shape, almost hiding the neck so that our faces stood on our collars like badly done puddings on upturned earthenware dishes. The ugly flat service cap was simply 'putting the lid on them'. In the early days of the war there was no such thing as being fitted for uniform, as I said earlier. Tunic, trousers, and puttees were literally thrown to the recruit after he had been 'sized' up in the time it took to walk from the door to the table where large, medium and small sizes were piled. However, there was no regulation against swopping, and bad misfits got sorted out sooner or later. We were glad of the short skirts or tails of the tunic, or would have been had we sampled the battledress of 1939-45. It kept loins, thighs and hips from too quickly becoming cold and wet. It had four pockets and an extra one in a corner for the field dressing, so there was no need to bulge anywhere and there was a place for all our bits of personal gear. In fact, active service proved the uniform not as bad as it looked.

When the recruits were supplied with arms and clothing they regarded with curiosity the thirteen items of woven webbing straps, bags and cases that had to be assembled. It was realised with a slight shock that these bits and pieces had to carry everything that a soldier possessed except the rifle itself and the clothing one stood up in. That is to say: bayonet and scabbard, entrenching tool and its handle, waterbottle, 150 rounds of .303 ammunition in thirty clips, mess-tin, hold-all with its personal cleaning gear, button-stick and powder, cutlery, 'iron rations', jack-knife, cap-comforter, towel, rubber groundsheet (6 foot by 3) and lastly (and voluminously) the greatcoat.

Recruits were shown how to assemble the parts of the equipment and, to their enormous relief, how to reduce the greatcoat to a neat, compact rectangular bundle which could be stevedored into the pack. Around the waist went a three-inch-wide webbing belt. At the back of it, permanently riveted on, was a pair of two-inch tabs which carried brass buckles or Ds through which the two-inch shoulder-straps were passed, crossing at the back, passing over the shoulders and hanging down in front. The aforesaid tabs extended below the belt to buckle into a pair of Ds riveted to the top of the entrenching tool case. The four ends of the shoulder-straps carried, on the left of the body, the haversack and, on the right, the waterbottle carrier, both of these having their own Ds ready to receive the ends of the shoulder-straps. The ammunition pouches also had their own pairs of Ds through which the shoulder-straps passed after coming over the shoulders and then passed under the pouches to haversack and waterbottle carrier. The entrenching-tool handle was fastened to the front edge of the bayonet scabbard by loops and a press-stud, and the scabbard hung in a frog which was looped on to the belt. The pack had two two-inch tabs sewn at the top corners at the back, and these tabs buckled through a pair of sliding Ds threaded on the shoulder-straps left and right at shoulder height. At the

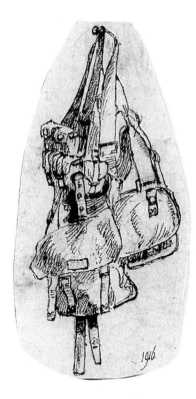

bottom corners, the pack was fastened by narrow one-inch pack straps to the belt, the straps passing through loops sewn under the pack, then crossing over the pack's front to its top corner behind. These straps could cross over and hold the folded groundsheet and, later in the war, the steel helmet when not in use. Below the pack was, sometimes, carried the mess-tin in its canvas cover, the pack-straps being long enough to go cross-wise over it, through a loop on the front of the cover. In the haversack was carried 'the unexpired portion of the day's ration', the iron ration or tin of bully beef, and the hold-all with its knife, fork and spoon, though it was often carried in the pack unless battle order was worn, in which case the haversack took the place of the pack, which was kept in the company stores for the time being.

When all was on, complete with ammunition and the 1½-pint waterbottle filled, it was a heavy load in addition to the 9-pound rifle but the equipment was so well designed that it carried well. It was incomparably better than the wretched leather gear worn by the New Army.

As an old camper, the entrenching tool appealed to me. In action it was used as both pick and shovel or its handle could form a little 'Spanish windlass' to tauten slack pairs of wires. When not in use the blade provided comforting defensive armour over one's otherwise vulnerable rear. Its more personal and domestic uses were many and various. It dug and afterwards covered up over one's private latrine, scraped clean and smooth the ground in dug-out and barn, chopped sticks and hammered nails. Its well-sharpened pick jabbed holes in a fire-bucket, and if the glowing bucket had to be moved, was used as a carrying hook.

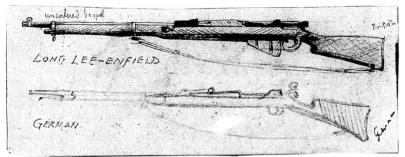

When arms were first given to us our NCOs drummed into us the phrase 'The soldier's best friend is his rifle.' Though ours were old-fashioned, we were proud of them and took a delight in learning their mechanism and keeping them clean. The rifle used by the Regulars in 1914 and throughout the war was the Short Lee-Enfield (SMLE). The Territorials, or at any rate our 143 Brigade, had the Long Lee-Enfield, and in March 1915 we went to Flanders with them as there were not enough SMLEs to equip both the New Army and the Territorials. The long rifles were withdrawn about June 1916, just before the Battle of the Somme, and in exchange we were given our 'new chum', who made up for shortness of stature by flourishing a gruesome length of bayonet. 'Shorty's' performance as a long-range target hitter was distinctly inferior to that of the old rifle, or so we thought, but the war had become a short-range duel from fixed positions so that that did not matter and 'Shorty' was much handier and easier to keep clean in trench warfare.[4]

In a big park in Essex in the autumn of 1914 a TF battalion is in training. The men are not yet all in complete uniform. Even the old Terriers are not all in khaki. Some are wearing their ceremonial dress or part of it, appearing on parade with, for example, dark blue trousers, red-striped, and a dirty old khaki tunic. Most recruits have new khaki uniforms but there are some in civilian dress.[5] However, there are rifles and webbing equipment for all. The rifles are of the long pattern but these young men are proud to have any rifle that is serviceable.

With the two exceptions of the Commanding Officer and the Adjutant, the Battalion is officered entirely by Territorials, that is by amateur soldiers. All the non-commissioned officers are old Terriers and a few of them are Boer War or Indian Frontier veterans. The Battalion has been brought up to war strength by men only recently recruited, who have done a fortnight's preliminary training at their home towns, enough to enable them to assemble in two ranks, to form fours and march off in step without falling over each other's feet.

The Adjutant is a dynamic personality. He is responsible for instilling into a crowd of young men that *esprit de corps* that more than anything else turns it into soldiers. He addresses an individual as 'Soldier' if he does not know his name, in which case he very soon gets to know it and never forgets it. After a man has been addressed at any length by the Adjutant, he feels the better for it, even if he has been reprimanded. Captain Johnson is tall, lean, sallow, dark, beak-nosed, wears a monocle but has far-seeing eyes and a far-reaching voice. He meets a recruit in the street near Headquarters. 'Soldier!' 'Sir!' 'What is your name?' 'Two-one-oh-four Miller, J., sir.' 'Well, Private Miller, why did you join the Royal Warwickshire Regiment?' 'Sir, all my mates were joining in Nuneaton.' 'Have you been in the regiment long enough to be proud of it, do you think?' 'Oh yes, sir! We all are.' 'How do you show it?' 'I dunno, sir.' 'Well, Private Miller, I'll tell you one way and you can think of some more for yourself. DON'T LEAVE ANY BUTTONS UNDONE!' 'Oh, sir, I hadn't noticed. Sorry, sir.' 'You will take care in future.' 'Yes, sir, I won't forget.' 'Nor shall I. I don't forget faces or names or THINGS THAT MATTER, however small. Carry on, two-one-oh-four Private Miller, J.'

On parade, mounted on his tall black horse, he is about to yell an order when he stiffens, pointing to a man who had hardly expected to be singled out from so large an assembly. 'That man there, rear rank, Number Eight Platoon. NO CAP BADGE! Sergeant Jones, I shall expect to see that man at Orderly Room tomorrow complete with cap badge for having the audacity to appear on parade PRACTICALLY NAKED!' When the occasion demands he has a copious flow of invective and vituperation which, spread over a host, hurts no man. In battalion training when everyone is present and his wonderful flow is not wasted, for he is a great showman, he draws on his store of Biblical reference, and the training is lifted to become a thrilling experience. On such an occasion his horse, trained like a police horse to stamp perilously near one's feet, whisks round on all fours or pivots alarmingly on two with equal facility. The pair ideally suit each other and move as one.

The Commanding Officer has bellowed an order, 'Battalion—form—LINE!' After a prolonged struggle, a line has been formed while the Adjutant has been dashing about with a wonderful display of horsemanship, finally to gallop with thundering hooves and flying monocle down the line from end to end. At this the line shudders visibly, then straightens like magic, and only just in time, as horse and rider wheel at the far end, the flank corporal of D Company holding his breath while flashing hooves seem to semicircle over his head, to come down with fearful precision a few inches from his feet. 'Your Commanding Officer ordered LINE and line I suppose it is, for the Almighty alone knows what else it may be, but oh, my good godfather and godmother, WHAT a line! A dog with a hind leg the shape of this alleged line would be a sorry cur! THAT MAN THERE! I don't want to see your face. Tuck your arse in, that soldier there. That BELLY there. TUCK IT IN, MAN!' Here the pair perform an amazing getaway, accelerating at the expense of the turf which flies into the faces of the front platoon. Very much sooner than it takes to tell, a line is formed and an electrified battalion awaits the next order.

After a stand-easy for a breather, the Battalion is formed into company columns. The order to advance is given and the companies are stepping out or stepping short to adjust their distances when suddenly the CO shouts, 'Prepare to receive cavalry! Echelon left. A Company leading!'[6] Now, instead of advancing one behind the other, companies assume a staggered line, spreading towards their left. The Adjutant is again performing feats of horsemanship as he charges across the staggered company fronts. 'DEAD MEN ALL! BROKEN AND PUT TO ROUT! The Good Book says, 'On the Fifth Day were made ALL CREEPING THINGS and by the Great God who created us all, YOU ARE THE CREEPIEST!'

The Battalion Provost-Sergeant was the sergeant of the Regimental Police whose job it was to see that soldiers kept the peace when off parade, left the pubs at the proper time and wore their uniforms correctly. At stated times he conducted defaulters' parade when soldiers were sent to him to atone for petty crimes with the sweat of their brows. As a raw recruit one of my secret ambitions was to sample pack drill and in due course I achieved it, finding that one hour was more than enough, though it was an experience which I have never regretted. What my crime was I forget, but it was not necessarily one of those indicated in this sketch which is a fair sample of what happened during our training in the sunny autumn of 1914.

Seven soldiers, in full marching order but without rifles, file through a gate and approach the burly figure of the Provost-Sergeant, who stands at ease, his silver-knobbed cane under his left arm in the middle of a small field. The straggling party has nearly reached him when suddenly he springs to attention and yells at the nearest man, 'You here, right marker. Halt!' and then to the remainder, 'Fall in on the left of the marker at the double. Halt! Answer your names.'

The Provost-Sergeant delivers every order and every homily in a loud, hoarse yell, without the least sign of strain or even effort, and without a pause for either breath or punctuation. There is seldom more than ten paces marched without a change of direction or formation.

'Into file, right turn. Quick march. On the left form squad. Forward. When you joined the Army you joined a body of MEN. If you behave like kids you TAKE THE CONSEQUENCES. About turn. By the left. Change direction left. Left form. Forward.

'When you joined the Territorial Force you joined a body of men who wash their necks and shine their boots. About turn. Into file, left turn. If you appear on parade like tramps you TAKE THE CONSEQUENCES. Right wheel. Into line, right turn. By the right. Change direction right. Right form. Forward.

'When you joined the Royal Warwickshire Regiment you joined a body of men. Number five, take that grin off your face and when the squad's dismissed YOU go marching on like John Brown's body—I said a body of men who know how to carry their beer. ABOUT TURN. If you leave your pub after a paltry half-gallon and disgrace His Majesty's uniform in this respectable town of Witham you TAKE THE CONSEQUENCES. About turn. Into file, left turn. NUMBER FIVE, you likely broke your poor mother's heart BUT YOU WON'T BREAK MINE. Left wheel. When you joined the Sixth of Foot you joined a body of men who when in the company of females conduct themselves with discretion. If you play the dirty dog in this respectable town—THEY'RE PROS FROM LONDON AND COLCHESTER, YOU DAMNED YOUNG FOOLS—BY GOD, YOU TAKE THE CONSEQUENCES. About turn. On the right, form squad. Forward.

'When you joined the County Battalion of the Royal Warwickshire Regiment you were allowed the honour of wearing His Majesty's uniform and so were your officers. When you salute them you salute His Majesty's Commission and Uniform, NOT THE BLOKE. If you think you are as good as he is and fail to salute then you bloody well ain't and you TAKE THE CONSEQUENCES. About turn. Into line, right turn.

'When you joined the Seventh Battalion of the old Sixth of Foot you were given the privilege and responsibility of carrying rifles. By the right, change direction right. Right form. Forward. If you don't keep your rifle clean you TAKE THE CONSEQUENCES. About turn. Into file, right turn. If you damned awkward squad are allowed on active service (God help England)—on the left, form squad—you'll find that your rifle's to shoot bullets out of at the enemy. About turn. Then if you can't shoot him for muck in your rifle barrel, he'll damned well shoot you and GOOD RIDDANCE. About turn.'

II

HOLDING THE LINE IN FLANDERS

Before the end of 1914 the Western Front had congealed into the shape which, with minor alteration, it would maintain until the high summer of 1918. The plans with which France and Germany had started the war had proved abortive, and the second German scheme, to break through to the Channel ports by way of Ypres, had been narrowly frustrated. In the process the British Regular Army had all but disappeared. Between August and December the equivalent of three infantry divisions (each comprising some 18,000 men) had been killed or were missing and more than enough men to make up two more divisions had been wounded, some of them so seriously that they could never return to the line. From the point of view of expanding the Army, the most serious part of this loss was in officers, of whom 1,530 were killed or prisoners of war while 2,097 were wounded. Of that rare breed, graduates of the Staff College, fifty-nine fell in 1914.

Five more Regular divisions were scraped together, one of which was diverted from France, and two Indian divisions, which had one British battalion in each brigade, were brought to France, but the French constantly required their allies to garrison longer portions of the front and this line could only be manned by employing non-Regular formations despite the elementary state of their training. Territorial divisions, led by 46th (North Midland), started reaching the front at the end of February 1915, a month that also saw the arrival of 1st Canadian Division, and five more TF formations, including 48th (South Midland), were in France before the first week in May. The first New Army division (9th Scottish) landed on 9 May. Initially each battalion of these new troops was attached to a Regular unit for practical experience in trench warfare.

It had been intended that TF divisions should undergo six months of intensive training before being exposed to continental campaigning but, although all of them had been embodied for at least six months, the shortage of Regular Army instructors, caused by battle wastage, meant that every one of them fell far short of the training standard that was required. Moreover the type of warfare in which they were to be engaged was something in which the British, and indeed the French and the Germans, were totally inexperienced—siege warfare.

It was sixty years since the British had last undertaken a siege and such skills as had been acquired at Sebastopol had long been forgotten, and neither did the material required for siege warfare exist. Even shovels, according to a senior Engineer officer, were 'worth their weight in gold'. There were no hand grenades. The only grenades available in England had been left behind since they were too expensive and too inefficient to take to war. Various improvised grenades, mostly consisting of guncotton with some kind of fuse, were employed but most of them were exceedingly dangerous to the thrower. The first efficient and reasonably safe grenades, a batch of forty-eight Mills bombs, were sent to France on 15 March 1915. There were no trench mortars, and forty Cohorn mortars, dating from the 1840s were bought from the French and used between March and May 1915. The first efficient trench mortars did not become available to the British until November of that year. Sandbags were in short supply, only a million being available in January. Before the end of the year the requirement was found to be thirty million monthly. Heavy artillery was largely lacking and in June 1915 the BEF could only boast 105 guns larger than the 18-pounder field guns, and for guns of all calibres ammunition was in short supply. In April the factories were only producing 10.6 rounds each day for each of the field guns so that orders had to be given restricting them to eight rounds daily. Only one round a day was being manufactured for the three 15-inch howitzers with the Army.

Both sides did little more than survive the winter of 1914-15 but, with the appearance of spring, thoughts turned to achieving a breakthrough in the siege lines which had been etched on the landscape from the Swiss border to the Belgian coast. The Germans, who had been forced to divert fourteen divisions, six of them cavalry, to oppose the Russians in the east, launched only one major attack in the west. In an attempt to test the effect of poison gas, they attacked north of Ypres on 22 April and, thanks to the defection of a French Algerian division, tore a great gap in an already tenuous front. Fortunately they had underestimated their possible success and were not ready to exploit it, their advance being checked by the gallantry of the newly arrived Canadians and a hotch-potch of British and French detachments.

The French were much more determined in their attacks, partly from their desire to take the weight off the Russians and partly since *l'offensive à l'outrance* bulked so large in their military thinking. In London the British government was also anxious to do what it could for the Russians but less convinced that the Western Front was the best place to do it. There was a tendency to favour knocking out Turkey and opening an ice-free route to Russia by forcing the Dardanelles. This they originally hoped to do by purely naval action but soon found that troops were needed to seize the Gallipoli peninsula. Thanks largely to poor leadership, at sea and on land, they failed in this enterprise but in embarking on it they had to divert troops and, even more important, supplies which were badly needed by the BEF in France and Belgium.

Field-Marshal Sir John French, commanding the BEF, was wholly opposed to Gallipoli which deprived him of artillery ammunition and, apart from other troops, of a Regular division (29th) which had been promised to him. He was under constant pressure from his French allies to take over more front and to co-operate in offensive operations, an enterprise his naturally sanguine temperament favoured with a view to cultivating the offensive spirit of his men. He was also anxious to regain the high ground in front of his existing line since this would not only permit observation over the German positions but would enable his infantry to dig trenches to a useful depth, since in the lowland positions to which they had been driven back in 1914 the water table was only a few inches below the top soil. He set his sights on the Aubers Ridge which rises a bare forty feet from the plain west of Lille, and in his first attempt (10-13 March) succeeded in capturing the village of Neuve Chapelle at the foot of the ridge. It cost 11,600 casualties (including 544 officers) but no further progress could be made and a second attack on the ridge on 9 May achieved nothing for 11,100 casualties (458 officers). A week later, in co-operation with a French attack on Vimy Ridge, he attacked Festubert and made only insignificant gains for 16,600 casualties (710 officers). The French lost 100,000 men.

It was in the middle of this flurry of abortive activity that Harry Ogle and the rest of the 48th (South Midland) Division arrived at the front. They were seriously undertrained but they had to be put into the front as there were no other troops available. Their first turn in the 'trenches'—usually breastworks above ground since water prevented deep digging—was done with each battalion under tuition from a Regular unit. Thereafter they were given a quiet sector of their own. 48th Division was lucky that their sector near Armentières was genuinely quiet but other TF divisions were less fortunate. 50th (Northumbrian) was sucked into the fighting at Ypres and lost 5,000 men, while 47th (London) Division had to be employed at Festubert and suffered heavily. For 48th Division the spring and early summer of 1915, though not without danger, was a period largely marked by discomfort.

The Battalion is embarking at Southampton on 22 March 1915 with all stores, equipment and transport. The men are nearly all aboard SS *Copenhagen*, while the big derricks swing out over the side and in again over the holds with a ceaseless rattle. Every available space appears to be occupied by khaki-clad men in full marching order and carrying life-jackets which they will put on as soon as there is room to do so. They have not yet begun to thin out and disperse between decks. They must await the order. There is no confusion but a good deal of the inevitable waiting about for orders that is one of the minor irritations of army life. Everybody with a stripe or stripes seems to be looking for somebody with a pip or pips, while the stripeless and pipless stay where they have been told to stay. Some find seats but are invariably dislodged because they sit in a fairway, or on a wanted coil of rope, or for some other seafaring reason. Two or three super-landlubbers perch on the very gunwale. Suddenly there is a commotion, a diminishing cry cut off by a loud splash, while a hundred voices yell: '*Man overboard!*' There are also cries of, 'It's Cashy', for Private George Cashmore was one of those who had perched on the gunwale. There is a rush to the side but already, as if they had been waiting like actors in the wings, two seamen have appeared. With a peremptory 'Make way' and with perfect composure, they separate the two ends of a very long ordinary ladder which is lashed to the bulwarks and in a matter of seconds it is over the side and its end touches the water almost at the same time as a lifebuoy. Cashy seizes the lifebuoy but the ladder is so close that he chooses it as more familiar and climbs up, his heavy greatcoat discharging gallons of water. He is soon near the top where he is seized by the two seamen and swung bodily inboard with the easy action of men who do these things as part of the day's work when soldiers are on board. The crowd cheers, perhaps a little derisively, but the noise subsides rather quickly, for a burly figure with gold lace on cap and sleeves has rolled up, quietly and apparently from nowhere, sailor-like. The officer's hands are thrust into his jacket side-pockets, his feet planted apart. Poor Cashy stands dripping between the seamen. 'Damned young fool!' 'Ye-yes, s-s-sir,' agrees Cashy. 'Dixon, take him below to sick bay, quick, and perhaps you'd better get a purchase on him in case he tries to dive through a port, as he seems fond of water.' The two disappear below, one to hot-water bottles, blankets and a tot of rum. By this time platoon commanders and platoon sergeants arrive but the fun is over.

The Channel has been crossed without incident by night and on a grey and chilly morning the *Copenhagen* is about to make fast at Le Havre. The troops have been up, washed, shaved and breakfasted this last hour and, with rifle and equipment all ready to don at a moment's notice, are on deck to watch proceedings. Every item of mooring has been noted and now all eyes are turned shoreward to the land of France and most ears are keen to hear the French lingo. Again the soldiers experience the inevitable waiting, while those in authority seem to be chasing each other about for orders. Nobody falls overboard. The ship had begun to discharge her mixed cargo almost before she was made fast. The men are in high spirits and as the company cookers are hauled into view and overhead, there is a cheer for each one of them. The transport horses, stout little hog-maned cobs, are led down the gangplanks with much stamping of hooves, and though they look askance at nearly everything, they are obviously glad of the presence of their drivers and give little trouble.

At last the order comes to go ashore and there begins a steady hollow clumping of heavy, nailed boots on gangplanks, suddenly to become augmented by their clatter on granite setts as the first groups reach the quay. Now the men are streaming by complete companies along the quay, across covered shed floors, across railway lines innumerable, along permanent ways, to bring up in a wide, granite-paved yard. Here is room to assemble in close company column and rolls are called. After another wait the Commanding Officer Major and Adjutant arrive, and soon after the Battalion moves off in

column of fours. Ahead is a red and white level-crossing bar, closed. From the left an enormous locomotive puffs slowly along with an apparently endless train of wagons. The troops are watching curiously and just as the monster comes abreast, it omits a little, thin treble 'toot!' suddenly and apologetically. The men who had been much impressed by the size and majesty of the engine, find this altogether too much for them and roar with laughter, rather to the mystification of the driver and fireman. But the laughter is followed by a cheer, taken up by every company and the Frenchmen acknowledge it by waving their greasy caps, and they grin with delight, shouting '*À bas les bosches!*'

Soon the Battalion is entraining at Le Havre for a destination at present unknown to the rank and file. One point of interest in such a move is that the whole Battalion, men, horses, transport wagons, wheeled cookers and all stores whatever, can be seen together. Everything and everybody is there and the train is in. Now, with the usual waiting to endure, a man can observe the trucks and wagons that are to carry him to the front. There is much that is unusual—the big locomotive, the funny little guard's or brakesman's box sticking high up at the end of the last truck. One of the things that strike him about his own train is that there is only one railway carriage, the rest being made up of closed horse-boxes and cattle-wagons, and open trucks. He reads the legend painted on the wagon nearest to him. 'Chevorks eight, ommies forty,' he says. 'What's that mean, Tom?' Tom says it means eight horses, forty men. 'God's truth! but you can't get forty men into this van, let alone eight bloody 'orses!' 'Don't be so daft it's eight horses *or* forty men, of course.' 'Then why the 'ell can't they write 'or' then?' But the matter is settled for them when away to the rear of the train they see that the transport horses are actually being led up the ramps into exactly similar wagons. A man glances into the wagon near him and says, 'I bet they've got more straw in them than in these what we're going in.' 'Well, what did you expect? You're not going to be'ave same as a 'orse in this wagon of ours, are you?'

Now it is time for the troops to board the train and up they swarm to their allotted wagons, much like schoolboys eager to sample something new. 'Them forty Frenchies wot they measured for these 'ere vans must have been 'alf-starved little buggers!' but all are settled in a couple of minutes. Now they crowd to the sliding doors. The horses are all aboard. The open trucks, with their sides let down, are receiving General Service wagons, company cookers and water-carts. Everything has disappeared from the paved yard, but there has to be some more waiting. There comes an officer who wears an arm-band labelled RTO for Railway Transport Officer and he carries a sheaf of papers. He joins the senior officers and seems to have a long gossip with them. He goes away and the senior officers and the Transport Officer of the Battalion walk along the whole length of the very long train, looking into every van and saying a few cheery words. Finally they climb into their carriage. A soldier in one of the wagons leans far out to look forward. 'There's no bloody engine! Come on, Number Twelve Platoon, get out and shove, or we'll be late for the war.' Presently an engine is heard puffing and as it moves into view the troops give a cheer. This is acknowledged by a wave of the hand and a shout of '*À la bonne heure!*' from the fireman. After getting coupled to the train, the engine gets under way and slowly gathers speed. When it is realised that the journey 'up the line' has really begun, a tremendous cheer is raised.

There is no settling down while the train rumbles slowly through the town, and every French man, woman and child receives a cheer and some of them send back charming acknowledgements, for it is yet early in the war. The houses are left behind, the sliding doors are partly closed for safety and the men settle down on their packs or on the straw—what little there is—though there is no room to stretch. The inevitable cards appear and 'pontoon' is played. There is much speculation as to where the Battalion is going. There are many stops, for no reason apparent, and on some of them men take a risk and leave the train, though keeping a wary eye on the driver, who sometimes waves a warning or toots the whistle. Strangely enough, nobody is left behind. Night falls and somehow it passes with some sleep, a few smokes and some re-shuffling. As dawn breaks and chinks of light can be seen at the ventilators, some curious early waker tries to see what there is outside, but his efforts are unpopular and, amongst muffled curses, he settles down again, taking out a cigarette for consolation. That gives others the same idea and lit matches disclose a queer scene of closely packed, greatcoated mounds and hummocks. Soon, as daylight filters in, a general movement and conversation begin. The train stops, officers come alongside, NCOs jump out, orderly men are appointed, and some sort of breakfast is made from haversack rations, tea and hot water.

After the train has got under way again, the men take notice of their changing surroundings. Some of the more observant notice that station names and other names seen on houses, vans, inns and signposts are somehow different. There are names ending in -kerque and -cappel, -becq, -beek and -brouk, -gheen, -zeele and -voorde. Also the language, what little they hear in attempted conversations shouted at level-crossings, at halts and to workers in fields and on canals, is different and Dutch-like.

It is after midday before the train rolls slowly into the big junction at Hazebrouk, and there is much shunting and waiting before at last it is on a single railway line leading due north. 'It's Wipers for a quid!' But about fifteen kilometres north of Hazebrouk, the train stops. Nobody stirs. Nobody asks 'Where are we?' Somebody reads the name on the station name-board. 'Winnie Zeely,' he says. Nobody is at all interested. By this time voices are heard approaching, doors are slid back and it is seen that already soldiers are out on the goods yard pavement. Soon orders are heard and a shout goes up: 'We are THERE!' 'We are where?' 'This ain't any-bloody-where', and then 'Shut up and listen to orders.'

The Battalion has really arrived, at the end of its railway journey at least, to the relief of all and, whether they have arrived at somewhere, nowhere, anywhere or even Winnezeele, they are glad of a change. Officers, one with red lapel tabs and red cap-band, are talking with the Battalion Headquarters staff and maps are being unfolded and pencilled. The Transport Officer, who was first out, hurries along to his beloved horses, and soon there is the bustle and clatter of unloading. Meanwhile companies have been formed up and now they move off in column of route and the march to billets begins, the men being glad to stretch their cramped limbs and step out, singing. C Company follows a guide along a road heading north-east and climbs a low hill, halting at cross-roads where No. 12 Platoon breaks away to follow another guide. He follows a side road or track which brings the platoon to a farm and the men enter the cobblestoned yard. To their right is a farmhouse and a barn, to their left are shippons and stables. At the far end are sheds and pigsties. In the midst is an enormous sunken manure pit, and the house is as close to it as are the shippons. Close to where the men stand is a big stone-built dog kennel shaped like a conical beehive.

The light is fading and, away due east, the Very lights of the Ypres Salient can be plainly seen, soaring and then slowly falling. Now there is much to do before tea is brought and a meal got together. But before No. 12 unroll groundsheets for their kip-down in the barn that night, first one and then another steals out into the field behind the barn till they are all there, standing silent. The lights seem to hold a strange fascination for them, as they rise, hover, and fall, slowly and interminably.

The Battalion is on the march in Flanders. It has been out of England little more than a week and has spent part of that time in a ship and another part in railway trucks. So the men are in high spirits because at last they are moving under their own power and, moreover, moving nearer and nearer to The Line. Their full marching-order is a heavy load and has been increased, quite unnecessarily, by a spare pair of nailed boots strapped on top of the pack. The road is one of little gentle hills and long, straight, level stretches. It is a *pavé* whose big stone setts are everlasting in wear but very bad for marching in nailed boots, which slip on them, especially on the camber and under heavy loads. The rank and file do not know where they are going but guess at Ypres until, instead of turning east at Steenvoorde, they go straight on south. It might be anywhere now but when they come to Caestre they

do turn east and march along the Armentières road. That border town, in the line, is their destination but with their load on this pavé they will be very glad to break their journey at Bailleul. That will make 12½ miles, not very far, but enough to start with. Anyhow, distances and times are not arranged to suit them but to fit in with complicated troop movements.

The road is lined on both sides with tall, leggy poplars and aspens, and goes forward by almost dead-straight stretches of three or four kilometres, punctuated by the ancient towns of Caestre, Flêtre, and Méteren and Bailleul. The last-named town, which the men call Baloo, is piled on a hill rising some 120 feet above the river Flanche Becq. Ten roads converge on it from all quarters, climbing up to the central group of noble buildings about the town square which tower fantastically against the sky as the troops approach the town. These buildings, and many others in this district, including some farms, have a decidedly Spanish look. The town was badly damaged later in the war but in April 1915 was untouched and only the younger men of its 13,000 inhabitants had left.

The Battalion has climbed the hill steadily to the town square and as they enter the square they march to attention, for French troops are marching out and now the sounds are of exchanged compliments against the heavy, measured background of marching feet. The companies are met by guides whom they follow to billets. C Company is billeted in a brewery recently occupied by French soldiers. Some men of No. 12 Platoon are allotted the task of removing and dealing with filthy latrine buckets and *L'entente cordiale* is seriously strained. However, whether the French do or leave undone their own dirty jobs, there is no job too big or too small or, it seems, too dirty for English soldiers, and this one is done.

Tea over, the men go out to see the town and are at once befriended by men of the Artists' Rifles, then being withdrawn to make into an officers' training battalion. They show the Warwicks the sights of the town, the best *estaminets*, *épiceries*, and the like, and the places to avoid. The newcomers have their first taste of vin, both rouge et blanc, both *chaud* and *froid*, of Grenadine and Malaga, of beer which is both thin and sour, and Byrrh which is not beer at all. Some find, in one of the narrow streets which converge on the square, the 'pillow lace' makers at work. The day being fine and sunny, the women are seated on chairs on the pavement, their pillow stools in front of them, dextrously moving pretty little turned wooden bobbins of different shapes and sizes which hang on cords attached to the pillow frame, over and under as the traditional pattern dictates. As they work they carry on a brisk and lively conversation across and up and down the street, with much shrill laughter, and the English soldiers, still rather shy, and who are fascinated by the women's sleight of hand, suspect that they may be the subject of the conversation. But he is a poor soldier who cannot quickly make friends with women, old or young, and soon they are all laughing together.

During their few days' stay at Bailleul there is a trench-digging expedition to Dranoutre [Dranouter] where our field artillery is firing a round or two and men learn to calculate distance by flash and sound. This place is behind that part of the front presently to be occupied by these same troops.

Now there is a rumour that the Battalion is going into the line at Armentières and away they go, along the Flemish border, still further east and closer to the line, singing 'For we all want to go to the fight, that's right'.

As we march into Armentières, night is falling, shops are lit up, the men are singing 'Mademoiselle from Armentières' and 'Oh! You Beautiful Doll' and cheering everybody and everything. French people come out of their houses and shops and throw open upper windows, and here and there somebody waves and calls to these obviously 'new' boys, so fresh and enthusiastic. Other British troops are in the town and some of them walk alongside to be friendly and to swap news. They are rather older men and look seasoned, tough and professional, as indeed they are, some of them being Old Contemptibles. One of the things that Territorials of our division at least will never forget is the comradely spirit and tolerance of our Regular soldiers.

Now the Battalion has marched right through Armentières, turning left at the centre to follow the Houplines road for a short distance. We halt outside a tall building behind a high wall, and presently we march through the gateway, breaking off by companies in a big yard. This building is a

HOUPLINES   Trench Shelter

convent school of three or four storeys and can accommodate a company on
every floor. C Company are high up but wash in the yard in a biscuit tin
which they fill at a slow-running standpipe. It is presumed that the departed
sisters and children *did* wash, but No.12 Platoon did not see any
arrangements other than the standpipe.

The next day the Battalion goes into the firing line at Houplines, where
the Durham Light Infantry hold a very narrow salient. These men are
Regular soldiers, many of them out since Mons, to use the current expression
to denote a veteran, and have endured trench warfare through the recent
winter.[1] They are receiving the Territorials for a few days as 'guests' or
apprentices on this their first spell in the line. How this was managed I don't
remember but I suppose that a proportion of the Durhams was withdrawn
for a time, leaving most of the NCOs and senior soldiers as instructors. It
made cramped quarters for all but nobody minded that.

The Regulars do their best to initiate the Terriers into the routine, chores
and mysteries of static warfare, and the Terriers do their best to assimilate
all the lessons, advice and good example. There is none better than the
Durhams' best and the Warwicks' Terriers have yet to prove themselves, as
they did later on, worthy to fight alongside the Regulars on equal terms.

In this dangerous, uncomfortable, hairpin salient they learn first how to
take care of themselves. The DLI point out that a mistake in the first lesson
may wash out the whole course for some unfortunate or careless learner.
They begin with a few DON'TS. *Don't* gaze over the parapet but use the

loopholes and, if you are not a sentry, you have no business to gaze about anyway. *Don't* loiter anywhere and, if you are off duty, get into your shelter. *Don't* volunteer like a stage hero for jobs you know nothing about. If you do you may wreck the job. On the positive side there is a lot to learn—how to improvise cooking and washing, to make the best of the rations provided, to use, make and maintain proper latrines decently, to keep trenches and shelters clean and dry, to keep oneself and one's mind occupied usefully and intelligently, and if you really have nothing to do, get down and *sleep*.

The raw troops soon realise that in these few days it is impossible to do more than get a glimpse of a fraction of what there is to learn. There are so many things to do in the dark and in bad weather, such as digging, sandbagging, revetting and duck-boarding, the making and fitting of loopholes and sniper plates, the maintenance of fire-step, elbow rest, parapet and parados. 'Over the top' there is barbed wire with its pickets and posts. There are saps and listening posts. There is experience to be gained in patrols and covering parties. And all the time the enemy, whom the troops are beginning to refer to as 'Jerry', is in the way, or trying to prevent you doing your job, or having a shot at you. The Durhams know him quite well, for some of them have fought him hand to hand, have been chased by him and have chased him to where he is now,[2] 'over there' but usually not to be seen. They are not at all afraid of him but respect him as a brave and capable soldier. The Terriers, in these their first trenches, and only 'borrowed' at that, do not yet know whether they are afraid of him or not, and many are afraid of being afraid. The Durhams can do nothing about that, except show a good example.

In this narrow salient, bullets seem to fly from all directions, but there is not much shelling for obvious reasons. At night NCOs and officers get a chance of using Very-light pistols and get used to seeing those of the enemy, and the men of No.12 Platoon remember how, not long ago, they watched them fascinated as they rose and fell in a much bigger and grimmer salient.

Pont de Nieppe is only two kilometres from Armentières where the Armentières–Bailleul road crosses the River Lys. Close to the bridge and on the left bank of the river was a brewery. It was too near the firing line to continue its business so the British Army took it over to convert it into baths for the troops. There was little conversion necessary. The River Lys provided the necessary water, the vat room provided the bath tubs and water pipes, a storeroom was emptied for use as a dressing room, and all that was needed then was the installation of a stoving and fumigating plant. The vat room contained dozens of big wooden tubs of perhaps 200 gallons' capacity, every one with piping for hot and cold water. Between dressing room and bath house were the rooms for stoving and fumigating clothes.

The hot bath was a joyful event. A bath was infrequent so that men's clothes and bodies got really dirty and infested with lice. In the line areas some kind of a piecemeal wash could sometimes be contrived but never a complete bath, without great and unusual good luck and then only a cold one. Marching companies of soldiers in fatigue dress, carrying towels only, were a familiar sight on the Armentières road or between that road and the more northerly villages of Neuve-Église and Ploegsteert. They marched briskly along, always singing, arms swinging high, towels tucked under shoulder straps.

Arrived at the Brasserie, the men filed into the big dressing room by a street door. Within, they stripped naked. They put their boots on again, bundled their clothes together, leaving on the floor or on the benches only their braces, belts, and service caps into which they put their personal gear. These were looked after by an NCO bath attendant. Next they pushed their bundles through a hatch in the store-room wall and trooped, stark-naked, looking and feeling ridiculous, on to the River Lys towing path. Within a few yards, fortunately, was the vat-room door. Every vat was big enough to immerse two or three men at a time. The water was hot and deep. Soap lost was only with difficulty recovered. It was not provided by the baths people and that was the only snag. The rest was undiluted joy. The big, steamy room with its great tubs and innumerable steam pipes and water pipes rang with the noise of many voices raised in song or badinage or in exultant whoops of sheer delight.

On one memorable occasion the noise was suddenly reduced in the quarter near the towing path, gradually to subside everywhere when it was realised that some very important people had arrived to view baths and bathers. In fact there were two, Mr Asquith, the Prime Minister, and Sir John French, our Commander-in-Chief.[3] Evidently we and our immediate surroundings were reckoned among the Sights Worth Seeing. Somebody raised a cheer and it was soon taken up by the whole bath house, those away at the back not knowing what it was all about but joining in for the fun of it.

After far too short a time in the vats, the men reluctantly went back to the dressing room via the towing path, where no doubt they looked a bright pink to the onlookers across the river. At the stoving-room hatch they were given their fumigated clothes, which smelt vilely of scorching. Then they dressed and paraded outside in the street with pleased and shining faces, ready and willing to tackle the war, including its minor evils, once again.

In any detailed account of the war of 1914-18, sooner or later the time must come to mention *them*, the inseparable companions of front-line troops, companions regardless of heat, cold or danger, who were indeed blood of our blood and parted from us by death alone. In summer, when of course less clothing was worn, they were bad enough. Unless we were wearing equipment on parade or on duty, we could at least tackle them from time to time by day and more thoroughly at night unless we were in the trenches. In winter they were intolerable and became a real danger to health and morale. They were at their worst when their victim was warm, perhaps near a brazier in a shelter, wearing thigh boots and equipment over a jerkin. In such a pickle men suffered torments for they could not reach them and could only scratch inadequately. After a spell of duty as night sentry, though it was a relief to take half-frozen hands to the warmth of a fire bucket in however wretched a shelter, it was an even greater relief to get back again to the cold fire-step where, after a while, they could be dealt with, as one grew colder, by an occasional kicking of one's own shins, or by rubbing, cow-like, against a revetment post. In the cold they would lay off, finding gooseflesh too tough.

In billets there could be no peaceful sleep without the nightly 'chat'. 'Chatting' consisted of hunting the beastly things, first in the clothing, then on the person, and killing them without mercy between opposed thumbnails. After a spell of several days in the trenches their numbers increased outrageously but little or nothing could be done until billets were reached. One practice was to singe all round the underclothing seams with a candle flame. Some men even cut off all hems. Outer clothing could, with difficulty, be kept free and was so kept by all except the few incurably dirty and indolent—and such people received attention from time to time at the hands of their comrades: when things began to emerge from these people's clothes and bootlace holes, it was indeed time to act!

Quite early in the war, stoving plants were set up at the bath houses but they were not numerous enough and a mere bath did not get rid of the nuisance.

No rank was immune (I have no personal knowledge above the rank of lieutenant-colonel) but every officer had a batman to look after his personal gear, and these men were cleanly and particular people, taking pride in their 'blokes'' turn-out and comfort. An officer's blankets were rolled in his own valise, whereas those of his men were rolled together in bundles of ten, promiscuously, and thus carried many passengers who were well distributed by the end of the journey, so that officers did not wholly suffer this major discomfort of unwanted companions.

In the line itself everyone suffered. Some men wore a string treated with a plasticine-like substance round their waists, hoping and sometimes claiming to achieve immunity, but it was not so. It was noticed that after a while they 'chatted' assiduously with the rest of the platoon. As one soldier remarked to his fed-up friend, 'It's the *little* things wot's sent to try us, as

Cooker

you may 'ave 'eard before. If it were just Jerry, you shoots 'im or 'e shoots you, and that's that 'an no ill-feeling. But these little bastards never lets up, except when your skin's too bloody cold for 'em to bite at.'

'Dear Mother,
   'We are billeted in a barn...'
That must have been a very common opening in letters home from the front, yet few people appear to have much idea of what it was like. Our barn billets were very much alike, differing only in size and state of repair. Farmers were paid for our use of them, I suppose, but how they could spare them at all is not easy to understand.

My memory takes me back to the spring of 1915. A platoon is marching up the main street of a Flemish village. It is met by a guide who falls in alongside the platoon sergeant and platoon commander, to whom he imparts information about the village, pointing to buildings as they pass them. The guide finally points to a wide passage under a half-timbered building alongside the road.

The order has been given to march at attention and the platoon wheels and marches in. As the farmyard within is occupied by the manure pit, a pump and a dog kennel, they halt in the passage. 'Number Twelve Platoon, halt. Left turn. Your billet is the barn in front of you. The garden and orchard at the gable end of the house and behind it is out of bounds. The pump must NOT be used for drinking, but it has other uses. The water cart is at Company Headquarters just across the road you marched in by and its water must NOT be used for washing. Company cooker and stores are in the same yard. I have instructed Sergeant Talbot to see that any serious cases of sore feet or toes must go for treatment to Sergeant-Major Cooper who will be at Company Headquarters at seven pip-emma. And WASH 'EM first! Sergeant-Major Cooper is a trained chiropodist—toe-nail cutter and corn remover to you—but he likes to see what he's doing without having to put on his gas-pad.[4] Battalion Headquarters is further up the road on the left. Keep your eyes open for it. Platoon dismiss!'

The platoon streams in through a side door in the passage. There may be a pantile or two missing or loose here and there and the wattle and daub of its timber-framed walls may be out of place, but holes can be covered with sacking or opened-out biscuit tins or whatever you can scrounge. The floor is of earth, trodden board-hard and swept clean by the outgoing troops and there are plenty of pegs and nails in the timbers upon which to hang one's equipment. The Pioneers have mended the big double doors and they open and shut tolerably well.

As the men begin to enter, one of the corporals stands by the door. 'Hunt and Hurlston, orderly men. Rogers and Ogle, draw rations. Foss, Lines, Parsons, and Wallsgrove, blankets.' In the barn the men are dumping or hanging up their equipment. 'Shears, save a place for me—here's my stuff—I'm off for the char.' 'Right-oh, Ernie.' Shearsby pulls out Hunt's groundsheet, spreading it out with one end against the timber wall-sill. Then he places the equipment, pack and all, at its head and folds the groundsheet over it to keep it clean and allow movement on the floor. Private Teed unrolls his to full length, removes his puttees and loosens his boot-laces, then lies with his head on his pack, blissfully inhaling the smoke of a Woodbine. Just then Lance-Corporal Plummer comes in saying, 'There's an old piece of tarpaulin over in Headquarters yard and it'll just do to stretch over those holes in the wall. Come with me, Artie, and I'll show you before the guard's mounted.'

Meanwhile orderly men and ration carriers are crossing the road with the big black dixie of tea and soon they are heard shouting, 'Tea up! Char!' By the time they enter the barn the platoon is ready with mess-tins or enamelled mugs. Before they are all served the blanket men arrive with their rolls of ten and throw them down while they get their tea. The two corporals lay out the platoon's rations on a groundsheet, dividing them into four parts, one for each section, and the lance-corporals take one each to divide between their men. 'What sort of pozzy[5] is it, Freddie?' 'Plum-and-apple as per bloody usual.' There are tins of butter and of jam to open, loaves to cut, cigarettes, pipe tobacco, matches and mail to distribute, and soon everybody

is occupied and there is comparative quiet till Corporal Middleton comes in with a big, shining square tin. 'There's a tin of hard tack here. Make up your iron rations from it, anything that's spoiled. Iron rations only, mind, and in case any of you lot start trading your bully tins for love or anything else you fancy, there's a kit inspection in the very near future.' Here Sergeant Talbot comes in, 'Now, my lads, what about those blistered heels and sore toes! Time some of you learned how to march. Sar'n'-Major Cooper's coming down the street now. Let's see yours, Jack. Better go across and take that boot for stitching. Mac's snob-shop's only across the street. Yours, Bert—good enough? Better safe than sorry, so go across. Any more? Right-oh! Nothing more tonight till orders. Cheerio!'

Two platoons of Territorials just out from England parade at dusk in early April 1915. They assemble behind a barn in the ruined village of Wulverghem [Wulvergem] in Flanders in order to be loaded with rations and trench stores to carry up to the firing line a mile away. This is their first visit to the breastworks on the little river Steenebeek near its confluence with the River Douve. Company Sergeant-Major Jack Sharratt, an Ancient of Territorials, who really has no business to be out on active service at his age, is in charge of the distribution of loads. Acting under him are Sergeants Palmer and Jones of Nos. 11 and 12 Platoons respectively, and amongst the NCOs are Corporal Bert Middleton of No. 12 and Lance-Corporal Freddy Plummer of No. 4 Section of that platoon. Amongst the private soldiers who are to bear the loads are Privates Gilliver Giles, Ike Steane, Ted Shearsby, Ivor Teed, Ernie Hunt, Frank Horswill, Jack Terry, Alfie Rush and Johnny Damp.

In private life these men and boys are all well known to one another. 'Old' Jack Sharratt, landlord of the Cricketer's Arms, served drinks to them all, Ike Steane painted their houses, Sergeant Palmer delivered coal to them, and his employer's son, Frank Horswill, was in his platoon. Teed was a tailor, Rush, Damp and Lance-Corporal Plummer worked at Flavell's Iron Foundry, Giles worked somewhere in Shrubland Street, Shearsby, Hunt and

36

Terry may have been clerks. All the NCOs and Giles and Steane were Old Terriers.

To a man they were brave and willing and did their duty as soldiers though not, especially in those early 'apprenticeship' days, in the disciplined manner of the Guards. What they did they did because they wanted to do it, not because punishment loomed as a permanent background. Such extreme, iron discipline, based on the blind, undeviating, inhuman inevitability of punishment is impossible with troops bound together by lifelong friendship and even kinship and it is argued that such a bond is no bond at all but the weakness of the Territorial system. Indeed, as time went on and the Old Pals' ranks were thinned by casualties, and new drafts were made up of troops unknown to each other and the NCOs, the discipline became tighter and more like that of the Regulars.

'Sergeants Palmer and Jones, get them men on parade.' Orders are shouted through holes in the wall. The men emerge, chattering cheerfully and in no great hurry.

'Nice evening for a stroll in the fields, Ted, among the sweet flowers.'

'Get a move on! Jump to it! NCOs, make them MOVE!'

'Hello, what's up, Gillie?'

'There's no bloody matches come in this issue. You got any?'

'Get a MOVE on!'

'Gil, there's not 'arf a bloody load 'ere. Look at that lot of corrugated iron. I'm not carrying that!'

'Nor me neither, Ike. Where's the rum jar? That'll do me.'

'Carrying party is reported all present.'

'Now then, Numbers Eleven and Twelve Platoons, listen to me. Every section has its own job carrying and its own destination. Every NCO knows where that is and if he don't know he's to find out. Every man carries what his section commander tells him and NO ARGYMENT!'

Here Privates Giles and Steane hold a whispered conversation.

'There's TALKING IN THE RANKS ON PARADE. That was you, Gilliver Giles!'

'*Private* Giles to you, you old windbag.' This though *sotto voce* is noticed.

'You're answering, you are, are you? Any argufying in the ranks with your Su-perior officer is a CRIME akin to mutinous conduct. YOU'RE ON ACTIVE SERVICE NOW AN' I CAN SHOOT YOU FOR MUTINY, PRIVATE GILES, IF I WANT!' If mere looks are reliable, this appears to be Old Jack's dearest wish. Private Giles, who has been trying hard to keep his face straight, sees in his imagination his middle-aged, paunchy, walrus-moustached sergeant-major chasing him round the barn with a Long Lee-Enfield in the gathering darkness. It is too much for him and he gives vent to an uncontrollable whoop of mirth in spite of the efforts of his pal Ike Steane to gag him.

'CRIME that man, Sergeant Palmer, CRIME STEANE AS WELL! Now get about your jobs and DON'T FORGET YOU'RE ON ACTIVE SERVICE NOW AND NO MORE ARGYMENT!' The old sergeant-major steps down from his pile of débris, muttering and fulminating. Sections are allotted tasks while Sergeant Palmer, having achieved a stern face at last, solemnly produces notebook and purple pencil, which he licks. 'Number and name?'

'Three-oh-three Fred-Bloody-Karno.'

'I said Number and Name!'

'Double-four-oh, Giles, G., Sar'nt.'

Now to Ike, 'Number and Name?'

'Double-four-one, Sar'nt.'

'Now, for Pete's sake, you pair of 'arf-baked idiots, bugger off, each under a couple of sheets of corrugated iron, yes CORRUGATED IRON IS WHAT I SAID, so poor old sar'nt-major can't see your damned impudent mugs, and keep out of his way until there's something else or somebody else to rile him. And keep your faces straight—THAT'S BETTER—while I'm speakin' to you, and your whacking great traps shut till you're out of earshot.'

On this, their first journey to the breastworks, there were rations in sandbags, a big stoneware jug of rum which bore the letters SRD, letters and a parcel or two; there were rolls of barbed wire, sandbags in bundles, a few ready-made duck-boards, a box of .303 ammunition and sheets of corrugated iron. From the farm the road turns eastwards to the line of the Steenebeek, a tributary of the Douve, but the troops used what was once a bridle track but had become indistinguishable from the surrounding ground, shell-holed here and there. Part of the track was duck-boarded for wet weather, but troops preferred to avoid the wooden tracks when heavily laden, provided that the ground was dry, as there was so much stepping on and off at breaks. From the Douve bridge eastwards the ground was swept lightly by rifle fire, mostly over-shots from the German trenches under the hill of Messines or Mesen, though sometimes a machine-gun sprayed the back areas 'just for fun'.

C Company had begun the journey and had covered perhaps half a kilometre when a few stray bullets whispered overhead or hit the ground with a soft *phut*. Suddenly there was a shout of 'HAH!' and the voice was the well-known one of Private Ike Steane. The shout was followed by the loud clonk of Ike's corrugated-iron sheets as he threw them down. In front of him was his pal Gilliver Giles and his equally well-known voice was heard in enquiry, 'Wot's up?' Those following behind Ike were held up as his

DOUVE TRENCHES
NR WULVERGHEM 8/5/1915

sheets of iron and himself and Gilliver and his sheets of iron were slewed across the track. 'Come on, speak up, you dumb ox!' cried Giles. Steane replied, more to himself than to Giles, 'IT IS!' 'Wot is?' 'It ain't!' this rather dolefully. 'What the 'ell ain't it? Make your mind up, you 'alf-baked perisher!' 'IT BLOODY WELL IS!' decided Ike at last. By this time half the party, with its varied loads, was tied in a knot round these two characters and there were yells of 'GET ON WITH IT!' 'Why the 'ell can't you paralysed cripples limp another yard or two?' But those nearest the comedians were loth to go and miss the fun, whatever it might be. Ike had been standing on one leg, but now sat down and began to take off a boot. It dawned on the rest (remember it was dark) that Ike had stopped a stray bullet. Giles now dropped his corrugated iron and addressed his friend, 'You call yourself a pal! Wot the 'ell did you come out here for at all if you're on your way back already? You rotten lucky perisher! Let's have a dekko. Sock's wet, boot's half full of blood. Where is it? Right in your heel, and it's not come out! That's a proper Blighty, that is. You've finished with the bloody war. How did you get it in your heel though?'

'Well, I turned round to ask Ernie Hunt about them fags and matches.'

'And you think soft Gilliver's going to carry the wounded 'ero 'ome? STRETCHER BEARERS! I'm coming with you as far as the barn anyway to see you don't pinch anything, you lucky old bugger!'

Stretcher bearers soon came up and bore the wounded hero away, his pal in attendance, and their friendly chatter gradually died away.

I am standing as day sentry on the fire-step of a bay in our breastworks labelled 'Grouser's Alley'. The neat little signboard is the work of Private Shearsby. It is nearly four o'clock in the afternoon of a sunny spring day with a slight westerly breeze. Up and down the line an occasional shot is fired. The sector is what is known as a 'Rest Cure'. Not that we need rest but we are raw troops only just arrived in Flanders and we are Territorials whom nobody seems to trust. Half-way up the opposite hill the brick houses and barns on the outskirts of the village of Messines show orange-red in the sunshine. They are somewhat damaged by shellfire, their rafters showing through holes in the roofs, and bits of wall have been demolished. As I watch them through my loophole, there is a whine overhead coming from far away behind and one of the houses seems to change into a smoke puff which from pale grey turns to pink as it becomes charged with brick dust. Now the smoke is blowing over the remains of the roof and the crash of the explosion is heard, followed by the sound of the gun that fired the shell, borne on the wind that blows from behind the village of Wulverghem. While the smoke is still drifting up the hill there is another whine followed by a round puff of whitey-grey smoke and then by an explosion on the ground with a sound like a hollow box being banged. The grey puff rolls up the hill over the fresh green of spring grass while a little smoke still lingers about a black hole. There are two more rounds at the same intervals, one making another brick-dusty cloud on a house further to the right, and the last one blowing aloft what looks like sandbags and timbers at about where the Messines–Ploegsteert road crosses the firing line. I hope it is not a 'short' for the trenches just there are only eight yards apart.

That seems to be all our artillery shoot for the day. Four rounds![6] Now it is time for Jerry German to take his turn and, sure enough, he begins as if taking his cue from our last eighteen-pounder shot. But overhead is a double whine, high up. I can't hear his guns. They are behind the ridge and the wind is the wrong way. But I can hear *crump-crump* as his shells explode over on the other side of Wulverghem. That means they are trying for our eighteen-pounders with their howitzers, firing 5.9 calibre shells. Two more, almost together, *crum-ump*. So it seems there is nothing for us in the breastworks today.

Feeling cramped behind my loophole, I relax and descend from the fire-step to stand up and stretch. At that instant, with startling suddenness,

DouVE TRENCHES.
WULVERGHEM
1915

comes a rushing, whizzing sound with a bang like a monstrous whip-crack at its heels. There is acrid smoke in the trench and a sheet of corrugated iron, full of holes, is standing up on end above a shelter. It waves gently in the breeze as if to attract attention to its plight. As I gaze at it a sandbag falls with a heavy thump over my loophole, accompanied by a rain of dirt which fills ears and neck. Meanwhile there have been a couple more whizz-bangs, one more a direct hit, and one well over. We crouch waiting for the fourth.

For some reason it does not come. The second direct hit has breached the parapet in the next bay where nobody was standing; the first has removed a shelter roof. There are no shouts for stretcher bearers and I return to my loophole, clearing away the débris of the sandbag. I hear voices and here come Lieutenant 'Jock' Howatt, Sergeant Jones and Corporal Middleton. The sheet of iron still waves absurdly over the scene until somebody removes the few sandbags which anchor it down by one corner. 'Good shooting!' says Jock. 'But who and where are the homeless, Sergeant Jones?' 'Ogle on sentry next bay, and Shearsby... Oh! here he is,' as Private Shearsby appears, to everybody's great relief. 'Lucky you weren't at home.' 'Yes, sir, I was on the latrine. If it hadn't been for those Number Nines the old Pox Doc...' Here Corporal Middleton delivers himself of a tremendous noise meant to pass for a sneeze. 'You were saying?' resumes the platoon commander, looking hard at Corporal Middleton.' 'Yes, sir, the, er, Medical Officer said Medicine and Duty, sir, and Corp. Lewis gave me some Number Nine pills and this afternoon...' 'Yes, yes, Shearsby, you need go no further. We are all the same after Number Nines. Well, sergeant, the parapet must be repaired at once, but keep well down. Use that colandered iron sheet to hide your movements. I don't suppose Jerry has any more ammo to spare. And see that Shearsby and Ogle have time to re-roof tonight instead of wiring tonight. I'll indent for corrugated iron, but meanwhile they can scrounge in the old barn after dusk for timber.'

As they depart, I hear 'Shears' rummaging about in the next bay and presently his voice in angry protest, 'Rotten square-headed German bastards have smashed our signboard!'

We three private soldiers lie out in no-man's-land. We dispose ourselves, one facing forward and the others left and right, with our loaded rifles handy to bring up to the firing position. Anything seen or heard by one can be passed on to the others by a tap of the foot. We are wearing our 'cap comforters' instead of our service caps. They are knitted woollen affairs like sewn-up bags which can be rolled up to fit the head or be unrolled to become scarves. With these pulled down to the eyes and tunic collars turned up there is little of one's white face exposed. The password is 'Lasses'. Our platoon-mates, some seventy yards behind us, are strengthening the barbed-wire defences in front of our breastworks. They are driving wooden posts into the ground with heavy mallets and it cannot be done quietly, even by muffling with a sandbag. Immediately behind us is a big shell-hole called a 'Johnson Hole' in tribute to the reigning coloured heavyweight boxer of the day.[7] All around us, except in the hole, is lush meadow grass, sweet-smelling with wild camomile, starry white on this not-so-dark night. To our right a little brook, the Steenebeek, makes an elbow projecting into no-man's-land and swings round, gurgling and plopping, under big pollard willows whose long leaves sigh in the night air. Close behind the willows and behind the brook runs our section of the trench, which here is a breastwork because dug trenches would quickly fill with water. Across the brook there is a single plank, removable of course, for easy access. The German trenches are rather over 100 yards in front of our Johnson Hole. They are at the bottom of the Messines ridge. A road crosses no-man's-land at an angle, bearing away to our left, joining the village of Messines, in German hands, with Wulverghem, in ours. There is little left of either village but ruins, in spite of shell shortage said to limit us to four rounds per battery per day; but both villages changed hands several times before the line became fixed. The shortage keeps our sector quiet at night, anyhow. We think the German troops here must be Saxons, they are so quiet and well-behaved, but we should like to know.

We three have been out and settled down some five minutes and so have got used to the gurgling of the Steenebeek, the plop of the occasional vole or rat, the whispering of the leaves or long grass, and can now concentrate on our job. That is to listen and look ahead and, if necessary, warn the wiring party to retire while we cover their retreat with our fire. Of course, there are other covering and wiring parties left and right of ours, so that there is no big risk that we might be surrounded and cut off. A dog barks somewhere up the hill.

Suddenly there is a muffled pop and a flare or Very light rockets up from the enemy line with a trail of sparks, bursts on its way down and, for a few seconds, lights up no-man's-land from trench to trench. If we look at the flare we can see nothing else, but we shade our eyes and watch the ground it illuminates. The soldier looking forward has noted the place from which it was fired. Evidently 'They' have heard a noise or two from our wiring party, who meanwhile feel self-conscious in the glare, since they cannot drop flat into the barbed-wire entanglements. Now the flare is burning out on the grass, which, for yards around it, is a vivid emerald green. Now it is out and the Warwicks' thump-thump is resumed. Otherwise all is quiet and we listen with concentration, our breaths coming slowly and deeply. After that flare we must be on the alert. A few minutes pass, then, with one accord, we kick each other. Right-hand man slews round a little forward and we two face the direction of the sound. Third man stays still to mind his own flank. Listen again. Knock-knock-knock. Of course! That means German wiring. On the principle of 'Live and let live' they take advantage of our preoccupation with our own wiring to do theirs. But we must look out for their covering party settling themselves down. They are sure to send one out and so far we have neither seen nor heard it. If we do, unless they are obviously seeking trouble, we shall let them alone, and they us. We are not a fighting patrol and in this sector we are not afflicted with a fire-eating General Staff. Work is in full swing, knock over there, answering knock over here like an echo, and no attempt to disguise or muffle the noise. There is a single rifle shot somewhere down the line. Work goes on. The ceaseless *crump-crump* of shelling round about Ypres can be heard plainly, an occasional rifle shot and now and then the stutter of a machine-gun.

Now left-hand man kicks and stage-whispers, 'HALT, who goes there?' The answer is 'Lasses', followed by a giggle and 'Bet you wish I was' and our Lance-Corporal Freddy Plummer strolls up, rifle at the ready. 'Come on, you lot, unless you'd like me to fetch you blankets and hot cocoa and tuck you in for the night. Party's nearly all in. You two go back. I'll stay with *you* till they're well away.' A pause, then 'Your turn now. Stop and wait before you lose sight of me.' I go back till he is just visible and wait, then we cross the plank and pull it in. All in now. A flare soars up from the German line, so they too are all in. Roll on, daylight.

There were growing pains for the Battalion in its spell in the line in front of Wulverghem. One evening the gurgling water of the little Steenebeek and the rustling leaves of the willows sounded more than ever like a prowling but garrulous German patrol. A nervous sentry fired into the darkness and shouted, 'STAND TO!' Then another fired, and another, and somebody shouted, 'FIVE ROUNDS. RAPID FIRE!' without naming a front, a target or anything. There was a frightful din and a few enquiring German shots in return but not from no-man's-land. Fortunately, the platoon commander hurried along and stopped the rot before another five rounds of scarce ammunition could be shot away.[8] He went out with a patrol and found nothing to cause alarm, though, of course, that did not prove that there had been nothing.

Shortly after this 'wind-up' we retrieved our honour by beating off a German fighting patrol, killing one of their number, when it attacked a listening post near the same place. For his part in this little affair one of our men was awarded the Distinguished Conduct Medal, and the Belgians awarded him their Croix de Guerre. Seeing that his listening post party was outnumbered, he sent his comrades back, covering their retreat by his own fire, killing one of the enemy and preventing the others from recovering the body, and only returning to our own trenches when the enemy had retreated and we had gone out to help him. Then we brought in the dead German. We laid him on a stretcher and had him carried down to Battalion Headquarters. There was a little cemetery at Wulverghem and there we gave him a property military funeral.

In May 1915 143 (Warwickshire) Brigade was in the Ploegsteert Wood sector, south-east of Wulverghem. Le Bois de Ploegsteert, le Bois de la Hutte, or

Plug Street Wood to the troops, in the southernmost corner of Flanders,[9] is a rectangular block of game preserve and other woodland, covering an area of roughly 2 x 1½ kilometres. The British front line in 1915 stood on or near the eastern edge of the wood. The little villages of St-Yvon (or St Ives) and La Gheer mark the NE and SE corners respectively, while La Hutte, and the little town of Ploegsteert mark the NW and SW corners. The Messines—Armentières road cuts off the NW corner from Plug Street Wood to a château on a steep hill on the middle of the northern edge of the wood.[10]

When out of the trenches the troops were billeted in farms, barns and huts in La Hutte, Petit Pont or at Neuve-Église, still further west. At the bottom of the château hill at a road junction was a little inn called Au Retour des Chasseurs. The château was said to belong to the Martells of 3-Star brandy.

The wood was intersected by long 'rides'. These were connected by shorter ones but not in any regular pattern that I can remember. The rides became muddy in wet weather and before our visit in the spring of 1915 a duck-board track system had been made from small timber cut on the spot. This was, of course 'round' or unsquared timber or 'half-rounds', the flat sides being nailed to the sidepoles, leaving the round part to walk on. As there were some two kilometres of this kind of track on every main ride from the main road to the trenches, coming in and going out with full load was a wearisome and foot-aching tramp. Reliefs were carried out at night and many were the lurches and stumbles over broken and missing 'rounds'. I came to know these awful tracks particularly well. Before the 7th Battalion came to the wood, two men per company had been chosen as guides for incoming troops, General Staff visitors and others in the Wulverghem sector and as far as St-Yvon on the edge of the wood. When the Brigade took over the Plug Street sector, we guides had to learn all the rides and tracks whatsoever in and about the woods. They had all been named by London regiments and the names had been painted on boards and nailed to the trees—Rotten Row (yes, indeed!), Regent Street, Piccadilly, the Mall, and all the rest of them. I have long forgotten which was which—all but one. That one was called simply, but no doubt with feeling, MUD LANE, in its own right. It was not really a ride but part of a road or bridle track from Au Retour des Chasseurs to St-Yvon village and was seldom used by troops as it was on low-lying ground. We soon got to know the routes and alternatives by both day and night, and conducted many a relief, officers, staff officers, sappers, signallers and machine-gunners. Meanwhile the tracks were repaired from time to time but the breakages overtook the repairs long before we left.

The opposing lines were rather close along the eastern edge of the wood and sappers therefore were always busy underground, mining and countermining. When a mine was blown and a crater formed on either side there was always a scramble for possession if it seemed worthwhile. The enemy lip of the crater had to be occupied if possible and put into a state of defence or at least denied to the enemy. With our usual extraordinary luck, nothing much happened while we were there, though early one morning there was a tremendous though muffled explosion and our bit of trench began to rise with creaking joints; but it subsided without disintegrating. It may have been a 'premature' of ours.

Though there was constant activity and almost incessant explosions of one kind or another all along the edge of the wood, yet, within its depths, when we first went there, pheasants were sometimes disturbed and birds sang.

III

HOLDING THE LINE IN ARTOIS

After the Battles of Aubers Ridge and Festubert in May 1915 the BEF spent the summer building up its strength and, before its next major offensive, starting in mid-September, sixteen more divisions—all, except 2nd Canadian Division, from Kitchener's New Army—arrived to swell its ranks. In mid-July a Third Army was created under General Sir Charles Monro (who was succeeded by General Sir Edmund Allenby in October). 48th Division was transferred to this new Army, joining VII Corps under Lieutenant-General Sir Thomas Snow and moving south to another quiet sector between Arras and the Somme, where Third Army held a stretch of the front separated from the main body of the BEF by French Tenth Army.

Both French and British High Commands still believing that the German front could be ruptured with a single decisive blow, an autumn offensive was planned, with the French Tenth Army assaulting the Vimy Ridge and exploiting towards Douai while First British Army (General Sir Douglas Haig) attacked on their left aiming, in the first instance, for the town of Loos and the mining country beyond. After a preliminary bombardment in which the British fired more than a quarter of a million field-gun shells and 22,000 shells from heavier pieces, the attack was delivered on 25 September and overran much of the front line of the Germans who were taken by surprise. There was a fleeting chance that a real breakthrough could have been made but Sir John French, as Commander-in-Chief, had resolved to keep the reserves under his own hand with the result that they were not available at the critical moment. The fighting around Loos dragged on until mid-October but the gains made were insignificant and the price paid was very high, 50,000 casualties apart from a further 10,000 in diversionary operations.

Meanwhile the French had failed to take Vimy Ridge at a cost of 48,000 men and had also suffered 85,000 casualties in another offensive in Champagne.

Nineteen-fifteen had been an unsuccessful year for the Allies. The BEF's battle casualties between January and December had amounted to 12,009 officers and 273,098 other ranks. Not all these losses were the result of engagements which would rank as Battle Honours. Trench warfare exacted its own steady toll of dead, wounded and missing. Third Army, whose task was restricted to holding a 'quiet' sector of the line for less than five months, suffered 7,500 battle casualties, one of whom was Harry Ogle.

During our stay in Plug Street Wood we found that though the trench and breastwork fire-bays were in fair condition considering the mining and counter-mining that went on, the shelters were poor. Quite a third of them had fallen in, were waterlogged or unusable in some way. I don't remember any deep dug-outs. There was much crowding and discomfort in the shelters. I was a guide at the time but was given the job of making a survey of the front-line shelters to fill in the time between guide duties. The time was filled in very completely.

I worked with long, narrow strips of fairly tough paper, pinning them together into a long roll as the plotting went on. Each little plan was numbered and named if it had a name. Some of the names were at least frank, some uninhibited and some downright obscene, but they were all faithfully recorded. Remarks (mine) were written under each one in words decent but, as my company commander remarked, 'incapable of any misinterpretation'. When a sector was finished, or perhaps a company front, the roll was handed in to Company Headquarters and thence to Battalion, the Company Commander wishing he could write, 'For information and necessary action, please'.

I claim for the 7th Royal Warwicks what I fully expect has been claimed by every battalion of the British Army. Wherever we went, in the line or out of it, we left the place better than we found it; sometimes we left it cleaner; sometimes both, or handier for getting about, or in better repair. There were few places that could not be improved. We improved them as defensive works; dug-outs and shelters were rebuilt; drainage was at least undertaken; communication trenches were duck-boarded, made passable and convenient. Wiring was kept up to standard, though never attempted on the German scale.

On 13 July 1915, one of my very few dates combined with place, the 7th

Royal Warwicks came to the village of Houchin,[1] a stage on our journey south.

On the northern side of the village was a wood, and close to its edge and not far from the houses the Battalion bivouacked for a few days. I have pencil sketches of the bivouac shelters and of the French soldiers who were billeted in the village. We soon made friends with them in the streets, shops and *estaminets*; some were artillerymen, very smartly dressed, and some French Territorials,[2] and nothing like so smart.

In the village was a bakery which we found by following our noses. It was well patronised by the Battalion and I still wonder how the baker managed to cope with the extra demand. He sold very long twisted loaves, some straight ones, some curved into an open ring or torque, and also enormous loaves of black or rye bread which the villagers cut with a special kind of sickle, holding the loaf in the crook of the left arm. But this baker's speciality was a very big pastry or flan with a filling of stiff, spiced custard. These were baked in rectangular tins at least 12 inches by 10 and the flans were about two inches thick. They were sold to us without wrapping. Their price I don't remember but the four of us in our bivvy managed to raise it. The villagers derived obvious amusement at the soon very familiar sight of the pastries being carried from bakery to camp with great care and conscious pride, or of groups by the roadside dividing them with a jack-knife for immediate disposal. Many of us had already sampled the big loaves of rye bread in Flanders and knew that it was good when new but dreadful when old (and it aged quickly) and it needed butter, which we lacked. At one *estaminet* I tried to cut slices of it with the sickle but, though sharp, the sickle *would* come through the slice instead of keeping steadily down for the whole twelve inches. Mademoiselle laughed at my clumsiness and took both loaf and sickle away from me, thereafter deftly cutting regular half-inchers, but she handed me the ones I had spoiled.

The village of Hébuterne lies to the south-west of Arras at a distance of about twenty kilometres by road. In 1915 the British front line lay to the north, east and south-east of the village, curving round it at a distance from it of between half and one-and-a-half kilometres, and between our line and that of the Germans was a wide no-man's-land of up to 500 yards. The ground between the front line and the village was cut up by long communication trenches and by support, reserve and old front and other lines disused. These had been captured by the French[3] and we took over from them to find many bodies buried only thinly under earth and lime, some being within a yard of the trench side. The place was swarming with flies and rats and there were innumerable empty bottles. The French had named the trenches and we took them over complete with trench names painted on boards. The

communication trenches, or to give them their much handier French name, the *boyaux*, had names of such heroes as Vercingétorix, Du Guesclin and Jean Bart, famous men such as Pasteur, of battlefields such as Jena or Austerlitz.

On our left flank, that is, towards the north, the trench system in the front areas was ill-defined, seeming to end at several points *in* no-man's-land. Where the German line was we private soldiers, and I am now fairly sure our officers, had not the faintest idea, for Jerry had saps, slits and hidey-holes all over that horribly wide no-man's-land as later we found to our cost. Right across our battalion front slanted the road from Hébuterne to Serre, a village which became notorious in the coming Battle of the Somme as a fortress which was practically impregnable and was never actually carried by assault. This road crossed at a fine angle and where it crossed our line at a well-known thorn tree there was a barricade, followed at about 150-yard intervals by two more and in between these barricades there was no definite defensive line that I can remember.

It was opposite the barricade by the thorn tree and some 150 yards in front of No. 12 Platoon's fire-bays in Tranchée Sourit that the Germans one night planted a notice board. A paper was pinned to it, bearing the exultant legend in very big, spiky German script 'WARSOVIE BEFALLEN. HURRA.' It was readable from our lines. We knew that Warsaw would probably soon fall but I believe that this was our first intimation that it had actually done so.[4]

There the thing stood and the more we looked at it the less we liked it.

Quite unofficially three or four of us decided to go and fetch it in, in daylight. The idea was to replace the board, facing the other way, with a counter-blast. There was nothing that we knew of big enough to reply to the fall of Warsaw but somebody found a *Punch* cartoon, one of Bernard Partridge's very worst with a primly disgusted Britannia and an irate John Bull and this had to do.

Four of us crawled out, keeping very flat amongst the lush grass, white clover and yarrow. That sweet-smelling herbage I remember more vividly than anything else in this escapade. I managed to loosen the post which held the board, ready to pull it down but not before a careful search for booby-traps. Meanwhile, Wallsgrove, Parsons and Cliff Dawkes lay within stage-whisper range as covering party. Next I tied a piece of telephone wire round the post low down and then pushed the slip knot as high up as I could reach with a slow movement of my arm held upright behind the post. We retired some 50 yards to the end of our telephone wire. A quick, strong pull and over it came. We flattened and waited for a fusillade of rifle shots from Jerry. He was not watching! I crawled back to the overturned board and placed it on its back so that no harm should come to the paper. The very inadequate, pompous *Punch* cartoon was put in place of Jerry's shout of triumph. Again, not a shot was fired. A few nights later the *Punch* John Bull was still out there. I believe that the Germans had a good look at it through field-glasses and decided that it was not worth fetching in. I think Jerry won that round.

Whether the maps of our sector were inaccurate, unfinished or non-existent I do not know but maps were urgently required. Why the proper men for the job were not set to work on it, I don't know. A private soldier was sent for by our Commanding Officer and ordered to make an immediate survey. He was Private Rogers, in civilian life John Rogers ARIBA of Leamington Spa, my old friend from Leamington School of Art. He named me as assistant so I too was sent for and ordered to help him as he desired. Whether I ranked as Assistant Surveyor, Armed Escort or merely Surveyor's 'bloke', I don't know. I held the end of a measuring tape supplied by headquarters, or held up a measuring rod (and very conspicuous it was), made notes of distance and angles, kept a very wary eye open for possible unwitting deviation into that unknown no-man's-land, and thought I was doing well.

We were given a free hand and no restrictions whatever except that the survey had to be finished during our tour in the line. We had freedom to come and go anywhere and at any time. We had to arrange our own billeting, rationing, timetable, everything. We had one boss and that was our Commanding Officer. We set up our headquarters in the south-eastern part of the village where a wet *boyau* passed through and under the remains of a row of small single-storied cottages. All but one were in ruins and that one was over the *boyau* so that it was somewhat incomplete as a dwelling. It had one 'habitable' room because, by some freak of circumstance, its roof was unbroken. We bridged the trench with a door and stepped into the room through a hole in the wall. In the room we found a broken chest of drawers, a broken chair, a bucket (bottomless or it would not have been there), a large wooden box, a straw bee-skep or hive, many empty bottles and some straw. John put a drawer upside-down over the beehive, stuffed straw into the chair seat, made a drawing-board from the bottom of another drawer, stuck a candle in a bottle, draped some ancient rags over the enemy-facing window and there was his office, set up. My box made me a desk and both of us a dining table, the upturned bucket and some straw a seat, and our bed was the straw, tolerably clean and dry, covered with our groundsheets.

The survey was rather exciting for we found it impossible to avoid exposure from time to time. The series of cracks of a ricochet against flints, or the sudden dull phut of a bullet in the clay told us plainly enough when we had been spotted. I was all for guesswork at some of the badly enfiladed stretches but John had the job done properly, bullets or no bullets, and in due course the survey was done, a map produced in our 'office' and handed in to the Commanding Officer well before the time limit.

It was with some regret that we said goodbye to our 'office' and went back to trench duties.

'Stand down and post night sentries.' The order has come at the close of a hot and breathless evening in the trenches recently taken over from the French at Hébuterne. The sky has been changing from overcast to dark while thunder rumbles nearer. Now it is abnormally dark for August and the first drops of rain fall with heavy resonance on my steel helmet[5] as I stand sentry with my mate on the fire-step. Suddenly the darkness of the sky is riven by a long, leaping, branching river of vivid light. I still see it on my eyeballs when the first crack of thunder follows as if driving it into the earth. And now the sky splits again and the storm rages to show that we soldiers hold no monopoly in terrific sound.

My job is to keep a watchful eye on no-man's-land, so I keep my head down to avoid the glare of the almost continuous flashes of lightning. It comes to my mind that in my childhood we used to clear the table of cutlery when a storm threatened and I give a sideways glance at the long prominent steel of my bayonet, close against my shoulder and helmet as another flash illuminates it and all around. We are now in a steady drumming downpour. In the flashes, against a brilliant emerald-green background, our wet picket posts and wire shine with an even greater brilliance, every barb shedding a glittering succession of drops. Glancing to my right I can see the steel

Pte John Rogers ARTBA Aug 1915

"Surveyor's Office" HEBUTERNE 1915

53

helmets[5] and wet groundsheet cloaks of the next pair of sentries standing out in the darkness as though whitewashed.

In the short intervals between the crashes and reverberations of the thunder I hear an ominous watery sound which seems to come from all directions. I am on the raised fire-step but, in the trench below, which has no duck-boards, is a little river, gathering rapidly from sources innumerable, all cascading into the trench. I am not the only one to be aware of it, for there are shouts from many quarters on my right. Here the fire-trench dips down into a hollow, slight but sufficient, where it is met by the long Boyau Jena. My French dictionary says of *boyau* 'i) Bowel, gut; ii) Hosepipe; iii) Narrow thoroughfare.' The dictionary explanation is beyond dispute. Things must be getting serious and though it is not my business, it very soon will be. My friend and funk-hole mate, Wallsgrove, with Foss and Hurlston and Rogers of next door, is out and trying to salvage kit by the glare of lightning flashes. This consists of our haversacks, a few sandbags and my Baby Primus stove, which has miraculously survived until now. They all refasten their haversacks to their equipment and fasten ours on as we stand at our posts. We tuck our sandbags under our belts and survey the watery scene by the intermittent glare.

Sergeant Clarke says, 'We are lucky up here. They are getting all our water though the Boy-oh Jeener into Trenchay Brisoux, and Trenchay Sour-it is flooded.' 'What'll we do, sarge?' 'Your job is on this jolly old fire-step and not swimming about.' By now the thunder is passing over, but the rain continues unabated. From another bay comes the well-known voice of Private Gilliver Giles the irrepressible: 'Sing of Joy, Sing of Bliss, Home was never like this, YIP-I-bloody-addy-I-ay.' He yells across no-man's-land, 'Sing, you square-headed bastards, SING!' No answer but a peal of thunder from the direction of Serre. Hurlston and Rogers have taken our places as sentries but we are now all on the fire-step, dripping and waiting for early dawn and the order 'Stand to', when we shall all continue to stand on the fire-step and drip. We sing 'We're here because we're here because we're here, because we're here', to the tune of 'Auld Lang Syne'. The storm passes and with it the night and over in the direction of Serre a bar of light grows and spreads. 'Stand to!' comes the order, which of course we have anticipated by many hours.

The clouds part, to disclose a thin crescent moon and, not more than four moon's breadths from it, the brilliant planet Venus. It is like watching a stage spectacle, a wonderful backcloth, and we might be waiting for the actors to appear. All is still and quiet. The dawn light spreads. Out entanglements are all glittering with jewels of coloured light strung out on silver wire. The rent in the sky widens, pale green deepening upwards to blue, where the moon floats on her back while the morning star is lost and found as bars of cloud

drift in succession. We have nothing to do but watch, held spellbound by the beauty of the dawn. But the mood is transient and we have parts to act ourselves, so down we come to muddy, watery earth with 'Stand down and post day sentries.'

'And wot the 'ell do we do now?' asks someone, not expecting an answer. '*You* can do wot the 'ell you like but *I'm* goin' home. I'm catchin' the next workman's tram.' 'Wot, an' ride on wet seats on a cold tram-top?' 'It doesn't look as though there's goin' to be any bloody breakfast, considerin' the state of Boy-oh Jeener.' 'Let's make up a party an' go and fetch it.' 'No fear! let them fetch it 'oos job it is. They'll manage, same as we would if we 'ad to.' 'Listen! There's cheerin' goin' on somewhere. There's nothing to cheer about but breakfast, so that must be them comin'—unless the bloody war's over.'

Shouts are heard in the distance and, not very late after all, with ribald comments, cheers, laughter and much splashing, a comic turn appears at the Jena entrance. There they come, the dixies slung on poles borne aloft by bare-legged figures not at all like the home-folks' notion of soldiers. Trousers and boots are slung round their necks and their grey shirts are kirtled high. 'Company Commander says we'll all be on the peg for indecent exposure.' 'Don't know what he means!' Breakfast is up and though the water swirls all around us and fills our shelters, nothing else matters just now.

I am standing on day sentry-go in a front-line trench. There is a lot to do to consolidate this line which only this week we took over from the French south-east of Hébuterne, but at the moment I am doing nothing but peer through a loophole. Through this loophole, which is about a foot and a half

wide and half a foot high, I can see just five wooden posts which support nineteen strands of barbed wire between them. I have counted them over and over again to keep myself awake. Two of the strands come close to my loophole, over its right-hand corner. There are seventeen barbs on them. If we let him, an active German lad could take a running jump into this sparse wire and out again with a couple of high-stepping strides after the manner of a hurdler, and he could be at my loophole. Even a cripple could get through it without too much trouble but his would be a noisy passage among the tins and bottles. Right in the middle foreground of my bright though ill-framed picture lie two empty tins, one jagged lid shining uncomfortably in the morning sun. There it must stay till nightfall. These are only the nearest of hundreds in the long grass.

All across my foreground are dog daisies, not looking quite at home in these untidy surroundings but, if I look at them through half-closed eyes, I can see little else, so brightly white and yellow are they. Little above the half-way line of the picture the tops of a row of about a score of trees, stretching right across, mark what I think must be the road to the little village of Serre. Near the middle of the row is a brick gable, rather indistinct because of the shimmering haze on the damp grass and because it is close to my eye level. I can see very little of the German trench line for this loophole is almost at ground level, badly placed for distant observation or shooting, and their line is... we don't know exactly where but up to 500 yards away, and very soon we must find out. It is a dangerously wide no-man's-land, with plenty of room for German mischief, such as hidey-holes, listening posts, long saps nightly pushed out further, booby traps and trip wires. Both sides are obliged to patrol endlessly and there is so much room that opposing patrols could, unaware, pass one another in the dark, or be confronted suddenly with one another under a Very light, a dramatic situation indeed.

The sun is getting uncomfortably hot on my shoulders and the flies would prevent concentration were there anything on which to concentrate. One of our biplanes drones slowly over the lines, not very high up, perhaps taking photos of the sector. The enemy 'Archies' have not fired on him yet as he is too close to their own lines. There are a few rifle shots up and down the line as if sounding notes of enquiry and sometimes a bullet hums overhead after a ricochet as snipers search for us, as we do for them. It is a bad place for *Minenwerfer*,[6] but they do not worry me, as sentry, for they are inaccurate, or so it seems, and may drop their 'Minnies' anywhere between the firing line and the village. On the whole the front line is safer from them than anywhere between. But the speciality of the fire-bays where I am standing, from the reception point of view, is the rifle grenade[7]—an exceedingly horrible fragmentation bomb. At present we don't seem to have the answer to it, though the trench mortar[8] men pay us occasional visits, leaving before the enemy retaliates, invariably and heavily on both front line and supports. We do not like trench visitors of any kind and make no attempt to disguise our feelings towards the TMs. As a sergeant of ours remarked, looking with unfriendly eye to his opposite number who had just arrived with his men and guns, 'If you pop-gun wallahs came and *stayed* with us, you might be welcome, but you pops and *goes*. There's some as grouses about them wot's all Take and no Give, but you lot's all Give and no Take.'

In August 1915 the *Leamington Courier, Darwen News, Northern Daily Telegraph* and no doubt other local newspapers gave the following information.

Casualty List 13 August 1915.
R. Warwicks Regt. 7th Bn (TF): Boote 2375, A; Lincs 2897, O: Ogle 2695, H; Parsons 2758, J; Wallsgrove 2759, F; Williams 2008, H.J.

After the great thunderstorm and deluge on the night of 9-10 August, the sun blazed down on flooded trenches and the long *boyaux* which linked them with Hébuterne village. With the constant passage of carrying parties the water first churned to liquid mud and that to a viscous glue, warm but smelly and abominable, and by the evening of 13 August it was a relief to get out of it and over the top into no-man's-land. Here was good, solid dry ground, herbage and sweet-smelling clover, if one got far enough out.

So thought Privates Ogle, Parsons and Wallsgrove, of the casualty list here quoted, as they began to pick their way through the barbed wire on their way out on patrol. Who else was with us I don't remember. The night was quiet, with only the occasional rifle shot. Suddenly Wallsgrove said 'Ouch!' Sparks flew amongst the wire and the new iron screw-pickets, whilst at the same time German rifle or machine-gun fire was heard, I am not sure which, though I think I heard only one report. My whole attention was taken by the state of my right leg which felt as though somebody had kicked it hard, right on the calf, inside and from the front, and it felt numb. I did not know then but at that same moment Parsons was feeling his wrist to find what had hit him and how much. Wallsgrove was in a fix in the wire and quite unable to stand on his left leg and when Parsons and I, who were both within touching distance of him, attempted to help him, I found that my leg was out of action too.

Meanwhile somebody had called for stretcher bearers and eventually Wallsgrove was picked off the wire while Parsons and I managed to get into the trenches somehow. I don't remember any more shots. Soon we were bandaged up and waiting for dawn, for it was impossible to move us with Boyau Jena in such a state after the flood. We had not been waiting long before we were joined by Private Lines who had been pulled out of a collapsed dug-out and was crushed somewhat. The night was fine and warm and we had nothing to do but wait. Joe Parsons and I sat on the fire-step with Frank Wallsgrove and Os Lines lying on stretchers close by. Frank, Joe and I had been students together at Leamington School of Art in 1911 and '12. We had also been the half-back line of Leamington St Albans Association Football team. We had enlisted together, trained together and generally went about together in and out of the trenches so it was not surprising that we should go out on patrol together. But that we three should be wounded at the same moment by the same bullet (or parts of it when it fragmented against a screw-picket) fired probably at random by a bored German sentry, was too funny to pass without comment. We laughed at first but soon tired of the joke.

It seemed a long time before dawn began to streak the sky and 'Stand to' was called, but at last it was light enough to attempt to carry three stretchers, Joe making his own way out, through the gluey slime. In the Boyau Jena it became impossible to use stretchers so Frank and I were carried pick-a-back and cradle-wise in the worst places. For poor Oswald Lines our stretcher bearers achieved the impossible after a heroic struggle. It was in the less difficult places that our slow progress was punctuated with 'damns and blasts'. It was squelch, suck and splash with feet unwilling to move at all, while the spare bearers, less deeply sunk, held the stretcher handles and the bearers moved forward another yard. Here they saved their breath for there was none to spare for cursing. The sun beat down on our shoulders and the evil-smelling vapour rose from the churned slime and stiffening glue of the *boyau*. When we met incoming working and carrying parties who were bare-legged for the job the combined efforts of both parties actually speeded the carry, though the apparent jamming and confusion, shouted instructions and general all-round cursing reached comic proportions, and good humour was restored. In some places the incomers squeezed not past but under the stretchers though where it was possible to make detours they did so, my intimate knowledge of the trench system helping them in that.

At last we arrived at the good, firm, simply heavenly duck-boards of the long Boyau Du Guesclin, where we halted and were joined by two more wounded, Boote and Williams and their carriers, making us six wounded plus about ten carriers. We all now had a rest, a smoke and a partial scrape-off. Soon we were toiling up Boyau Vercingétorix and the final slope to the village and the First Field Ambulance where we were cleaned and bandaged afresh. The following day an ambulance van took us to Second Field Ambulance Station at Louvencourt [15 kilometres south-east of Doullens] and from there we went to Beauval Casualty Clearing Station [5 kilometres south of Doullens].

I have no recollection of the First Field Ambulance nor of Second at this time though I was there later in early 1916 for a few days, but there there were friends and if the disability was slight one soon went back to friends. The Casualty Clearing Station was a very different affair. It was the place from which there was no return. Having once arrived there, a sick or wounded soldier went down the line, to a Base Hospital at Rouen, Boulogne or Étaples. At CCS a man became a regimental number, visibly labelled with the name of his disablement. Of course in very many cases this was necessary, the man being unable to speak for himself, but even walking wounded were regarded as casualties, not men, with no right to speak about their disablement at all, unless required to do so. On the whole this worked well enough, but it might not.

At Beauval CCS, where I arrived on 15 August, I remember indistinctly the suffused orange light of a big marquee and densely packed stretcher cases on the ground. There were orderlies, RAMC officers and others in white overalls. I think it must have been here that orderlies tied Casualty Labels on our top tunic buttons, and got mine wrong, though it may have been at Louvencourt or even Hébuterne. Wherever it had happened, it was here that I first noticed it and called the attention of an orderly to it. I had been wounded in the right calf by part of a rifle bullet which penetrated deeply and remained in but I had been labelled for superficial something or other, while Frank Wallsgrove was GSW for gunshot wound. I said, 'Mine's wrong, for we two were hit by the same bullet.' 'Can't alter your label, chum. Anyhow it doesn't matter. It'll get proper attention.' We were already being packed into a train so nothing could be done and I didn't worry about it.

Joe Parsons had got no further than Second Field Ambulance as he had little more than a scratch on his wrist. Boote and Lines had disappeared and I don't know where they went. Frank and I had to insist on being kept together and that was no easy matter for us, for nobody seemed to care about human relationships. It was only by a sort of savage insistence that two friends, though in the same category, could have their stretchers kept side-by-side or end-to-end. There were so many possible points of separation and a helpless private soldier has no power, save that of his own personality, to influence stretcher bearer, station orderly or RAMC man. These people were good at their job but their humanity had inevitably been 'case-hardened'. Frank and I had simply to cling to each other's stretchers and sometimes use main force, or as much as we could exert, on the lifting orderlies for the various carries to and from trains. But we were not separated, though at Rouen there was some anxiety when our stretchers were being slid into ambulance vans and one of us looked likely to have to wait for the next. But again we managed it, or the humanity of the orderly prevailed, and at No. 6 General Hospital we were carried in together. On being handed over to the hospital orderlies we were promised adjacent beds and, at last, we were actually dumped on them, congratulating ourselves on no mean achievement.

An orderly came along (it was then dark night) and threw a nightgown and a towel at me. 'Bathroom. Down that passage. On the right. Any of them.' 'Don't think I can get there. Can't walk.' 'Let's see your label.' 'Label's wrong.' 'What do you know about that? Go on.' 'I know a bloody sight more about it than you do, chum, but I'll see what I can do.' It was not easy as the leg was quite out of action and my orderly friend had no time to watch, but that bath was too good an idea to miss and not to be compared with its alternative, a miserable blanket bath. I crawled to the bath, managed to get in somehow and wallowed happily in the hot water, with my wounded leg held aloft. On crawling back I found Frank tucked into bed. Our case-sheets were clipped to boards which hung on the wall behind our beds and, so far, the items from our tunic labels had been copied out on the case-sheets. The next morning the customary round of visits was made by the Medical Officer on duty with Matron and Sister of Ward and an orderly or two. I tried to explain that my label was wrong and Frank backed me up but we were simply ignored. My wound was dressed as a surface wound. This day, 17 August, was my twenty-sixth birthday.

Day by day the same routine was followed and we both repeated our story of how we had shared the same bullet but only Matron appeared to attach any importance to what we said. After a few days Frank was sent to England and I was not to meet him again until after the war. Meanwhile my leg was badly swollen and at last Matron got the medics to listen to her suggestion of an X-ray. The operation was on 26 August and I returned to consciousness to find a twisted, almost spiral, piece of nickel and lead lying on a tuft of cotton wool on my locker. I was rather touched by this evidence of humanity or dry humour but was delighted to have proof that my story was true. It is difficult, in fact impossible, not to feel bitterness against the MOs who delayed X-ray examination so long. To them we were just cases. To me at the time they were pompous asses, perhaps young, inexperienced and overworked but far too conscious of their rank and power over us other ranks. However, put them all against the saving of life and limb accomplished by, probably, the very same people and surely the balance is in their favour. But how I *hated* one of them at the time.

Matron was a regular, efficient, kind and friendly, interested in us as persons but had no favourites. As the wife of a high-ranking general, perhaps she could afford to be independent in outlook. I had also a friend in one of the orderlies, a Darwen man whose intonation I recognised immediately as East Lancashire and when I answered him in 'Darren' dialect he was delighted. Thereafter he brought me the *Darwen News*, the 'Last Pink' or *Northern Daily Telegraph* and, on more than one occasion, a generous wedge of 'Gradely Darren Sadcake'.

After the operation, time in the ward went merrily. We played cards, wrote letters, argued, listened to gramophone records and, as we gained strength, took over floor polishing. A 'dot-and-carry-one' would sit on a folded blanket while one or two sound-legged ones would tow him along. I was soon up and about on crutches and time seemed to speed away. A buzz went round that there was going to be a sudden clearing out of all possible cases to convalescent camp to make room for casualties expected in a coming push.[9] We thought 'con-camp' should be a nice place to stay, so we were not alarmed in spite of our orderlies' warnings.

The Rouen Convalescent Camp must have been designed to make soldiers

desire fervently to get away from it, even back to the very line itself. There was a wire fence all round it. Inside were bell-tents and marquees. At the entrance were wooden huts for reception rooms, office, dining rooms, general stores, cookhouse and MO's block. We slept in the bell-tents. I don't remember how long I stayed. It may have been a week, certainly not less, but whatever it was it seemed too long. I still had a slight limp but very soon found that on occasion I could disguise it. The routine consisted of camp chores without end. The NCOs were of the typical 'Base Wallah' type who bawled all day for fatigue parties. They searched us out from all nooks and crannies and there was no escaping them for long. Granted that we must have been an intractable crowd, I can't imagine that any decent man would look for a job at 'hazing' his fellow men. We scrubbed floors, benches,

LADY EGERTONS
COFFEE SHOP. ROUEN.

TROOPS REJOINING UNITS FROM HOSPITAL, & NEW DRAFTS,
WAITING FOR TRAIN. ROUEN

table-tops, steps and tent floors. We struck tents and repitched them, restruck and repitched them until the bully tired of bawling at us. We suffered very visibly from lameness, stiffness, deafness and shock at fatigue times but, once inside the MO's hut, were smart and soldierly. This MO was no fool and a humane man and I don't think he sent anyone up the line who was unfit to go. But he seemed to see our point of view and kept us only until the call came for drafts to be sent on (or so I suppose). One afternoon we fell in behind a band and marched into a pine wood not far away. Here we fell out, sat about or played like children amongst the trees and bushes. This was my one pleasant memory of that camp.

One day we, the 48th Division men, were paraded and told we were going to be sent to the Divisional Base Camp at or near Le Havre, which meant 'Up the line you go.' We rejoiced.

At Rouen railway station a group of Royal Warwicks and others waited for a train to take them to Le Havre. The Warwicks were Brown and Rainbow of D Company, Taylor of A, and Ogle of C, all of the 7th Battalion. They sat in Lady Egerton's Coffee House or Canteen,[10] a large wooden hut which looked grim outside but inside was gay with the flags of all the allied nations, hanging from rafters and spars. There were men returning from leave, men from hospitals and men in new drafts. Some sat at tables writing letters or field postcards, or drinking cocoa. Others just sat patiently until some NCO should come in with shouted instructions. The four Warwicks were wondering how to raise the price of something to eat to augment their scanty haversack rations when Taylor wandered off towards where could be heard the raucous, interminable patter of a Crown and Anchor bloke and his mate. After some ten minutes, he returned with a few francs; Jack was no fledgling in the ways of these army entertainers. His mates asked no questions.

Crown and Anchor men could always be found on the fringes of army life. They operated in big transitory camps like Base Camps and Overseas Depots whose population was not only mixed but 'here today and gone tomorrow'. Likewise they were to be found at big railway junctions, seaports docks and Reinforcement Camps. The ones I remember were no ordinary men. Even as children they must have been unlovely and unloved. I never saw one in the three regiments in which I served, yet I was never to make a railway journey or Channel crossing or be in one of the big camps I have mentioned without finding one or more. I cannot imagine them in the line. They were much too cute to get there. There was no 'dough' to pick up. You can't keep on plucking your pals. Their method had to be pluck and go. In civilian life they must have begun early as newspaper boys, then hangers-on, tipsters' boys, go-betweens, frequenters of back-alley precincts, fetch-and-carry boys on racecourses, for ever on the alert and able to sense a policeman through

a block of houses. Their patter was continuous, spoken with a voice always raucous but untiring and effortless, and the voice was indeed the first requisite of the game. The pattern of the patter varied but consisted of threadbare clichés, adages, proverbs, quotations misquoted or brought up to date, snippets of pidgin French, remnants of Indian Army slang and imitation Hindustani, all repeated again and again as new faces appeared—'Now, my lucky lads. Roll up, roll up and try your luck.' There they were, invariably an entertainment but always making money at top speed.

After a while the four Warwicks drifted away to watch a party of Gurkhas who squatted round a little charcoal-burning brazier and made chapattis, which smelt good. There were shouts for South Midland men and others, and they bundled into a train, keeping close together. They did not exactly *love* one another but they *knew* one another, having shared active service life since March, with all its hazards and varied activities.

At Le Havre a bustling NCO marched them and others to No.18 Base Camp, Harfleur, the same place to which they marched when they first came to France. It was a very big camp of bell-tents, marquees and wooden huts of all kinds and sizes. There were YMCA and Salvation Army canteens and a cinema, a real old 'flicks', showing everything as though in a downpour or snowstorm. Part of the camp, that to which the Warwicks were directed, was on a hillside where the tents were pitched without much regard for slope. In the morning there were two heaps of men in a tent, or partly in and partly out; one, a heap brought up against the tent pole and the other, less fortunate, bulging the lowermost tent wall with sundry arms, legs and rears outside where the pegs had come out.

From this camp fatigue parties were made up daily for work at the docks at Le Havre. They were marched down the hill to the main road, then piled into a line of tramcars which hurtled them down to the docks at breakneck and unnecessary speed. They wore fatigue dress, which is simply full uniform without equipment at all, not even a belt. They hooked their mess-tins on one of the tunic hooks which normally kept the webbing belts in place. The wheeled cookers with their cooks arrived soon enough to prepare dinner. Arrived at the dock gates, the men were lined up by their own NCOs and made into parties as required by Royal Engineer NCOs. Fortunately, the Warwicks had an excellent sergeant, Pat Brereton, with them, and the four pals, and other little groups or couples, were never separated. The REs then conducted them to their various jobs. These consisted of unloading war stores or rather of trolleying what the stevedores and derrick-men unloaded, to warehouses and stacks.

The war stores the Warwicks handled while they were there consisted of rolls of barbed wire, sheets of corrugated iron, rolls of wire netting, of 'expanded metal' for revetting trench sides, iron screw-pickets, angle-irons, iron girders, light railway metals in sections, timber and great bundles of sandbags—all old friends of a sort. There were also great bundles of clothing sewn up in sacking and cases of canned goods. The work was arduous and the great derricks stopped swinging only when the midday cease-work whistle blew. Then there was a tremendous rush to where the wheeled cookers were gathered. The soldier dock labourers were allowed one hour for the inevitable bully-beef stew and for a smoke if they were lucky. After their scanty dinner they settled down behind the shelter of the big seawall embankment to risk their hard-earned scanty pay on a housey-housey card. There was the chance of 'coming up', perhaps on a 'buckshee card', that is a free card given sometimes by the operator, and which, if it gave him a House Full or 'Top of the Whack' would make his private soldier's pay look barely worth picking up. If there was no luck there had at least been a little of this apparently endless Base Camp existence spent and the day of release brought nearer in a pleasant and exciting way. The fact that on that day they would begin their journey up the line again did not disturb them. The line was 'where they belonged', their temporary home, the real one being unobtainable except by a fortunate Blighty wound bad enough to get them back across the Channel (and not *too* bad, of course, but some folks were hard to satisfy). Home was where their families were but, after all, their *friends* were up the line.

At such big depots Base Wallahs flourished at their detestable worst. There was something about a true Base Wallah that was hateful and those most hated were the NCOs who had most to do with the constant stream of troops going up to and down from the line. He was sometimes an old time-serving Regular or even an Old Contemptible but was none the better for that. He was efficient at his job, otherwise he would lose it and join the pool of men

awaiting a posting up the line. He did nothing that would provoke a legitimate complaint and was fairly safe if one was laid, for his services were valuable. He had to play safe. He had to be seen, and especially heard, in the big Base Camps, in the huge aggregations of hutments and tents around the parade grounds, sometimes on the staff of smaller reinforcement camps, convalescent camps and the like. Usually a sergeant or at least a corporal, he was older than most, his face more or less empurpled; he was thick in the neck and jowled, his eyes bloodshot, his voice raucous and loud. He had a shifty, darting glance, an air of suspicion and an unconcealed look as if to say, *'I'm all right, damn you.'* Overseas he was tolerated with a fair amount of humour, for the men he bullied knew that they would soon be moving on. At home in England he was hard to bear and made posting overseas an event to which one might even look forward with some degree of consolation, if not relief. The Base Wallah had the effect of making soldiers glad to get up the line again. There, whatever the conditions, they were out of the sound of the everlasting *bawling*, of the raucous, insolent cliché, the insufferably boring homilies, the boasting, the stamping, the grisly jests about Germans, the veiled or open threats of punishment, the insults to decent men.

In 1915 men from 48th Division's Base Camp at Le Havre were sent not directly to their own battalions but to a reinforcement camp near Elverdinghe [Elverdinge] at an equal distance of about 3½ miles from Poperinghe and Ypres. Why this camp was there when the division was south of Arras I do not know. The grouping of men at such camps were called Entrenching Battalions though that near Elverdinghe was of no more than company strength in November 1915. They were employed on trench and other repair work on the Ypres defences *behind* the line. Their stay at the camp might be anything from a few days to a few weeks, depending upon the call for reinforcements.

Brown, Ogle, Rainbow and Taylor of the 7th Warwicks had heard rumours that they were going into the Salient and thence—'if you survive', as a sergeant kindly put it—to their own battalion. The journey to 'Pop' was the usual horse-box crawl and they slept most of the way. The train stopped at Poperinghe, where ordinary civilian life seemed to be going on amongst crowds of soldiers. They were directed, along with others, to their camp and marched along a *pavé* road which was bordered with ditches brimming full while a cold drizzle fell. They could hear the rumble and clatter of ammunition limbers and General Service wagons approaching them from both directions, and when the bouncing, slewing vehicles came alongside they had to break ranks to let every man look after himself. In the distance they heard the everlasting *crump-crump* of shellbursts. They could see, straight ahead in the grey northern sky, four black smudges which lengthened downwards with a wriggling caterpillar motion till four black

Elverdinghe
bei POPERINGHE

rings detached themselves, wobbling downwards. These were German 5.9 howitzer shellbursts, 'Woolly Bears' or 'Handcuff Kings', timed by fuse to explode over crossroads or any well-used stretch of road. The four Warwicks and their companions did not greet these familiar sights and sounds with joy but nevertheless had a strange feeling that they were 'back where they belonged'. A guide fell in with the party well this side of the Woolly Bear crossroads and when on the right they saw a windmill amongst a group of houses the guide said, 'That's the bloody place.' Soon the tops of bell-tents appeared at the near side of the houses. It was not a big camp. There may have been a score of tents on an acre of ground. In front was the deep road ditch running full. Along the northern side another ditch would have emptied, if it could, into the road ditch. Instead it slopped over to the camp.

The whole site, except perhaps one corner, was a morass. It had been set up in summer, of course, and now the campers had to make the best of a very bad job. From the road gate great bundles of brushwood had been laid so that, in theory at least, men could enter and leave camp without getting water over the boot-tops but in practice some of the bundles tipped sideways and the duck-boards laid on them were incomplete in many places. Some of the wooden tent floors were almost awash and the pegs were always coming out.

To dry themselves and to cook what they bought from a little shop by the windmill, men made stoves and ovens of biscuit tins, when they could get them, which they placed on little platforms of clay on the wooden tent floors at the entrance to the tent. From the stove to the outer air was a tin pipe lagged with clay. This ended a couple of feet or so away from the tent wall in a vertical pipe or chimney with a jam-tin cowl. For the majority, all this was far too much trouble and risk but the four Warwicks had quite a good stove. There was no shortage of water when the tent seemed about to scorch.

The little general shop by the windmill sold groceries at high prices. Some said the shopkeepers deserved all they made for hanging on so near the lines[11] and supplying so many wants. Others were less complimentary. The Warwicks bought Quaker oats to cook on their stove, for it did not take long to cook. Fuel was a problem and any bit of wood, wet or dry, was precious.

Trench-repair and construction parties went up to and beyond Brielen and Le Château des Trois Tours[12] and to many other places by day or by night as required. By day they marched in small parties separated by long distances, for German observation balloons were watching the roads and there was no cover from shrapnel. When the Handcuff King appeared close, men prostrated themselves, sometimes as close to the brimming ditches as possible; but most old hands knew it was of little use and that lying flat exposed more of themselves to risk. There was no steel helmet there. They were a mud-bedraggled crowd, those Warwicks, Worcesters, Gloucesters and

Ox and Bucks, but one day their numbers were not only augmented but enlivened and adorned by a very small detachment of Coldstream Guards, perhaps six or eight under a corporal. They had a tent and did the same chores and fatigues as the others. They arrived clean, kept clean and it was maintained by some that they did not even get dirty with work. They kept clean on the roads, so far as that was at all possible, because their discipline did not allow them to break ranks without an order. As their corporal apparently recognised no Handcuff Kings, he just kept on marching and his men did likewise without alteration of pace or step. To have left the ranks would have counted as absence without leave, or worse. On their return, spattered with mud from the hurrying limbers, they got themselves clean before they did anything else. The corporal had found a large log or fallen tree and they rolled it to the comparatively dry corner already mentioned. On this they sat, with groundsheets, brushes and button sticks, and achieved a turn-out fit for a ceremonial parade. When somebody remarked, their reply, after a good look at 'The Others', and a loud guffaw in unison, was simply 'Passes the bloody time, don't it.'

Late one afternoon a shellburst set fire to hay and straw in a farmyard near the camp. In this place there was a store of .303 rifle ammunition. This the men did not know when they were ordered out in haste to douse the blaze but by the time they were entering the farmyard some of the boxes were alight and cartridges were exploding in volleys. Fortunately for the firemen they had been stacked only a few here and there and most of them were soon dragged to safety but it was an exciting affair the few minutes it lasted. The already burning boxes had to be left to burn out while the men took cover after hastily removing the straw. There were no casualties but the Flemish farmer carried on in a manner shocking to hear until a Flemish-speaking officer took him aside and said or did something to pacify him.

The heavy rains of approaching winter seemed likely to turn the camp area into a lake. It was decided to set up a new camp on a dry site close to a pinewood on the other side of the road and nearer to Poperinghe. The advance party consisted of the camp Sergeant-Major, camp Quartermaster-Sergeant and Privates Brown, Ogle and Taylor of the Royal Warwicks. Two tents were pitched near the farm. The first requirement was a headquarters hut. This was designed by the two warrant officers, who also did the biscuit-tin roof of which they were very proud. After the site was cleared and levelled, it was pegged out to about 12 foot by 16 foot. Then the workmen were given a big felling axe and sent into the pinewood to fell larch saplings for framing poles and rafters. The corner posts were hammered in to about 5 foot in height, then horizontals were tied to them at ground and eaves levels. The ridge pole was supported by poles inclined towards each

W.H.BROWN
J.TAYLOR Fect
H.OGLE Xa. 1915

Beginning
of
Camp
between
Elverdinsh &
Poperinghe.

W. POP___ HE.

J.Taylor. K. 1916
in attack on Pozières
W.H.Brown. K. 1916 in
Stokes Gun Accident

ROYAL WARWICKSHIRE

72

other from the gable ends like old-fashioned English crucks. To the outside of the framing were tied bundles of 3 foot straw, making a close, thick wall. Inside, the spaces between the close-set verticals were filled with wattle and daub made with clay, twigs and straw, and this inner wall was, at the gable ends, continued up to the ridge. The exposed top ends of the straw bundles were each given a little roof of biscuit-tin sheet bedded into the clay wall above the straw. At the sides of the hut the bundles were protected by the overhang of the roof. This was made entirely of biscuit-tin sheets and included the porch, which was set diagonally at a corner, the 'valleys' between porch and roof being properly 'swept' by bending and hammering. The windows were in the gable ends. There was a biscuit-tin chimney with a cowl, set in the middle of the roof, near the ridge, the WOs having managed to scrounge one of the little cast-iron, bucket-shaped stoves from somewhere. The sergeant-major was disappointed with his chimney at which he had hammered away with a homemade mallet on a tree stump for half a morning, making a wonderful job of the jointing, but when he came to fix it he found that he had not allowed for the pitch of the roof so that his chimney stuck out at a very decided angle. However, after gazing sadly at it from several points of view he said, 'Well, my lads, I'll stake my crown[13] there isn't another like it on the British front. Anyhow, there the bugger stays.'

This job was like the gift of a Boy Scout holiday to the three Warwicks. They worked in an atmosphere fragrant with resinous pine and with wood smoke, for a cooking fire of larch chips and twigs was kept going under a shelter of branches. They had their rations at midday with the friendly warrant officers, who saw that they lacked nothing, including smokes, which they themselves enjoyed. They were thankful indeed to be away from the abominable camp in the morass for the greater part of the day.

The job was barely finished when a draft was made up for the line and they were in it. Sergeant-Major said goodbye to them, adding the well-known, 'Up the line you go, my lads, and the very best of luck.'

I remember little of the return journey to the Battalion except the French railway carriage in which we travelled. This was, for us, an unusually luxurious way of getting about or so we thought when we first boarded the train. Our compartment was a double one. In the place where the dividing wall between two ordinary compartments would have been there was a pair of seats, back to back, with a fairway around both ends and, above them, a big strong luggage rack. Seats and racks were all of slatted hardwood rather widely spaced, this being the fashion in tram seats in those days though I had not seen it in railway trains before, all our previous journeys having been in horse vans. The seats were supposed to be shaped to the body curves but, as Jack Taylor remarked after we had all begun to fidget, 'The Frenchies

"UP THE LINE — WITH THE BEST OF LUCK

are rum folk. They speak different, they act different and, damn me, if their arses aren't different! How're you getting on, Jack?' Jack Rainbow replied, 'I ain't, I'm getting off.' He stood up and continued, 'I'm worn about me pin bones. They seem to get wedged between these blasted slats when they aren't getting worn down on top of 'em. I'm going to sit on the arm of the seat, to get a change of ache!' Billy Brown was already trying the big luggage rack above our heads, sharing it with some fair weight of equipment, and there he stayed until smoke and general fug forced him down. There were no corridors and no conveniences, and no one knew when the train might stop or go on again when it did stop. Anyone who could not wait had to use the open window.

We were travelling south and, as we heard that the division was still in the sector between Arras and Albert, we expected to be turned out at Louvencourt. Whether this was so or not I do not remember but we had several kilometres to walk to the Battalion. They were not at Hébuterne but at the neighbouring village of Foncquevillers to the north of it. Of our walk I remember only the end of it when we saw the first gable of the village which announced in large letters BYRRH.

It was 20 December 1915, Christmas week, and we were in good time to spend it with our pals wherever we might be on the Day. There were *Daily Mail* Christmas puddings in tins, which had already arrived and were waiting in the quartermaster's stores in 'Fonky'. That was the first news we heard.

We had first to report to Battalion Headquarters. The Adjutant greeted us cheerily as befitted the season and, perhaps, also the occasion. I happened to be the last one out and thought the Adjutant had fixed me with an eye, as if to say, '*That* fellow's back. I'll find him a job.' On Christmas Eve we were out of the firing line and in the village to C Company's great joy. I was told I was wanted at Battalion Headquarters. I reported and an orderly told me to go to the cookhouse. I brightened up. As I entered, the cook barely looked up in recognition, slung a brace of pheasants at me and said, 'Pluck them stinking bastards and DON'T BREAK THE SKIN!' They were high birds and had very tender skin, and I thought they ought to have been plucked or, better, buried long ago. I handed them back to the sergeant cook and hung about, obviously waiting for something, but he, holding the birds at arm's length, cried, 'Christ! You'd better 'op it before Jimmy Adj's nose brings 'im in 'ere. 'E's not 'arf proud o' these, or was!' The Maconachie ration[14] I was going to indicate as payment for my labour and ordeal was between me and the back door, waiting to be picked up. There was not much room up my tunic (loose though it usually as in those lean times[15]) because of the Ideal Milk tin that happened to be there, though all Cookie could see, if he was not still gazing at the wretched birds, was my perfectly correct back view.

La Haie Château

Foncquevillers is a village about 18 kilometres south-west of Arras. To the troops it was Fonky Villas or just Fonky. The British front line stood along its eastern outskirts in 1915-16. Opposite and a little south is the smaller village of Gommecourt, then, and for a long time afterwards, in German hands. The opposing trench systems were 500 yards apart, narrowing at the western corner of Gommecourt Park to 200 yards, then widening again to 500 yards toward Hébuterne. Behind our village and lines were the back-area or 'rest' villages of Souastre, St-Armand and Bayencourt. Nearer to Fonky and about half-way to Bayencourt was the Château de la Haie where sometimes we went in reserve. Close in front of the château was a system of strongpoints which looked anything but strong but had to be manned. Wet and unpleasant they were, though free from all German unpleasantness except shrapnel and gas.

In Fonky itself the support lines were on the borders of the village and the houses were being smashed up by *Minenwerfer* in the German lines. These *Minenwerfer*, literally 'mine throwers', were big clumsy trench mortars. They lobbed, with a very high trajectory, missiles which looked like five-gallon oildrums into our trenches and into the village. We spoke of the missiles familiarly but not affectionately as Minnies. They could easily be seen in the sky before they descended, slowly turning over. They fell with a dead bump and then, sometimes after an uncomfortable delay, went off with a tremendous roar. As the roar subsided, the accompaniment of falling pantiles could be heard, gradually trailing off until one might think all was over; but invariably there was another slither and tinkle, sometimes minutes afterwards. A glance aloft, if we were uncomfortably near, would show still more tiles precariously balanced, to fall in their own good time.

Fonky had what had been a fine old church, dated 1683 in ironwork on the western face of the tower, of which not one face was intact. I managed to make a very quick colour sketch of the church after a shell had destroyed

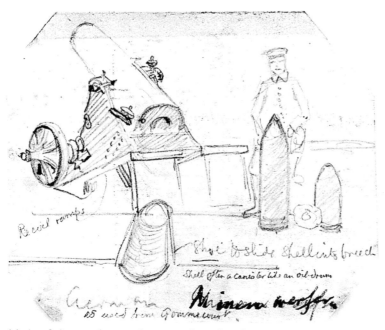

Recoil ramps

Shoe to slide Shell into breech

Shell often a canes or like an oil-drum

As used here Gommecourt.

Minenwerfer

two-thirds of the south-west buttress, but the place was not one to linger in. There was still a small section of roof left over the nave at the eastern end but it was being reduced day by day. The churchyard was a tangle of fancy ironwork and rank growth. Opposite to it was a farm, partly in ruins, with a large pond, walled at the roadside, in which we washed our gumboots on the way out of the trenches, though never really thoroughly because of an urgent desire to get round the next corner. Along the main street was a light railway of wooden rails and sleepers but it was not used in our time. There was a large deep well with winding gear all complete which provided the company cooks with good water and exercise. Also in the main street, continuing from the more northerly village of Hannescamp, was a line of tall concrete openwork pylons, once perhaps carrying power lines or designed for that purpose and interrupted by the war. During our stay they carried a tangle of telephone wires. They were said to have been put up by a German firm of engineers just before the war. They could be seen striding into and out of Hébuterne southwards.

When the 48th Division first came there was quite a number of house roofs intact but by mid-1916 most of the tiles were off, the walls down or tottering and the troops underground.

After an eight-day spell in the trenches No.12 Platoon, now strung out in twos and threes, makes it way into the main street, in which their billet is about half-way down, on the left, or leeside when the enemy shellfire is

Franqueville[?]
Dec. 1915

78

considered as it has to be even in these early days. The billet was the cellar of the village brewery. The upper works were being gradually shelled or minnied away, but down there it was dry, warm, dark and, perhaps, the safest place in the village. The Platoon gropes its way down the steps at that side of the building which faces a yard, lights a candle which some public-spirited man has had the forethought to save and keep handy, and by its light and that of the cellar gratings, identifies its packs. These have been brought out of Company stores and contain the men's greatcoats, shaving gear, towels, spare underwear (if any) and their marching boots strapped outside by the narrow pack-straps. Now they pull off their gumboots, put on their marching boots and return the others to the gumboot store a few doors up the street. Rolls of blankets are next obtained from Company stores across the brewery yard and thrown on to the beds for distribution. These beds are of wire-netting stretched on timber frames. In this cellar they make a continuous platform down the sides and at one end. The cellar is lit, dimly, by what light can filter down from the street grating and through the haze of smoke. Men keep their candles for night because candles are scarce. On the brick floor are a couple of braziers (mere drums of iron pierced with holes by means of an entrenching-tool pick) and two or three large square biscuit tins with their tops cut out so that they can serve as wash basins. The braziers are used chiefly as seats and so are the biscuit tins but, when available, fire and water are allowed to play their proper parts in them.

The cellar smells not only of cellar, which is the same the whole world over, but also of sour road mud which, without care, would ooze through the gratings, tobacco smoke, shaving soap and odds and ends of smells from the street which come and go, there being no hindrance. The ceiling is arched, with brick probably, but its blackness has never been investigated. The walls match the ceiling except where they have acquired a sort of dim lustre from the contact of webbing equipment and packs.

The Platoon spread their blankets over the sagging wire-netting and get out their mess-tins and enamelled cups while the orderly men climb the greasy steps to the yard where the company cooker stands. The east wind wafts the comforting and appetising smell of frying bacon through the gratings and soon, with a cry of 'Tea up! Char!' the orderly men come carefully down to dump the dixie on the floor, its inverted lid-like tray filled with the still sizzling bacon and plenty of fat, for the authorities, whoever they are, here or at home, have not yet conceived the unspeakably mean device of commandeering the soldiers' bacon dripping.

At first this billet sported more rats than was reasonable but we found that on the floor above this basement-cum-dugout was a pile of rotting grain which accounted for the powerful stink of the place as well as the presence

of too many rats. In order to get undisturbed sleep in the early days we used to fire volleys from three rifles into the runs under the foundations. The ensuing peace gave us time to get to sleep, though not for long and, until the stinking grain was removed, the rats were a nuisance and the reek of cordite awful.

No.12 Platoon did not, of course, always occupy the brewery but did so often enough to regard it with some measure of affection as (touch wood) a safe retreat in a village disturbed by *Minenwerfer*. The cellars were not easily rid of gas but that, in those days, was not frequent. Royal Engineers might have been inclined to work out the probable load, daily increasing as shell damage transferred weight from walls to brick arches, which those arches could bear, compared to the weight of vats and hogsheads, but Royal Warwicks never worried.

In those days there were many stray dogs in the village and they behaved in the manner of seaside dogs, attaching themselves to any person or party who would accept them for the duration of a spell in the front line or in Fonky. Some were taken into the firing line and were said to be very useful and intelligent in the listening posts, giving warning of movement by growling, but never barking. One day an order was read: '... this practice must cease forthwith', and our poor little friends were officially left behind. Yet, strangely shaped and lively sandbags were seen after that day, being carried in and out of the line.

Sometimes we occupied Le Château de la Haie and the system of strongpoints in front of it. In 1915 the château was almost untouched by

La Haie Chateau

shellfire except shrapnel which burst over or near it. It was remarkable for its towers, spires and turrets but most of all for its extraordinary dovecote. This was a little tower of brick, banded ornamentally with cream-coloured freestone. Its shape was like a little octagonal lighthouse with a balcony reached by a spiral staircase in a projecting turret while round the base was a cluster of small storerooms. I made several sketches of it and its detail. In the plantation behind the château were several deep dug-outs made by the French, but in wet weather these were invariably flooded and, as no pumps were provided, we hated them.

In January 1916 we suffered the disablement called 'trench feet', caused by continuously wet and cold feet. Rather later waders or gumboots or 'Boots, thigh' became the proper and only wear for the trenches. Our trench shelters were the old French *abri* of wooden posts supporting rafters which bore sheets of corrugated iron. On these were placed sandbags filled with the material dug from the trench. By the time we took over, these shelters were in a poor state and by mid-winter many were useless. Some had the remains of timber-framed beds covered with wire-netting. These beds sagged and had ever-larger holes from day to day, and a fall through them meant a wetting. At one time we crouched round coke-burning braziers which gave off dangerous fumes. After a few casualties, coke was withdrawn and we enjoyed charcoal for a *very* short time. Then came an issue of coal which continued but was scarce. Whatever we had, we suffered scorched knees and half-frozen backs, anyway. There were a few pumps to clear the worst of the low-lying places but when the pumps worked the water flooded back. In any case the pumps were nearly always choked or frozen or lost underwater.

As the weather got worse greatcoats became unwearable in the trenches through sheer weight of water and mud. Long capes were tried but were a nuisance and very easily torn. The only possible wear was the rubber groundsheet, 6 foot by 3 foot, or the cape-cum-groundsheet given us later. Under it we wore a big leather jerkin over ordinary service dress and thigh boots. Officers wore 'British warms' or heavy trenchcoats of proofed fabric. I disagree completely with modern critics of our rubber groundsheets and capes. As an officer later in the war, I was never so well protected as I had been in the ranks and never wore anything so handy to put on and take off, to turn back over the shoulders, so easy to dry and clean and with so many uses.

I was acting as orderly to our platoon commander on a tour of trench duty at Foncquevillers. We had passed the ruined church and were on the road which led to the communication trench. Lieutenant Fowler was saying, 'Now about those shelters. You think the whole idea of the French *abri* is bad. I'm inclined to agree with you. They are too big, holding too many men and

they're vulnerable *because* too big—there is a limit to the amount of earth one can pile on top. But there they are and the orders are to repair and use them. Now, you've got a notebook there...' At that moment a pair of runaway and driverless horses with a GS[16] wagon came galloping towards us, scared by a Minnie that had gone off among the houses. Without any hesitation the officer dashed across the road ahead of the runaways and ran alongside with a rare turn of speed in spite of his flopping trench-waders. Seizing the loose rein of the near horse, he bore down on it and within seconds both horses slowed down and stopped. As they were held panting, the driver came running, thankful to take over an undamaged outfit. The officer told him off for leaving his horses unattended or untethered, took his name and number, and we continued our tour and our talk. 'As I was saying, take a notebook and survey the lot, noting condition and probable requirements. Begin tomorrow after Stand-Down.'

I stand with another English soldier in the front-line trench that in daylight affords a worm's-eye view of Gommecourt Park but this is a dark night and our thoughts are upon the expected relief. I, especially, am longing for it as I feel poorly. I have hardly the strength to rub my right leg with my left boot heel, so that my balance is upset and I lurch against my pal. We hear the welcome voice of our platoon sergeant—'Relief's come.' 'And time too! We're staying in Fonky, aren't we?' 'Yes, but not in the brewery. We're in a barn. Anyhow, that's under cover where we can get our clothes off and deal with these little devils.'

At last the handing-over is done and we splash out of the communication trench into the open where the road gives firm standing and then we wade through the roadside pond to get the rest of the mud off our thigh boots. I find the drag of the water strangely trying and have to concentrate hard to avoid falling forward. I stagger up the bank and back to the road. My pal takes my arm, 'Come on, we don't want to waste time here.' I had hardly noticed the familiar crack of rifle bullets on the brickwork. We get round the corner into the main street of Fonky Villas. By this time I am moving as in a dream and my pal has taken charge. Presently I am under cover and someone is pulling my waders off. I hear our platoon commander's voice, 'You're a bit under the weather, old chap. Wake up and swallow your rum. It's only a drop but careful now! Corporal Colledge, see that he reports sick.' I fall asleep under the influence of the blessed rum. Later on I stagger off to sick parade where Corporal Lewis of the RAMC takes my temperature, then tells me I am for Second Field Ambulance and must wait here for the ambulance to take me to Louvencourt. Meanwhile some kind friend has handed my rifle and ammunition to Headquarters store. I doze. The motor ambulance arrives and I am slid into it on a stretcher. The driver or his mate says 'Three more trench flus. No wonder, you lousy lot!'[17] A weak voice replies, 'You shut your trap, Bill, or I'll set about you *and* your mate!' 'That's taking advantage, we're non-combatants, you know! But it seems you're a long way off dead yet, Jack.'

The ambulance took us to Second Field Ambulance at Louvencourt, fourteen kilometres south-west of our front-line trenches at Foncquevillers. There was a railway station there so that more serious casualties could be sent to the Casualty Clearing Station at Beauval by train. Fortunately trench flu did not come into that category, to my great relief for I had already had more than enough of being nobody's child after my leg wound in August 1915. The Field Ambulance building must have been the village school. With its big rooms and windows it had that familiar look. I am washed and put to bed. My clothes are removed to be deloused by stoving.

After a couple of days or so my temperature went down and I began to sit up and take notice of things and people. I wrote a few letters and was wondering what was happening to my friends who were in other regiments. This would be about mid-morning and someone said, 'Here are more casualties.' The door opened and RAMC men brought in two men on stretchers, there being three spare beds in our ward. There followed, on foot and with his arm in a sling, a black man. We had a Negro in our battalion and they could be seen in almost any battalion, so this was nothing for comment. An orderly motioned him to the vacant bed next to mine and he

84

approached, grinning and showing his white teeth, giving me a friendly how d'ye do. I grinned back saying, 'Morning, brother, you seem to have stopped something.' His grin faded suddenly and so did mine as recognition dawned on us both. We were both breathless and serious with joy. It was my friend Ted Pullen, my colleague (long ago it seemed) at Bridge Street Boys' School, Redditch, and now Lance-Corporal E.H. Pullen of the Gloucesters. His face and hands had been well blacked with burnt cork or something for a trench raid on the enemy line, I forget where, but probably in front of Mailly-Maillot.[18] He told me he had gone over with a few Mills bombs and a cosh, had survived the raid but had been pipped on the way back by a bullet in the forearm. This was our first meeting since the beginning of the war. We were preparing for a real chin-wag when Ted was called away for a wash and to have his wound dressed. It was not long before he was back looking both pleased and sorry, for he had to join the hospital train then actually waiting at the station. We had no more conversation—just a very heartfelt farewell and he was gone. We did not meet again for he was killed in action later in the war.

We trench flu cases stayed for perhaps a week or a little more. This Field Ambulance serves our division so here one can meet men from other regiments and services and can enquire about mutual friends, swap yarns, grouse, write letters, read, or just lie quiet. There follow a few days of convalescence during which we take short walks and find our feet again and enjoy the wearing of clothes now free of all the things that brought us here. Then we march back to lousy old Fonky, or equally lousy Souastre or Bayencourt or wherever the battalion may be.

Jack was an Irishman from Athlone. How he came to be in the Warwicks I have never heard but, knowing Jack, I do not think it could have been by purpose or design of his but by accident, having 'drink taken' perhaps. But, once in, there he was and we and he had to make the best of it. I had heard of him in training days at Witham but did not actually get to know him until the Battalion was at Foncquevillers and thereabouts. In Fonky and Bayencourt things and people were closer together and people like Jack were noticeable. It was said that Jack and the Provost-Sergeant might be regarded as inseparables but he moved with distinction in other spheres, being a keen and fierce first-bayonet man. Any sort of Occasion had to be celebrated by him, let them pay who can and will, not that he himself was averse to paying. The trouble was that his pay as a private soldier was not enough to see any real celebration through. A celebration might end in a sort of universal challenge during which the Provost-Sergeant appeared close on turning out time, as was natural, and said mildly 'Come on, Jack' and the two departed more or less arm in arm. If peaceable, as he usually was, Jack was deposited

FONQUEVILLERS

48

at his barn or billet and, if not, in clink. Then once again he appeared, deeply contrite, before Authority to suffer admonition, reprimand and so forth according to the magnitude of his shindy.

Every so often he reformed and became a miserable man but, sooner or later, his reformation had to be celebrated with the inevitable result. He was a devout Catholic and invariably entered any assembly, be it in billet, barn, *estaminet* or dug-out, with 'God save all here'; he crossed himself on all proper occasions and was superstitious to a wonderful degree. When worked up on any arguable subject, and he was prone to argue, his language became lurid even by active service standards. While we sat spellbound under his tumultuous flood of invective, vituperation or inspired 'cussing', he would come to a sudden and dramatic stop, mouth open, eyes wide, hands upraised. Then his face became mild, contrite and his whole body slackened in deep dejection. Then with great fervour he exclaimed 'God forgive me those drrreadful worrrds!' This usually ended the performance and Jack stalked off, where stalking was possible, though in a dug-out it ended with, 'And now, for the love of Jesus, have you such a thing as a cigarette about you?'

During our winter stay at Foncquevillers a lad of C Company shot himself in the hand. There may have been other cases but this was the only case that I can remember of a self-inflicted wound or SI. I knew him very well as a normal and in fact extra cheerful fellow. Fonky was looked upon as a 'rest cure sector' in those days and, though it was actually an uncomfortable sector, wet, muddy and 'Minnied', it was no more so than very many other places. Poor Ted must have felt very cold, wet and lousy, far from home and 'damn-well fed up absolutely' that morning as he cleaned his rifle. He was sent off to a SI hospital and afterwards court-martialled. The sentence included the notorious Field Punishment No.2 and Ted was to be seen on public exhibition for a certain period every day for I forget how long, tied to the wheel of a limber or a watercart in Headquarters yard.[19] True his bonds were only of darning wool, or something like it, and loose at that, but the indignity and intended degradation were obvious. He bore his punishment cheerfully and with a dignity unexpected and I never heard that he complained.

After his period of detention ran out we received him back amongst us without demonstration or comment. His left hand was of no further use for holding a rifle so he was made a company cook, as if to say he was degraded, which was not true. The fact is that cooks were usually chosen from men who had been in the butchering trade so that the best use could be made of meat rations. Ours in C Company were first-class and Ted made quite a good cook and was happy in the job. His particular chum was Lance-Corporal Tom White. How they came to be close friends in the first

E. Underhill
Fonegsville

Alec Hunter
at Fonley

place is a mystery but the SI business made the bond closer. Ted was at least as blasphemous as the average soldier of the day whereas Tom was never known to swear, was a teetotaller and non-smoker who never criticised his pals and did not pretend to be any better. Under his influence and that of his cookhouse comrades, Alec Hunter and Jack Bradshaw, both men of exceptionally good character, poor fed-up Ted took a new interest in life, such as it was, and was a pleasant and amusing companion. Tom White did not survive the Battle of the Somme and Ted was for a long time inconsolable though his fellow-cooks did much to cheer him up,

Scene. Packing cases, bales of goods etc, in front of a couple of bell-tents in a field.

Occasion: 7th Battalion Royal Warwicks out of the line.

Time: Morning, early in April 1916.

Characters: Platoon Sergeant. Captain Quartermaster. Private Soldier.

'Sir!'

'Yes, Sergeant Talbot?'

'Sir! 2695 Private Ogle, C Company to make a request.'

'Hah! Humph! All right, sergeant, leave him to me.'

'Now then, what do you want?'

'New uniform, if you please, sir.'

'What's wrong with what you've got?'

'Dirty, sir, and torn in places, though I have mended them.'

'*Who* dirtied it and tore it?'

'Time and weather, sir, and crawling about on recce, and wiring, sir.'

'Is it your first issue?'

'Yes, sir.'

'There's plenty of wear in it yet. It's no worse than the others.'

'But I'm going on leave on Tuesday, sir.'

'You lucky devil. Your quartermaster can't go on leave. Can't do without quartermasters! There *are* things we must do without though. The Battalion must do without *you* for a week, and *you* must do without a new uniform.'

'But, sir, I'm going to be married this leave.'

'Hell's bells! What next? The more fool you! What, on a private soldier's pay?'

'Not entirely, sir. Education Committee makes up the difference.'

'*That* won't break 'em! But you're lucky. Now look here. I've work to do if you haven't. The girl you are going to marry, God help her, is going to "Take you for richer, for poorer, for better, for worse, in sickness and in health AND IN YOUR OLD UNIFORM!" Dismiss.'

I arrived at Snitterfield[20] on 5 April 1916 on seven days' leave, which included travelling[21]. Muriel and I were married at Stratford-on-Avon registry on 6 April, travelling from the Schoolhouse in Thomas Timms the carrier's trap with Muriel's father and mother. Uncle George Hazell Smith came by car from Leamington. Before the arrival of the trap Muriel smartened up my old uniform by removing the frayed edges of the puttees with scissors.

We spent our honeymoon at 1) Manchester, at my sister's house, lent for the occasion, and 2) Hoddlesden[22] with Uncle Harry and Aunt Alice Ogle.

Muriel saw me off at Waterloo Station. There was a large crowd of soldiers going back from leave, of people seeing them off, and sightseers. There were different sorts of groups behaving in different ways according to their kind, and many pairs not having much to say to one another. The artist Richard Jack painted this scene and perhaps we are on it. After the train went out, so slowly but so surely, I looked at the big, fair artilleryman who sat opposite. He said, 'That your wife?' 'Yes.' 'Just married?' 'Yes' 'Bloody fool! I've done the same! Shake.'

IV

THE BIG PUSH

1915 had been a bad year for Allies. In the east the Russians had been driven back 180 miles east of Warsaw, in the south Italy, the newest Ally, had lost hundreds of thousands of men in gaining a few useless square miles of mountains. In the west great French offensives and smaller British attacks had gained nothing of significance at massive cost. Nor had the peripheral operations prospered. The Dardanelles campaign was in process of being abandoned. In Mesopotamia a British army was besieged at Kut with little hope of relief. The Serbian army, what was left of it, had been driven from its homeland and was being evacuated to Corfu. There was general agreement that a great effort must be made to finish the war in 1916 and major offensives were planned on the Russian, Italian and French fronts. To the south the Italians made a short advance with more heavy losses only to be counter-attacked in flank and forced to yield some ground. To the east the Russians launched a great offensive on a 200-mile front, drove Austrians and Germans back for twenty miles or more, taking 400,000 prisoners but were unable to exploit their success. It was the last victory of the imperial armies.

The attack in the west was conceived as a joint onslaught by thirty French and eighteen British divisions on a front astride the Somme in the early summer. Sir Douglas Haig, who had succeeded Sir John French as Commander-in-Chief of the BEF in December 1915, would have preferred to launch this offensive on the Ypres front and later in the year, but had no effective say in the decision. His orders from London enjoined him that 'the closest co-operation between the French and British as a united army must be the governing policy'* and in any case the French were very much the senior partner in the alliance. They deployed ninety-five divisions on the Western Front while Britain, with a population roughly equal, fielded only thirty-eight at the New Year of 1916 and, including Canadian, New Zealand and Australian divisions and troops from South Africa and Newfoundland,† fifty-seven by the end of June. Moreover the French army had all but shot its offensive bolt. By the end of 1915 its frequent offensives had cost it more than a million dead and missing, and almost as many

---

* In August 1914 the orders to Sir John French had merely urged him to 'coincide most sympathetically with the plans and wishes of our Ally' but not to risk his army 'where your force may be unduly exposed to attack'.
† The two Indian divisions had been sent to Egypt from France before the end of 1915.

wounded, while the British had lost only half a million casualties of whom some two hundred thousand were dead or missing

With this in mind, Joseph Joffre, the French Commander-in-Chief, was insistent that the joint offensive should take place astride the junction between the French and British armies, a point then located near Maricourt, a mile or two from the north bank of the Somme. This meant that there was no practicable strategic objective for the Allied armies unless the nodal railway complex at Cambrai be included, though no French or British believed that, since it was at least twenty-six miles from the existing front, it was likely to be captured. The objective on the British front therefore was a long, low ridge, little more than three hundred feet above the Somme plain. In fact, the undisclosed intention was to destroy the morale of the German army by a smashing if limited defeat.

What effect the combined offensive might have had can never be known as the Germans made a pre-emptive strike. On 21 February they launched a huge attack on the vital fortress of Verdun in an attempt to 'bleed the French army white'. For the rest of 1916 the defence of Verdun had to be the main preoccupation of the French army. Their resistance cost them 362,000 casualties but, in the Verdun sector, they inflicted more than 336,000 on the Germans. The scale of this great battle meant that the French contribution had to be reduced from thirty divisions to thirteen.

As a result, the Battle of the Somme became a predominantly British operation though largely conducted in accordance with French wishes. Of the nineteen divisions committed to the opening stage of the battle, four were Regular formation, though largely diluted with recruits, four were Territorial and eleven were New Army.★ The Regular divisions had all seen a good deal of active service, one of them at Gallipoli, but of the others only three had taken a major part in offensive operations while a few more had been drawn in to beating off German attacks. The remainder, while composed of magnificent human material, were in a state of training where they were fit only for static warfare in the trenches. There was little time for retraining them and the assault tactics they were taught—the advance in a series of waves, each consisting of a long line of men at intervals of two or three yards—could only have succeeded if the artillerymen had been right in believing that the preliminary bombardment would both destroy the German barbed wire and reduce the defenders to a state in which they would be incapable of offering effective resistance.

The gunners were wrong. Although the front to be attacked had been pounded by more than one and a half million shells (many of which failed to explode) much of the wire remained uncut and impenetrable, and more than enough German machine-gunners remained alive and active to render the first advance a massacre. Only on the right, where the French attack took the Germans wholly by surprise, was any substantial gain in ground made while, on the British right, an advance of about a mile was made on a

---

★ Since some reshuffling had taken place within formations, it would be more accurate to say that, of the 228 infantry battalions involved (12 per division), 48 were Regular, 38 TF, 137 New Army, 4 South African and one Newfoundland.

front of three and a half miles. On the rest of the sixteen-mile front only small lodgements in the German front line could be made and not all of these could be maintained. The price of this assault, a price inflated by the extraordinary gallantry of the young troops taking part, was 57,470 casualties on 1 July alone. Of these 21,392 were killed, died of wounds or were missing and never subsequently found.

On that desperate day Henry Ogle and 7th Warwicks were lucky. 48th Division was in corps reserve and 1/5th and 1/7th* Warwicks were detailed to hold a two-mile front between the left of Fourth Army, who delivered the main assault and the right of VIII Corps (Third Army) who made a detached attack on Gommecourt. The Warwicks' orders were to simulate an attack but to stay where they were. In the days and months that followed they were to take a full part in the long process of battering a way through the heavily defended German position.

In June 1916 the VIII Army Corps[1] was making ready for what we called, at that early stage, 'The Big Push'. 143 Brigade (with others, of course) was brought out of the front line and we were billeted round about Doullens. The 7th Warwicks were in barns in and about Gézaincourt. Though we in the ranks did not know it at this time, we were to return to Hébuterne where we had been in 1915 for the opening of the battle which we imagined would drive the Germans out of France.

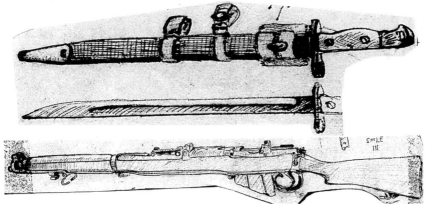

Our time was fully occupied with field training, practice in the use of Mills bombs and rifle grenades, Lewis gun and Stokes gun[2] practice, and in acquiring and getting to know the Short Lee-Enfield and long sword bayonet. We marched to the Citadel at Doullens for firing practice and the testing of our 'New Chum' with the Armourer Sergeant and his men in

* Although Ogle continues to refer to his battalion as 7th Warwicks it had officially become 1/7th. Like other Territorial battalions, it had spawned Home Service and Holding battalions known as 2/7th and 3/7th.

attendance. The Citadel was a huge fortified multi-angular enclosure with very thick, high stone walls. Defending the walls were wide, deep, paved and walled moats. It was, of course, out of date as a fortress but the dry moats gave us short-range rifle shooting. Not far from our billets was a place considered safe (from a civilian's point of view) for live grenade throwing and for instruction in fusing and detonating all kinds of grenades, including captured German 'stick' and 'egg' bombs.

We had a very able and enthusiastic Bombing Officer[3] who taught us not only how to prepare and throw grenades, which most of us already knew, but how to be bombed and survive unhurt, which we did not know, nor ever did, in spite of his enthusiasm. What we did learn, or rather what we had thoroughly drilled into us till it became impossible to forget, was the ever present danger of these weapons to the instructor and his class, and how to deal with the emergency when it might arise suddenly. We found that we could lie on the ground 'fairly close' to a Mills bomb when it exploded because the angle at which fragmentation occurred was unexpectedly wide, though a lot depended on the hardness or otherwise of the ground. As most of us had experience enough of bombs and bombing and being bombed, the whole exercise was simply a dangerous game invented to give us confidence in the handling of the things but no *over*-confidence. So we got used to the *bang* of the Mills and the *bing* of the German 'tin can on a stick'.[4] And I am sure that we all remembered 'Never, under any circumstances whatever, conduct bomb instruction indoors, and when out of doors never anywhere within range of people, animals or buildings.'

We also had a Bayonet-Fighting Officer who was not at all a success. He tried to be a bloodthirsty hell-of-a-man and to make us likewise but he had an unfortunate face, figure and temperament. When he screeched, gibbered and almost foamed at the mouth as he bayoneted those big unresponsive and unresisting sacks of straw, we became helpless with mirth till his fury seemed likely to result in disciplinary action against us. However, we pulled

COURTAULD
HALL
DOULLENS

ourselves together and went though the drill with all its parries and thrusts, and charged the fat-bellied enemy to our long-suffering officer's entire satisfaction. Whether his red face was caused by his own exertions or by our frightful language as we jabbed, I don't know.

One memorable day the brigade marched to a secluded place to watch a demonstration, by selected men of all four battalions, of the capabilities of the Stokes gun. The scene reminded one of an outsize football ground with spectators crowding up to touch lines each side but none at the ends. Instead at the far end were targets and at the near end four Stokes guns in line at intervals of perhaps twenty yards. I was all the more interested in this display because my friend Billy Brown was in our own Stokes gun crew. The signal was given and the guns opened fire. We could see the little shells up in the sky about as far as a lark soars, turning over and descending while the next volley ascended, till the sound of their explosions came in a thudding staccato from the target area. In the midst of the excitement there came a bright flash and bang at the wrong end of the range and when the resulting smoke had cleared we saw men lying on the ground and others rushing towards them. How many casualties there were I do not remember, but Billy was one of them. This put a tragic end to the show, for careful examination of ammunition and enquiry into the drill had to follow. It seems that a shell being put into the muzzle may have met one coming out. It was a very quiet march back to billets that day.

There was no time for a thorough examination of Doullens but we found old-fashioned streets, houses and inns. At least one of the inns had an arched entrance passage for coaches to its cobbled yard. Around the yard were inn buildings, some with a galleried upper storey with outside staircase. I found a Courtauld's silk mill built over the River Authie and made a pencil sketch of it. I don't remember the church. We were more interested in the little shops and inns. In Gézaincourt our platoon was billeted in a good, clean barn. Nearby were the farm buildings and a few cottages with gardens in front. The road had wide grass verges on which goats were tethered and occasionally we bought a mugful of milk, but the cottagers could not spare much. We spent much time on our brasswork, on our new rifles and in clothes mending and darning in general readiness for the Big Push.

A week before the Battle of the Somme began, two men per company were chosen from volunteers to 'run' as messengers between their Company HQs and Battalion HQ or between companies. I was pushed into the job as a matter of course having been John Roger's assistant when we surveyed and mapped the trench system in 1915 on our first visit to the sector. John was turned down because he was a stammerer. Runners took written messages and also memorised them on the occasions, which became more and more

VERCINGETORIX C.T. HÉBUTERNE

frequent, when the field telephone wires went dead or 'dis' by shellfire.[5] Linesmen often traced the disconnection and repaired it while we runners were actually on the run so that we might arrive, hot, breathless and feeling rather important, to be told that our news was stale.

We runners often really *did* run, not because we were so named, nor even because of our Devotion to Duty but for our lives. We were aware that we might run into danger rather than out of it but the whole question of whether to run or not to run, to fall flat or remain standing, had long ago been given up for the individual to answer for himself.

I thought I knew that extensive and complicated trench system well but soon found that it had received additions and had suffered deletions by shellfire, that some sections had fallen in through neglect or disuse and some new sections had been dug for greater convenience or for detours. It consisted of three main thoroughfares or communication trenches, *boyaux*, all three beginning from a wide master-boyau like a sunken road which led towards Hébuterne, changing its name from Boyau Vercingétorix to Boyau Du Guesclin about a quarter-mile before the cemetery. It branched off to the left or east to Boyau Jena, Jean Bart and Randon in succession, each increasing in length, with Jena about 1,200 yards. Boyaux Vercingétorix and Du Guesclin totalled quite 1,600 yards. The others ended on the support line and were interconnected by other *boyaux* in irregular fashion, each about 400 yards long, the nearest one to the supports being a fortified trench with wiring. The shortest route to the supports gave us quite a mile 'run', not counting twists and turns.

We were withdrawn from the companies when it was realised that our main use was going to be between Company and Battalion Headquarters and that for the distances involved eight men would be fully occupied. We were given a small 'elephant' or Nissen hut to sleep in. As this corrugated iron affair was close under the mouths of the guns of a 60-pounder battery which daily increased its rate of fire sleep seemed very unlikely. In any case we had to sleep when we got the chance for there were no regular hours for anything. When we *did* get down to it, we slept, even with the ground shaking over us. The hut was under a steep bank in the side of a sunken road or *remblai* [embankment] developed over long years by the French system of ploughing. I don't remember much about its position except that the shock of the ceaseless gunfire failed to keep us awake and that the battery was close to the raised bank or plateau on which Hébuterne was built. As the tempo of our bombardment increased so did the counter-battery fire from the Germans until so great became the din and turmoil that at times an occasional bursting high-explosive shell was not heard though it was seen as a sudden blinding flash amongst the smoke. To say that we got used to it or were unafraid would be untrue, for the scene, especially at night, was terrific. Long tongues

of flame leapt up from the mouths of the guns. From aloft at irregular intervals down came gushes of flame, reddening the smoke from bursting shrapnel shells.

As we made our journeys, all our own artillery fire, except the occasional 'short', passed over our heads and *could* be regarded as little more than noise, leaving our senses alive to the enemy frontal fire from Puisieux-au-Mont or enfilade from Gommecourt. By the third day of the bombardment we seldom heard the once familiar screaming approach of the 5.9s. We were aware of their arrival only when the earth erupted somewhere within our very limited range of vision. We had in mind the old soldier's saying that no two shells fall in the same place, with its comic variant 'A shell never falls twice in the same place' and while the 5.9s or whizz-bangs arrived in volleys we kept on almost into the smoke of the explosion.

Shrapnel advertised its coming (if we chanced to be looking in the right direction) in the usual way, by wriggling black 'Woolly Bears' emerging from black smudges in the sky but we could not pretend to keep a look-out both aloft and below and could only hope that their rain of 'hot and heavy' might fall when we were on the safer side of a *boyau*. To maintain the best route to any particular spot in a trench system under fire needed a thorough knowledge of it, with all the forks, crossroads and T-junctions firmly memorised. But more than that was needed. As someone observed with grim humour, 'We've got to keep our heads if we don't want to lose them.'

About the fourth day of the bombardment[6] I was sent for by Battalion Headquarters and told to report to the Commanding Officer. When I arrived he was ready to go up to the front line and told me to go with him. On our return many hours later he told me to be ready at any time to go with him as orderly or escort. Another company runner was put in my place but I remained with the gang in the elephant hut. I thought this was going to be an easier job but I had not reckoned 'Jimmy's' keenness and anxiety in what was his new command. Lieutenant-Colonel J. M. Knox had been in command for only a short time before we came to Hébuterne for the Big Push and, though he had known most of us since training days at Witham in 1914, he was evidently anxious that we should make a good showing alongside famous Regular troops. He was still more anxious that the Battalion should survive the enemy counter to our preliminaries without unduly heavy casualties or loss of morale. He was lucky in the former and there was never any doubt about the latter, yet, during the last three days, he often looked across the mile-wide hollow towards where Tranchée Sourit seemed to be going up in the air and muttered, 'Poor old battalion! Come on, Ogle, let's have a look at them.'

Meanwhile quantities of grenades, trench mortar shells, Stokes gun ammunition, and .303, were being carried up the long *boyaux*. The shelling increased in both directions but we gave far more than we received. There was a steady trickle of wounded but it was obvious that we were very lucky. The continuous thunder of artillery and shelling seemed to fill our day. During the final two days we moved under a curving and almost visible ceiling of iron which moaned and shrieked and roared, trailing sparks and emitting tongues of flame when it opened to deluge all with shrapnel.

On the night of 30 June-1 July our numbers were augmented by New Army men of the 31st Division.[7] The trenches were jammed full of men, ours and theirs, ready to go 'over the top'. We wore bright pieces of tin fastened above our battle order to flash in the sun for identification by our aircraft.[8]

On the morning of 1 July there was already a pandemonium of gunfire. It was close to 7.30 a.m. and every gun on both sides must have been in action, for the sound intensified to one gigantic drum-roll, shaking the ground. At exactly 7.30 there was a dramatic, awful, pause when, as our close barrage lifted, there was a shrilling of whistles and some fifteen miles of assault troops moved forward into no-man's-land.

By nightfall we were back in our old trenches with no gain of ground. The Germans were well protected in deep and well-drained trenches and dug-outs until the barrage lifted and we got into no-man's-land. They had their machine-guns in action in enfilade of us as we advanced towards the objectives between Gommecourt and Serre. They had also unexpected pits and holes and hiding places in the wide no-man's-land. Further south, the attack on Beaumont-Hamel was a spectacular failure.[9] Of that day I remember nothing except the ever-recurring rattle of the German machine-guns. I believe this is the only action, big or little, of which I have no detailed memory. I do not remember even the relief of the Battalion which must have taken place that night.[10] On 4 July we were in Couin and were paraded to hear General Sir Aylmer Hunter Weston's message. Amid many other things he said, '... the 31st New Army Division and the 48th Territorial Division,[11] by the heroism of the units engaged, have proved themselves worthy to fight side by side with such magnificent Regular divisions as the 4th and 29th. There can be no higher praise.'

At Couin I was promoted to lance-corporal. Old friend Ivor Teed, now Sergeant Tailor Teed, fatter than ever and less friendly as befitted his rank, sewed on my single stripes.

The 48th Division was very soon on the move again, southwards to the centre section in front of Albert, where the 'brilliant success'[12] of 1 July had resulted in an enormous loss of life and little to show for it. We travelled on the London General Omnibus Company's double-deckers,[13] their once gay vermilion saddened to mud-colour, and windows boarded up. We got out

Cown 1916

at Bouzincourt, a little to the north-west of Albert, and from a bell-tent camp we marched next day through Albert and a little way beyond it on the Bapaume road, near which we bivouacked for a meal and until dusk allowed us on the exposed road again. We were on the way to what had been the village of La Boisselle. On the way the Battalion entered a wide quarry where Lieutenant-Colonel Knox addressed his beloved men, wishing them Godspeed in the coming ordeal.

A pre-war map shows La Boisselle as a small village at a fork on the Albert–Bapaume road where a side-road leads to Contalmaison. Most of the village was built on both sides of the latter road and a short street at the far end joined the two making the village plan a narrow triangle with the church about the middle of the short base. Standing so, La Boisselle must have been a place of meeting, parting and tarrying, for the country folk and not a mere thoroughfare. In fact, it was all that we mean when we say village, with church and houses, priest and people. The British front line on 1 July 1916 stood in front of it and the German front line and supports passed through it in such a way as to make it a fortress.

The British bombardment began on 24 June and culminated at 7.30 a.m. on 1 July when a land-mine made a crater 100 yards wide and 30 yards deep among the German defences.[14] Even so the fortress did not immediately fall. 'Hard fighting on those days (4 and 5 July) ended with the village in British hands,'[15] says a historian of the war. Then the German guns added to the destruction.

By 10 or 11 July nothing remained standing, nor even was allowed to remain lying where it had originally fallen in heaps of rubble. An aeroplane photograph might have shown the blurred main lines of the village but to

the infantrymen there was nothing to indicate that there had been a road junction, for the roads seemed to have disappeared. There was nothing to show that there had been houses and of the church the stones that had fallen as debris had been blown up again and mixed with those of the nearer houses and then covered with earth and fragments from incessant explosions. Only a few dozen iron grave-crosses remained to mark the spot as La Boisselle. These stood or lay at all angles or twisted together or festooned with barbed wire or lay about as they had been hurled promiscuously over the village. Grave kerbs and the remains of bricked vaults were blown apart and scattered and many old brown bones and tattered grey rags with them. Across the wreckage was a fearsome tangle of German barbed wire, some of it on its criss-cross supports or in loose coils hopelessly involved.

Entangled in or sprawling across the barbed wire, slumped over the remains of trench parapets, or half-buried in the ruined trenches, were corpses, both grey-green- and khaki-clad; and over all lay a covering of chalk dust and flies which never had time to settle before being raised by the next explosion. Amongst the wreckage crept wreaths and coils of heavy smoke which hardly vanished before another shell obscured the scene and added worse confusion. The days were hot and windless. The dead remained where they had fallen or suffered alternate burial and disinterment by shellfire.

It became possible to view the remains of the village as one approached by the Albert–Bapaume road down Tara Hill. Taken altogether as a spectacle, it was unimpressive, for continued shelling progressively renders everything at last to a kind of uniformity. But its dreadful details, becoming apparent with nearer approach, began to make an impression which one realised could never be effaced. There was nothing to contemplate in this stilled maelstrom that suggested the works of man as a creative being. Deserted or ruined villages cause feelings of sadness but this was beyond tears, beyond immediate feelings, though all who passed through it knew that for the rest of their lives they would shudder at the name of La Boisselle.

The Battalion entered the village by the cemetery, which was identified by the twisted and bent iron grave-crosses amongst the wreckage. For some reason unknown to us we were held up and spent much of the night in it. When we did emerge we entered a trench which must have been on or near the main Albert—Bapaume road. It seemed to have become the main thoroughfare for troops entering this area and, naturally, it was thoroughly shelled at intervals with the certainty of causing dislocation and casualties. We came to a halt in a part that had lost all semblance to a normal trench. It had been blown in and blown out many times and the once level duck-boarded bottom, perhaps ten feet below parapet level, was now covered by an up-and-down beaten path which in places rose until the trench afforded no cover, and beaten hard only until the next shellburst covered it anew or gouged it out again. In many places were mounds which indicated corpses, with here and there an exposed knee or head. Across the parapet and parados were bodies either lying where they had fallen or slung there out of the way. I never had a strong stomach and smoked Digger Mixture in a corn cob until my mouth felt like pickled leather. The proportion of British to German dead at this point was about six to one. I think the proportion in the whole area La Boisselle-Ovillers-Pozières was about three to one. No doubt many Germans were deeply buried under the debris and in the great crater but I speak of what I saw and could estimate. In one place was a number of dead Loyals.[16]

On our arrival at La Boisselle, about the beginning of the second week in July, until 23 July, when we captured part of Pozières ridge, the situation had the appearance of a lull at first, gradually working up to a climax. We reckoned that after the awful loss of life on 1 July it was intended to proceed by carefully planned local attacks. The successful ones were pressed on with and those unsuccessful and likely to prove too costly were called off and pressure exerted elsewhere, but pressure never ceased.

The Germans occupied the Ovillers and Pozières ridges north and north-west of us, and a lot of the ground leading up to them was dominated by their fire. The straight Albert—Bapaume road ran under the parallel with the Ovillers ridge and climbed by a gentle slope to the ridge at Pozières, and all our fighting took place with this road as a central feature. Yet I seldom saw it, for so much of our advance was along trenches to bomb-stops,[17] the trenches zig-zagging in puzzling fashion, while all over-the-top attacks but one were failures. The successful one was a surprise night-attack when we linked up with the Australians on our right flank and drove the Germans over the skyline.

All this was easily defendable terrain and the enemy had machine-guns in plenty. If we attacked towards Ovillers we could be seen and fired upon from Pozières, and all advance towards Pozières exposed us to enfilade from the Ovillers ridge. There were no buildings, hedges, trees or upstanding features on this ground that I can remember, no cover except the trenches left by the enemy or dug by ourselves. We were subjected to fairly heavy shelling by 5.9s, whizz-bangs, shrapnel and gas, this last being a dreadful complication with the gas protection then in use. The German field artillery apparently fired their whizz-bangs over open sights, possibly from behind the ragged fringe of trees on the edge of Pozières cemetery, so accurate was their direction and timing.

The assembly for an attack in the open by a company was a fantastic affair, having to be done in almost full view of the enemy and therefore in a pandemonium of shell explosions and machine-gun fire, our heads covered with sticky, sweaty gas-bags inadequately mica-windowed, steel helmets crammed on top, so that nobody could really see or hear. Then the junior NCOs had the responsibility of keeping in touch with their platoon sergeant, of keeping their men in touch with one another, often without knowing exactly what was expected of them. One might have to advance or retire, halt or climb over the top, by hand signals almost impossible to see, or by whistles or shouted orders, while, if gas was about signals *had* to be visual. One had to seize the moments when the cessation of shellbursts coincided with the cessation of machine-gun fire, an unlikely event and then of short duration. In action no man could fall out to attend to another's injury. Stretcher bearers could not be used until nightfall when an over-the-top journey could be risked for some distance.

As a lance-corporal in C Company I took part in an attack which failed in its opening stages and had to be broken off. It may serve to illustrate how little the private soldier knew of what was going on in these battered trenches. His section commanders and corporals[18] acted under the immediate orders of the platoon sergeant who received them from the platoon commander and so on up the chain of command we used to hear so much about in training days. Whether this affair was designed as a company attack only or the beginning of something bigger, I never knew. There was a trench, very badly knocked about, which led towards Ovillers, branching off the main communication trench. Its regular twists and turns indicated that once it had been a fire trench with bays but it had lost all semblance save that. In places it was completely laid open by shellfire and open to enfilade from the direction of Ovillers. It ended in no-man's-land in an uncertain petering-out.

From what I could gather we had to attack from this trench either by going over the top on a company front by whistle signal, or by filing from the open end and then fanning out; but there was no confirmation of either. Our objective if we made a frontal attack seemed fairly clear, for there was a line of shovelled-out chalk indicating a trench of some kind parallel with ours, perhaps a hundred yards away or rather more. But the fanning-out idea suggested an objective at right angles to the end of our trench, otherwise how could we fan out? In any case it was just a choice of dying in line or in a bunch before the fan opened. It did not seem to matter.

Communication was extremely difficult in any of these tortuous, wrecked passageways. This one was deeply holed in some places, completely blocked in others, so that to advance one became exposed and had to wriggle over the hummocks. Shelling had already begun and soon it became apparent that the movement had been observed and the shelling intensified. A machine-gun, unexpectedly near, opened fire, enfilading the trench, taking toll at unprotected corners which had already been laid open by shellfire, and all this before the whole company had got well into the trench. The machine-gun fire was now augmented by whizz-bangs and we were reduced to a slow crawl, making a dash at every exposed spot. I found myself at length in a laid-open place which afforded an extensive view and I had one of my rare glimpses of the road, which seemed to ride well above its surroundings. But that information was no help in this predicament, there being no cover at all. A body sprawled across my path, two more were huddled against the side, and when I resumed my crawl in a hurry, another, round the corner, occupied what fairway there was. I managed to wriggle across to the lee-side and motioned the first man of my close-following section to halt under cover, for an order had been passed down. Meanwhile it seems that a lieutenant (Farmer, I think) led an assault from the end of the trench, upon God knows what! He actually got some 50 yards out, I was told, possibly surviving so long because the German machine-gunner was too surprised to fire at first, but then the officer fell and disappeared. Those who followed all fell, some before they had well started. It was obvious that nothing could survive above ground in a local attack without artillery support. By day there could be no surprise. After much anxious waiting, fortunately under much reduced shellfire, an order came from the rear to retire. It was somewhere about this area, though not in this trench, that I remember seeing the red lapel tabs of a staff officer and he it must have been who called off the attempt.

There was a rumour that Farmer was alive and had been seen moving, but he was nowhere visible and we retired. He was seen again late in the afternoon and during the night he was brought in, or returned, with other survivors.

Ovillers as a village had practically disappeared and the fighting there had become hole-and-corner work with bomb-stops here and there and bombing excursions from them to make small advances in order to secure more and more of that dominating ridge. My platoon sergeant, Talbot, was in civilian life a greengrocer of Warwick. His shop was near the Westgate Tower and must have been well-known to many Warwickshire people but 'Tolly' did not live to return from the war.

One morning when it was very misty and there was no immediate action, Sergeant Talbot sought me out and said, 'You and me are having a dekko over there', pointing into the mist along the top. 'Put your chaps ready for covering fire if the mist lifts sudden and have bombs ready.' I did the necessary preparations at the bomb-stop and joined him.

'What's the dekko for, Sarge?' 'I'm looking for my uncle. I know he was up here in that attack and he's been reported "missing believed killed".' We reached the remains of a wide belt of wire amongst numerous shell-holes apparently on or very close to the crest of the hill, for the place was very flat. Indeed, at one time we actually looked down a reverse slope but only for a short distance as the mist closed again. The wire was no longer taut but stood in curling loops and tangled coils in utter confusion. Our dead lay amongst it, hopelessly involved in it rather than on it. Recognition was going to be difficult and all I could do was to help Tolly turn over those whose faces were hidden, and hold back strands of wire. The flies made a close-textured curtain as they rose, time and time again, and our hands were black with them as we lifted. I think my face must have paled for Tolly looked at me and said, 'Go on then, get it up!' We continued the search when I had recovered and, as Tolly remarked, 'combined business with pleasure' by collecting as much ammunition as we could carry. Much or most of it was in bandoliers packed in leather pouches and we simply slung them over our shoulders. Time and dispersing mist beat us in the search and we returned to our bomb-stop.

During a spell out of the line at Ovillers, the brigade was drawn up in hollow square in a quarry. In the middle of the square was a small group of officers, NCOs and drummers and one figure who was already little more than a ghost. A minute ago he had been a private soldier in a regiment of the line, wearing that regiment's badges and buttons embossed with the Royal Arms. Now he stood deprived of badges and buttons and of all honourable military identity and was under sentence of death. He was to be shot at dawn the next day. Some sort of indictment had been read out to us on parade to the effect that he had been guilty of cowardice in the face of the enemy. I was one of many who sympathised but acquiesced, unable to think of a working alternative. Now he was drummed out of the service and marched away to wait for the dawn. The parade was dismissed to its various encampments and our battalion marched back to Bouzincourt.

That afternoon I was sent for by the Sergeant-Major and warned for a duty, the nature of which he would not at the moment divulge. He sent me to gather my equipment and take it to a bell-tent and I was told on no account to leave it without his permission. The morning's ceremony had made a deep impression on me and now my spirit was heavy with foreboding. On entering the tent I saw by the face of the man already there, another lance-corporal, that he too knew all too well what this duty was. The Sergeant-Major came in almost on my heels and confirmed our fears. We were detailed as members of the firing squad, two per battalion, for the execution at dawn the following day. We got our clothing, arms and equipment in order, but what else we did I cannot remember. Before Lights Out we heard orders being read in other tents and the Sergeant-Major himself came in and read them to us. As he entered he caught my eye and looked fixedly at me and then began to read. What he read I forget but with a shock I heard the words, '2695 Lance-Corporal Ogle, H., C Company, to be Corporal.' Then he said to me, 'You are posted to D Company. Report *at once* to Sergeant-Major D Company in D Company's lines.' In answer to the anguished enquiry he saw in my eyes, he nodded and half-smiled, saying quietly, '*That* is washed out for you. Get along *quick* and forget it.'

Over a battered trench sagged the metals of a narrow-gauge railway.[19] This seemed to be a place which the Germans thought should be thoroughly shelled as often as possible. It was easily seen from the ridge and there was no doubt that our men had been seen moving up. Before No. 16 Platoon of D Company passed it they were held up by whatever was going on in front and at that moment a barrage descended on them. There was no moving forward and they did not think of moving back. They had to stay there. The trouble was that about this crossing was a number of dead Loyal North Lancashire men, some in the trench, some half in and half out. Many were partly covered with earth trodden down upon them, and amongst these dead the living were obliged to crouch. One of the platoon cowered against the trench side, his eyes now staring, now tightly shut, his lips moving. In between explosions he could be heard chattering incessantly and moaning, 'God in Heaven!'

Suddenly the barrage lifted, or there was a lull in it, and the voice of Sergeant Hextall rang out, 'Come on, my lucky lads, over the top and let's get some of these stiffs out of the bloody way', and he led the way over the broken trench side with a GS shovel, all of us being provided with them on this occasion. A corporal followed him over, with a few of his own sections who were nearest, giving a hand to the frightened one—not that he was the only frightened man there. Whether it was Hextall's rousing call and his fearless lead, my proffered hand or the sheer relief at having something to do, nobody knew but he leapt up with a will. Helped by those in the trench (and they remained there only by their sergeant's firm order) those outside heaved up some dozen bodies by their equipment. There was no lack of shell holes and into these we hastily dragged the Loyals, throwing over them a very thin covering of earth, then shovelling and kicking down the crater rims over them. It took very little time but already shells were beginning to fall, again at the far side of the railway, Jerry having noted that our men were still there, and one fell over the heads of the burial party, exploding forward without anyone being hit. They were soon in the trench again, but Hecky remained to knock in a rough cross made from a rifle with its bayonet thrust into the ground, and a fragment of wood bound with wire, there being plenty of these materials about. He drove it firmly in amongst the craters to indicate a cemetery, then turned and jumped into the trench without haste. Many of that party must have thought of the man recently shot for cowardice and how something to do and someone to see that it was done might have saved him.

When Ovillers was taken[20] and the Germans driven off that part of the skyline, there still remained Pozières and the shallow valley between the Ovillers ridge and the Albert–Bapaume road.[21] The 7th Royal Warwicks, with the Australians on their right, accomplished this drive on the 23-27 July by a big surprise attack by night without any preliminary bombardment, or at least nothing to suggest a following attack.[22] It was a complete success. Later the Australians captured that part of the village lying further east, as far as the windmill on the main road which held out until 3 September.

One early evening D Company was crowded into a narrow trench with

very small hollows or 'funk holes'. Dennis Jones, my fellow corporal in 16 Platoon had drummed up a brew of tea by means of a Tommy's Cooker when Sergeant-Major came along bearing that well-known herald of action, a rum jar. Lieutenant Cayley and the big, cheerful, bombing officer were both there. The plan was simple. Our objective was the trench system that lay to the left of that familiar line of ragged trees on the Pozières crest, north of the Bapaume road and defending the western edge of the village. As the platoon commander said, 'Just string out in a line at about arm's length in no-man's-land without a sound. Keep in close touch with your section commanders from then on. I blow my whistle and off we go.'

When our Mills bombs were given to us we crept out and equalised spacing. Bayonets were already fixed and magazines charged. We lay down to wait for the whistle. The night was fine, warm and strangely quiet. When at last it came, the sound of the whistle was low so that others could be heard left and right, their slightly different tones blending unexpectedly for the bare second that the whistling lasted. We rose in silence in the dark and moved steadily forward, intent on keeping abreast and in touch. Everything now depended upon local control by junior NCOs, or so we junior NCOs imagined, and it was just as well that we did and felt so important and responsible, whether we were or not.[23]

I could hear nothing at first but the low clicking of entrenching-tool handles and brass tag-ends of equipment, and here and there a sniff or the clearing of a nervous throat. After a glance left and right for alignment we gathered ourselves for an increase in speed, for the German trench had become plainly visible as a whitey-grey line[24] in the semi-darkness. Mounting excitement brought our speed up all along the line to a dash and in a few seconds our first grenades began to explode right in the trench. The German wire I can scarcely remember, for action had begun. Right in front of my two sections a red signal flare soared up from the German trench. It located their sentries for us and there was another volley of Mills bombs and we leapt into the trench while the flare gave us light. I found the trench very deep, perhaps eleven feet, and well appointed. There was little rifle fire and only a few stick-grenade explosions, for we had the enemy completely surprised, but when I found that I was close to a large white flag with a red cross on it draped above the entrance of a deep dug-out, I wondered whether he had collected his wounded here for us to look after, left a few expendable troops and cleared out to defend a position behind or in Poziéres itself. Then I guessed that this was about the spot from which the red flare had been fired and peered cautiously round the near entrance post with a Mills bomb ready. As I did so another red flare, fired from the bottom of the steps, narrowly missed me but struck the trench wall in front, making a wonderful illumination. This was *not* properly conducted Red Cross business so, taking no risks, I lobbed my bomb down the steps, first giving it a few seconds. I heard a bounce or two and then it exploded. It must have hit a supporting post about half-way down, bursting there, fortunately for those below.

I followed it down and found several Germans in charge, or pretending to be in charge of a dug-out full of wounded. They were not stretcher bearers or Red Cross men of any kind because there was a clatter of rifles and equipment on the floor as I reached the bottom step. These men had their hands up in the light of a torch someone was holding. I saw them out by the light of the still burning red flare, followed them and drove them out towards our line, and was lucky to find my sections taking part in a scrimmage. This was short and sharp as already the Germans were streaming back across the way we had come with their hands up, anxious to avoid their own shelling which they knew would rain down on them very shortly if they were not quickly in the supposed shelter of our trenches. I had no time to speculate on the strange behaviour of the gang in the dug-out. Possibly they were waiting in safety until a counter-attack put us at a disadvantage, when they might emerge and take us in the rear. But our action and further advance was too quick for any counter-attack to develop.

By the time we had cleared this first objective, dawn was breaking. Our attack had concentrated on an area where a communication trench led towards Pozières on the hill top. The area seemed to include a support line and other complications, which must have been dealt with either by another company or by a second wave, or perhaps abandoned by the Germans when they saw the strength and speed of our attack, but of that I have no recollection. What I do remember is ridiculous. Glancing left I saw an object like a sentry box or a night watchman's shelter in a side trench. It was a latrine and on it, his hands raised, sat a bald-headed German. We left him sitting on his humble throne, his attitude suggestive of a blessing on us as we passed.

With the rapidly increasing light the German machine-gunners were finding targets as were also a few riflemen, but as hand-to-hand fighting was still going on there could be no indiscriminate firing and, at the moment, there was no shelling. But progress by bomb and bayonet up the communication trench was too slow so we got out and raced along both sides of it, upon which the Germans still left in it promptly gave themselves up and joined the procession towards our lines. This gave us an immediate advance for some distance up the slope, but at the top there was an obstruction or bomb-stop from which a machine-gun was opening fire. When our Lewis gun team outflanked them from the Australian side they fell back out of sight and we realised that we had reached the beginning of the crest. This must have been at the place where a fourth-class road or track running north-east from Ovillers joined the Pozières–Thiepval road. From this spot the lesser road continued at the other side to Courcelette, and another led down to Mouquet Farm, though of course we did not know this at the time. On our right, that is, looking south-east, were the ruins of Pozières and a fringe of blasted trees, that ragged line that had so long beckoned from the seemingly unattainable skyline, and from which so much of our trouble had come.

The Australians had halted at this line of tree stumps and our D Company, of which my two sections were further forward, halted at the place from which we had dislodged the machine-gunners. The other sections were left and right of this but I have no clear memory of exact locations other than mine. Nor do I remember how we two corporals had kept in touch with each other or even with our own sections. As we had told them, they had followed our lead and with a great deal of luck we found we were all, or nearly all, together at the bomb-stop and mainly to the left of it. Casualties had been remarkably few. For once we seemed to have forestalled the machine-gunners and escaped the shelling.

From where our trench ended we were now looking across a metalled road, the surface of which was about level with our heads. It was not trenched across at this place or anywhere else within view. Across at the other side of it on our left was the entrance to a trench. Right ahead were earthworks or a breastwork of some kind looking down on the road. All this put us at the disadvantage of having a very restricted view, and there was not even a parapet to stop a bomb or a ricochet. The section of road was exposed to fire from many directions without giving us any field of fire at all.

Lieutenant Cayley led a party of volunteers, perhaps rather more than a dozen, of which some of my sections formed part, across the road and into the trench opposite. There were Germans in it but after a few badly aimed shots they fled in the direction of Pozières,[25] abandoning much equipment. This trench was a short one or connecting link between others and had funk-holes at intervals but no dug-outs. It was rather shallow as if hastily dug. On the parapet were several German spiked helmets or *Pickelhauben* in their grey canvas covers, and other gear lay about but no arms. I knew that our men cast covetous glances on these souvenirs and on the way back later I noticed that nothing was left. Action seemed to have ceased so we pushed on further. At our end of this trench one looked down upon the scene of the last few weeks' fighting. At their end of it we looked down upon a gently sloping valley, this trench bridging the divide.

Suddenly rifle shots and then a burst of machine-gun fire brought us to a halt. In the shallow trench we had run along with our heads exposed too much in our eagerness to see what was going on, but we saw that the Germans who had fired on us were within bombing range. We had our Mills bombs ready and, suddenly rising, let them have a volley. There was no counter-fire and we dashed from our trench to a wider one with a fire-bay, where three Germans lay dead. There was no machine-gun and no gunners. Close by, on a fire-step was a tall aluminium mess-tin of steaming coffee, aluminium cups and bags of pie-crust biscuit. The guncrew had retired after firing the one burst and had escaped our grenades. Their emplacement was in the next bay behind and to one side of the dead riflemen. There was no sign of the machine-gunners. I looked over the trench side or parados and was amazed to see a few German bivouac tents of a pale orange colour, perhaps two hundred yards away down the slope and *in the open*! Beyond, if I had known anything about it, I would have seen, and probably did see Mouquet Farm or its ruins, taken later on after severe fighting by the Australians.[26] Our attack must have taken the enemy very much by surprise for him to have tents left out like that. Also, our shelling must have been entirely local and confined to the trench systems. Half right and a little behind us as we looked down the slope, were the ruins and shattered trees of Pozières. While we gazed about we pocketed the bags of biscuit and drank the coffee, good soldiers taking their meat and drink when it is offered. It was not *Malz* substitute[27] but real coffee made from ground coffee beans. At that time and much later also, German sections carried a little coffee mill.

Rifle shots began to come from our right and we heard the recall whistle. We made for the narrow, shallow *Pikelhaube* trench and, with shots increasing every moment, made haste to get across the open space on the road before the machine-gunners came up again for their revenge. I drove the men of my sections before me and saw them reach cover. I made my dash across the road behind a man, not one of mine, who suddenly fell. I dodged him, slithered past and into the trench. I looked back to see if the man had picked himself up but he lay still. He was not far away, though our road crossing was at a long slant, so I got out and went back for him. I found myself helping Lieutenant Cayley, who must have been following behind. I believe Corporal Harvey and perhaps another came out or were out. Together we lifted him while someone was shouting, 'Quick—machine-gun opening up!' There were rifle shots, badly aimed again except the one that hit our friend and that may have been by accident. But the machine-gunners were either too late or missed us, for we were all in the trench before the first burst of fire was over. The wounded man had a bullet hole right through him, in at the small of the back and out through the belly and his small intestines were protruding. Stretcher bearers soon took charge of him before we could do him any harm as we might easily have done.

Fire from ahead had ceased again and probably the enemy abandoned this point in order to man the defences of Pozières village. Lieutenant Cayley sent me to get in touch with the Australians on our right flank, here somewhat open, to find their company commander, gather information and inform him of our dispositions. I found them a little way beyond the ragged tree line and asked a Digger NCO to take me to his company commander. He promptly shouted down the line, 'Jim! You're wanted!' and presently Jim appeared. I wanted to greet him as a fellow-countryman, but military etiquette as I knew it forbade such a free and easy bonhomie between captain and corporal and my courage failed me.

Night fell with D Company in the same position, but with patrols out all the time. Our sections regaled themselves on what little hard tack they had left, some of the captured pie-crust biscuit and a tin of lemon marmalade, very sticky-sweet and thirst provoking. The chlorinated and petrolified water in our bottles was almost enjoyable after that meal. The night passed without incident though we were all ready for the expected counter-attack, with Lewis guns mounted and commanding the likely spots.

The Battalion was relieved on the following day [28 July], in daylight because, now that the Germans had been driven over the skyline, movement could be made along and down the Oviilers southern slopes and so down to La Boisselle. Down there was a signboard painted with black and white chequers and there were men with similar shoulder flashes, which meant that the 31st Division was relieving the 48th.[28]

It was very hot and dusty—stench and flies everywhere. My tobacco was all gone and nobody had any water left. At La Boisselle we had to wait. We had a look at the famous deep dug-outs. They were deeper than any shell of those days could penetrate. There may have been up to thirty feet of solid chalk above them. Their walls were matchboarded and furnished with cupboards, shelves, pegs and rifle racks. There were tables constructed on the spot, but the seats, or many of them, were of slatted wood shaped to the body curves and so exactly like those we had seen in French trams and railway carriages that they must have been taken from them and transported here on the narrow-gauge railway. There were bays and alcoves and tiers of roomy bunks in recesses off the main galleries. In some were lifts which raised a machine-gun with crew all ready for us the moment the barrage lifted for our assault on 1 July. I had no time to explore these but what I did see gave me still further insight into the strange German mind. Here also, in one or two quarried excavations in the chalk, were quantities of salvaged rifles and equipment and some of our men were persuaded to change their excellent woven webbing for the wretched, clumsy leather as worn by the New Army. This rubbish had heavy leather pouches for ammunition, one over each front and side and which bore heavily on one's bones and was ridiculously inefficient in action, for the ammunition was in cotton bandoliers. The leather was horrible when wet and soon deteriorated.[29]

V

'NAPOO BIG PUSH'

Disappointing and expensive as the opening of the Battle of the Somme had been, there could be no question of breaking off the offensive. Haig was under continuous and intensive pressure from Joffre, the French Commander-in-Chief, to pin down the German troops in Picardy; and while the British commander could and did resist Joffre's detailed wishes on how the battle should be conducted, the British were still so much the junior partner in the alliance—having little more than half the number of divisions on the Western Front that the French deployed—that French strategic wishes had to be complied with. Therefore, on 1 August Haig declared to the War Cabinet his intentions:

(a) To maintain a steady pressure on Somme battle.
(b) To push my attack strongly whenever and wherever the state of my preparations and the general situation make success sufficiently probable to justify me in doing so, but not otherwise.
(c) To secure against counter-attack each advantage gained and prepare thoroughly for each fresh advance.

Proceeding thus, I expect to be able to maintain the offensive well into the autumn.

This decision, which the War Cabinet endorsed, reflected the realities of the situation. Since the front ran from the Swiss frontier to the Belgian coast there were no flanks to be turned and, thanks to the defensive skills of the German command and the courage and professionalism of the German soldiers, a breakthrough was highly unlikely. Thus, with politicians and public firmly set against a compromise peace, victory could only be gained by grinding down the enemy's strength, by *une guerre d'usure*, a war of attrition.

Perhaps the only piece of good luck that Haig had during the Somme Battle was the reaction of the German command. The German Army Commander facing the British attack decided that the rather unimportant ridge which the BEF was threatening must be defended at all costs, an attitude strikingly reminiscent of that of Adolf Hitler nearly thirty years later.*

On 3 July General von Bülow issued a General Order:

* Hitler fought and was wounded at the Battle of the Somme.

The decisive issue of the war depends on the victory of Second Army on the Somme. We must win this battle in spite of the enemy's temporary superiority in artillery and infantry. The important ground lost in certain places will be recaptured by our attack after the arrival of reinforcements. For the present the important thing is to hold on to our present positions at any costs and to improve them by local counter-attack.

I forbid the voluntary evacuation of trenches. The will to stand firm must be impressed on every man in the army. I hold Commanding Officers responsible for this. The enemy should have to carve his way over heaps of corpses.

The Germans did their best to obey these orders and fought with the staunchness and skill which is the hallmark of German armies in the twentieth century, but they were remorselessly forced back and in the process suffered, over the four and a half months of the battle, substantially more casualties than the British and French.

Despite its disastrous opening, the Somme was a British victory on a grand scale. It did not make a breakthrough; two more years of hard fighting were needed before the German Army was sufficiently ground down to give up the fight, but it inflicted on them losses which, in the long run, they could not afford. Nor were these losses only a matter of quantity. The largely amateur British Army inflicted irreparable damage on the still professional Germans. In the words of Crown Prince Rupprecht of Bavaria, commanding the Army Group responsible, 'What remained of the old first-class, peace-trained German infantry was expended on the battlefield.'

A German regimental history commented, 'The tragedy of the Somme battle was that the best soldiers, the stoutest hearted men were lost. Their numbers could be replaced, their spiritual worth could not.'

For those in the trenches this overall, long-term picture was far from apparent, especially when wet autumn weather set in, reducing the battlefield to a sea of mud, and when each hard-won advance took them into country which had been pounded into a morass scattered with ruins, the more so since they knew that the enemy was being driven back into comparatively unravaged ground. Each time the British edged forward their fighting troops moved further from undamaged billets in which they could recuperate in their short periods of rest while the Germans got closer to such facilities. Certainly Ogle grumbles about the conditions in which he and his comrades were doomed to fight, but the astonishing feature of this part of his memoir is how little he complains, how little he blames the senior commanders who, in the opinion of so many historians, many of whom have no experience of war, got him into the appalling conditions which he had to endure. It is true that 48th Division and in particular 7th Royal Warwicks did not participate in some of the most lethal episodes of this period of the war but even in defensive situations, such as the position near the Butte de Warlencourt, the conditions were barely tolerable by even the lowest standards.

After the Pozières attack the 7th Royal Warwicks marched to Bouzincourt where a train of London General Omnibus Company's buses was drawn up under the roadside trees. Somewhat dazed by our luck, we were told to board them and did so, cheering like schoolboys off on a holiday. There was some competition for the bus tops, then of course open, for the lower-deck windows were boarded over. However, we managed to see the countryside by taking fair turns, though some didn't care about it, preferring to sit and dream. Many displayed souvenir *Pickelhauben* and other worthless loot and though many of these were taken into our rest village, I do not remember seeing any carried out. Whenever our buses went through a town or village we cheered and sang.

We were singing when we entered the lovely little village of Mesnil Domquer.[1] The tranquil beauty and homeliness of it brought out many an involuntary sigh and the song faded out when the bus slowed down and finally stopped. As our 16 Platoon bus drove in, Sergeant Hextall had peered at the white painted name board and announced, 'Boys, we've come to Mess Tin Domino!' We cheered and laughed and felt that whatever Harry or the French or anybody called it, it was good. When we were told to get out we did so with joy. There was a smell of grass where our bus wheels had rolled over a verge; there were garden flowers, farmyard and barn smells and the baking of bread. The village nestled amongst trees, all in the full, rich green leaf of high summer, and was bright with cottage gardens and orchards. Most of the houses were low and whitewashed and the roofs were of mellow red pantiles, and whole. There was a little church with a very little wooden turret with a spirelet, right in the middle of the village. Also close to the middle was a pretty orchard surrounded by cottages and barns. Into this orchard Corporal Dennis Jones and I led those of our men who preferred 'camping' to a common kip-down in the barn. I had foreseen a use for a once bright orange-coloured German bivouac sheet of strong cotton with its three-jointed poles complete in brown canvas case. Others had the same idea and some made bivvies in the usual way from rubber groundsheets, making use of orchard trees in place of poles.

Once again we saw and talked to women, children, cats and dogs. Some even found cows and horses and talked to them. The horses were mostly rather ancient nags that had escaped the remount officers of the French Army. The only males in the village were old men. We tried our French on them all, to their delight and mystification, and one of our ex-farm boys complained that the horses did not respond to orders and were just as French as the people. Some of our men could not keep away from the farms and began to do odd jobs and to help in the routine work with an immense amount of gesticulation and chatter. They would willingly have stayed there 'for the duration'. One morning after a pay parade a long line of LGOC

MESNIL-DOMQUEUR

buses drew up at the other end of the village which faced *away* from the line. A holiday was declared and we boarded the buses for a day trip to Abbeville, only about a dozen kilometres away. We cheered and sang our way in.

This busy old town, dominated by its great soaring church, and with streets of tall, old-fashioned, many-gabled houses, was crowded with people in gaily coloured dress, mostly women of course, but there were many French soldiers in their light blue to be seen amongst our khaki. We enjoyed the mere spending of money, knowing that our fare home was paid and transport waiting to take us back. Most of it was spent on fancy cakes, on wines and liquors, and some looked at souvenirs displayed to catch soldiers, but only the Australians could afford them. Some spent money on girls without exercising the discretion advised by our old provost-sergeant and, as he said, 'took the consequences'. After this outing time went quickly by on smartening-up and general re-fitting for another spell in the line. All too soon we were 'back were we belonged'.

We went back to the Somme battle area with the town of Albert as centre. As we marched in we passed warehouses said to be full of scrap iron collected by a French 'ole-cloes' man reputed to be a millionaire. Long before we entered we could see the church with its famous tower surmounted by the leaning Virgin and Child. It was a battered ruin but although the roof had nearly all fallen in much of the walling was still standing. The base of the tower up to nearly midway had been blown out and the tower must have relied upon the façade and part of the nave wall to keep it up. Though it must have been in a dangerous condition, civilians and soldiers passed along its front and under the leaning Virgin all day long. This huge statue originally stood, of course, upon the very top of the tower but after a direct hit on its pedestal it toppled forwards and downwards, bending its core of iron rods embedded in concrete until it hung over the roadway some hundred feet below, head downwards with the Babe held in the Virgin's outstretched arms. The iron rods had curved into an arc of almost a semi-circle in extent and the figure had come to an unstable rest making an angle of some 40 degrees with the tower front. Rumour said that when it fell the war would end and naturally the troops wished anybody's artillery good shooting![2] The church was very big, ornate and pretentious, built of bright red brick banded with cream-coloured stone in a style that might be described as ornate hybrid. There were traces of Italian Romanesque, Spanish Moresque and Mediaeval Fortress. The tower was heavily pinnacled, turreted and machicolated, surmounted by a round tower which had supported the statue. At one end of the building a sort of glasshouse or winter garden had been made but of course much of it had been smashed up. Parts of it had since been repaired and made into a bath house for the troops. There was a wonderful shower bath which squirted hot or cold water from above, beneath and all around.

Sixteen Platoon was billeted in a street not far from the church. It was a mean street without gardens, but behind it were open spaces, cleared of wreckage, where troops could parade. I never liked Albert. It looked mean, sordid and industrialised at the expense of decent living conditions.

The brigade re-entered the line [13 August] in the Authuille Wood area on the eastern slopes of the valley of the River Ancre. The ground between Authuille, in the Ancre valley, and Ovillers-la-Boisselle (to give the village its full name), on the heights, consisted of two spurs running south-westwards, divided by a deepish ravine up which climbed a fourth-class road. This road began at Aveluy on the Ancre[3] and joined the Authuille-Ovillers road about midway between those two villages. The Authuille spur was wooded, the Ovillers one was a grassy chalk hill. The old

British front line lay along the short northern edge of the wood and partly on the road. Opposite this northern edge or a little to the north was the formidable German trench system with concreted works, known as the Leipzig Redoubt, which made a salient feature following the contour lines.[4] Directly north, two kilometres away, was Thiepval, and fighting was still going on there as well as at the Leipzig Salient. The ground was in a frightful state, for the assaults of 1 July had made no change here and shelling on both sides was continuous.[5] The fighting was piecemeal work and it looked

as if a big full-scale all-out attack would be necessary to reduce the Leipzig Salient unless movements west from Pozières made the enemy abandon it. It was an awful place.

I was there on ration-carrying parties only, lucky to be out while my comrades went in, the custom then being to leave out a small portion of every company every time the line was occupied in battle. It was no holiday. I have no recollection of where our transport lines were, but for this sector they would probably be on the roadside between Aveluy and Bouzincourt. The 'details', as we were called, put up bivouac tents of groundsheets alongside the horse lines and the bell-tents which housed our stores. Here also were the company cookers and water carts. By day we had little to do but sleep and eat.

The Battalion was in the line near the north-eastern edge or corner of Authuille Wood. The approach by way of Aveluy was by road and communication trench which skirted the southern side of the wood along a steep slope. At the top the slope eased off after the corner of the wood was reached and the turn north led to a broad spur on which the Germans had made the Leipzig Salient works.

It was on the night of 17 August, my twenty-seventh birthday (and a parcel from Muriel had arrived that day), that our party set out with rations and stores for D Company in the line. We passed the thundering big guns in the valley and began the climb. The Battalion was due out the following night.[6] It began to look as if Jerry was expecting our relief to take place on *this* night, for well-placed shells fell on the way up and there had been none the other nights except those intended for the battery of heavies.[7]

D Company was in the front line, such as it was, and after some scrambles we reached their headquarters to find their part of the sector in that state which we had come to regard as 'quiet'. But this was not to last any longer, for we had hardly delivered our loads and assembled to return when we heard the well-known distant whine, increasing in volume and intensity with fearful speed, then deepening into an overwhelming roar, as a salvo of 5.9s plunged into the ground in front of the fire-trench at an angle, the nearest shell bursting exactly under the parapet. The resulting crater breached the parapet and filled the trench. The four explosions were almost simultaneous and heralded a barrage which must have been designed to catch the relief, which they evidently expected, when our trenches would have been full of arrivals and departures. Had the trench not been completely blocked by that nearest explosion, I and my party would have made a dash to get away before the debris had ceased falling. But while I hesitated to reckon our chances of finding only one obstruction—for of course we did not know then where the other shells had fallen—we heard a frightfully sudden *whizz-bang!*, followed in rapid succession by three more which all skimmed the parados and exploded just behind. The first or nearest had exploded on the other side of the blockage with a blinding flash. Next came the shriek and droning roar of another salvo of 5.9s descending nearer to the communication trench by which we had just come and by which we hoped to depart. These explosions must have covered the noise of a gas shell or two (they were always sneakers), for from the support line came the *ding-dong-dong-dong* of the gas alarm. This all happened in less than half a minute of time while we crouched at the bottom of the irregular ruin of a trench, three men near me and half a dozen out of sight round the corner of a bay. There was nothing we could do but wait for a lull long enough to get away in.

I was more than usually conscious of the extraordinary sounds of this barrage, for such it was, because I was forced to inaction and could give them some attention. In a noise-free couple of seconds I heard the throaty *wuffle* of what the artillery called anti-personnel 5.9s or shrapnel and, perhaps a hundred feet overhead, the night sky was rent by four lurid gushes of fire in a row and the shrapnel bullets rained. A sentry was huddling into a corner of the bay on debris which served as a fire-step, still keeping a look-out. His mate crouched by him, keeping down, there being no sense in having two heads exposed. Sergeant Hextall now picked his way past, amongst our crouching bodies, saying something to me which was lost in the din of explosions. All was now merged into a continuous pulsation of sound and a shaking of the ground while the air was thick with acrid smoke, chalk dust, flying flints and oddments, amongst which horrible jagged shards of iron cut their way with the peculiar, irregular humming note caused by their curvature.

There now occurred one of those strange lulls when for a few seconds there were no explosions. Instead, at full power was the tremendous, awful, mad music of the shells in their flight, ascending and descending, with all the different notes caused by the differences in speed, size and shape, whining, screaming, droning, roaring with full-throated resonance, at various altitudes, near and far. At the same time in this dreadful lull, which was far more terrifying than the explosions, it was possible to be conscious of, rather than to hear, the tremendous, throbbing drum-fire of all the guns engaged on both sides in barrage and counter-barrage and in bombardment of the batteries taking part. But under such mental stress this divided attention could not be maintained. Also heard in the lull, close to the ground, was the crescendo and diminuendo of innumerable speeding bullets, whistling and skimming the parapets with deadly precision, hitting flints and screw-pickets with whiplash cracks and loud zongs. Behind this immediate and nerve-racking whistling was the irregular staccato of the machine-guns, increasing in volume as the gun in its swinging traverse pointed directly, decreasing as it swung away, or suddenly overlaid by the nearby heavy hammering of our own ever-watchful Lewis guns. Underneath it all could be felt the heavy earth-shaking thudding of, perhaps, unexploded shells. Then once again all these undertones were obliterated by the resumed din of explosions.

This abstracted appreciation of all the terrible sounds that, combined in one gigantic frenzy, make this immaterial aspect of a barrage, was at once absorbing, thrilling, frightening and not to be endured. Action, any action, became necessary. When in command of men it may be possible to do something about it, such as a shouted word to one or a warning wave to another but to crouch and merely endure is dreadful.

When a human voice is heard for a fraction of a second by chance during the infernal din of a barrage the effect is dramatic and unnerving. A shout or a cry may have a beginning but no end, an end only, or it may even have neither end nor beginning—a mere fleeting middle of human sound but known at once for what it is because so unlike all other sounds. Such was Sergeant Hextall's voice as he passed me.

I was lucky to be in command of a few others, and on similar occasions I was also lucky to have specialist responsibilities (as when I was runner on 1 July), to concentrate on my job to the exclusion of at least some of the monstrous sounds around me. Throughout the war I had such jobs, otherwise I might easily have been overcome in some way by paralysing fear. I saw a lad change in a few seconds from a pathetic trembler to a soldier at the mere suggestion of responsibility, by my yelling in his ear, 'You're Senior Soldier when my number's up!'

We had not much longer to wait. Away on our left the uproar seemed to increase. Suddenly it was all over. It may have lasted five minutes, probably much less. Had there been a relief in progress the casualties would have been heavy. As it was there were but few exposed—pairs of sentries, a Lewis gun team and my ration party—and I think we got only the thin fringe of the shelling. There were shouts for stretcher bearers from several quarters elsewhere but we had come through untouched. We were all ready and lost no time in getting away.

After one of the spells in the line the Battalion went back to a camp of bell-tents on high ground overlooking a valley. It may have been Bécourt or Fricourt. The ground was pitted with shell-holes but leaving enough room for tents. There was no attempt at concealment and no cover. There were no orders against fires or lights, and fires were lit here and there and candles in the tents at night. We in D Company were drumming up a brew of something when a German plane was heard droning overhead, while there was much shouting of 'Lights out!' and 'Put those bloody fires out!' as if consciences had been awakened to the foolishness of such carefree illumination. But it was too late, for there came a rushing noise followed by an explosion and a huge fountain of earth spouted up between two lines of tents. Fortunately the tents and the lines were widely spaced and the bomb fell exactly midway between the lines, injuring nobody but holing a few tent tops. The next bomb fell outside the camp—a shockingly bad aim—and there were no more. This was the first occasion that I can remember on which German planes bombed troops in camp. Everybody was strangely scared and there were no more fires, or even candles, by order—but no orders were necessary.

Le Bois de Bazentin-le-Petit was a mutilated and horrible corpse of a wood, for a German trench-line of supports went through its southern end and the front line skirted its south-western edge. At the far side the village of Bazentin-le-Petit was completely demolished and between it and the German front line was a frightful tangle of broken trees, charred branches, barbed wire, smashed dug-outs and shell-holes, among which the surviving trees—if, reduced to bare poles, they can be said to have survived—leaned at all angles or stood erect but topped with a mop-head of splintered, slivered timber.

The first visit of 7th Warwicks to this dreadful-looking place was some weeks after its capture[8] and the battlefield had extended northwards. The Battalion occupied the old German front and support lines outside the wood.

The German line, their second line of defence, ran in a general north-westerly direction though, or in front of Guillemont, Longueval and the Bazentins, then up behind Pozières. From the corner of the wood we looked across a valley and up to the crest where Pozières windmill used to be.

These trenches were hopelessly smashed up and our 'shelters' were merely groundsheets stretched over material dragged from the general wreckage of the trench and wood, covering holes squared out by entrenching tool and GS shovel. There must have been some deep dug-outs still usable but I have no recollection of them. Perhaps there were enough for our various headquarters and signallers and no more. For the less fortunate rank and file it was a wretched place indeed. Close by ran what had been the Longueval–Contalmaison road which skirted the wood on its southern side and was now being cleared and laid with railway sleepers. Mametz Wood was only five hundred yards to the south-west and half-way between it and Bazentin Wood was a battery of heavy howitzers.

These monster 15-inch howitzers were ponderous masses of machinery and castings, with levers, hand wheels, recoil devices and a crane for hoisting the big shells into a sort of shoe or shovel and thence to the breech.[9] A gunner invited me to watch the shell begin its journey to the German lines. I had to stand well behind and plug my ears. I was conscious not so much of the tremendous noise of the discharge (in fact I thought that of the 60-pounder was more unpleasant) as of the sound made by the shell as it emerged from the muzzle and climbed into the sky. I felt as if in a tube of sound. It was a sound made up of giant, unlubricated screwing as the shell spiralled away, of rushing wind as the air closed in like thunder behind it, of screaming and whining as fragments of its copper driving band cut the air in its wake. As I looked up I could see the shell, a perfectly visible black, elongated speck near the top of its trajectory, which was very high, then as a round speck when it showed its base in my line of sight, then again as an elongated speck for a fraction of a second. Then it disappeared on its downward flight. On a still day, supposing at that moment there were no other noises, the final explosion might be heard, a mere *hrrumph!*, seven or eight kilometres away, probably near the road between Butte de Warlencourt and Bapaume. I tried to memorise these monsters for a sketch but found some newspaper photographs of a battery in action sometime afterwards and 'lifted' them into my sketchbook.

The men of D Company were ration carriers by night, getting some rest and sleep by day in the beastly wreckage. Early one sunny afternoon three corporals climbed out and stood on the wooden road, so firm and clean, looking in amazement at a *marquee* which seemed to have sprung up overnight at the very corner of the wood. There had been rumours of a YMCA canteen in the neighbourhood further south, which we took to be this side of Albert, but *this* was too good to be true. It could not be a canteen here! They quickly ran along the firm corduroy track (how good it felt to run again) and reached the apparition which was real enough after all, with its canvas, poles, guys and runners, all in order. They stood in the opening speechless and then began, all at once, to laugh. The YMCA men, at first mystified, soon understood and joined in the merriment.

The canteen had a trestle table-counter stacked with *everything*, or so the corporals imagined, that could be eaten or smoked or mixed for drinking. There were biscuits, slab cake, dates in fancy boxes, dates in blocks, figs, chocolates and sweets, oranges, tins of sweetened milk, of cocoa, bottles of Camp Coffee (with the Highlander sitting in his tent), Hoe's Sauce and Tomato Ketchup. There were tins of sardines, of herrings in tomato sauce, of salmon, of sausages. Piled in pyramids were packets of cigarettes—all brands, even Three Castles—and there was Players Navy Mixture, Three Nuns tobacco and Carlyle. Our folks at home were not forgotten, for there were envelopes and notepaper, pads and pencils. It was a wonderful sight. Why had they not appreciated all these good things before? And now, when they really did, funds were low. Someone suggested a 'tarpaulin muster' and they put all they had on the table. It looked unimpressive, meagre indeed, and not even clean as it lay there on the scrubbed white boards. The YMCA men entered into the spirit of the occasion and were helpful now they understood the resources of their customers. 'Something sweet in a tin, say, Bartlett pears; something savoury—herrings in tomato sauce, perhaps?' 'Certainly!' 'Smokes?' 'Yes, Woodbines in a tin—we mustn't forget the lads.'

ALBURY St. John's

128

As they chose these wonderful things, the ground shook to the discharge of the monstrous guns not far away.

The three men stood outside the marquee, their treasures in their hands while there in front of them again was the wood. Said one, pointing to it, 'That's a *fact*, that is. I can see it and smell it. But this behind me, is it still here? I don't believe it!' 'You mean to say that tin of herrings is just imaginary? Let's put it to the test, here and now.' Without any more palaver they gathered each an empty wooden box and, sitting resolutely with their backs to the corpse of Le Bois de Bazentin-le-Petit and with paradise before them, opened a tin.

Exactly when the 7th Warwicks stayed at Allery I can't remember but the fact that we gathered cobnuts from the hedges there should fix it as autumn, probably October, 1916. It must have been a rest interval between two spells in the Somme battle which, though it had slowed down, went on and on in complete disregard of the loss of life and the agony of body and mind of those who went 'in' and 'out' while the weather worsened. It was so memorable and delightful at Allery that the immediate before and after are blurred memories compared with it. I have an idea that its full name is Allery-sur-Somme but I do not remember any river in the pictures in my mind. It does not appear on my war maps but it is probably just off the bottom on Lens. Had I not two sketches made there I might come to regard it all as a mere pleasant dream sandwiched between nightmares.[10]

There was a pretty and ancient church and I made a sketch in watercolour of its well-worn priests' doorway. There was a very comfy and welcoming *estaminet* where two nice girls tried to improve our French and learned some mixed English, and another, also nice, made delicious coffee and omelettes. I made a sketch showing this girl attending to the kitchen stove and through the doorway are men of our battalion seated at a table in the light of a hanging oil lamp. The short cotton 'curtain' hanging from the edge of the mantelshelf behind the men adds a touchingly homely note.

Sixteen Platoon's barn-billet was near a row of whitewashed cottages in a leafy lane which was hedged with hazelnut bushes. We gathered hundreds of nuts, carrying them in small sacks, sandbags in fact, provided by our billet hosts for whom we collected the nuts. These kind people were handloom weavers and were then weaving sandbag material from the jute provided by the French government. Their looms were like those I remember as surviving in East Lancashire about 1907. They were built into the framing of the cottages, that is to say with the main posts pinned to the joists of the floor above. The looms (two, I think, in one cottage) were close to the two windows. The weavers sat in the window recess in the thickness of the wall and the seats were worn smooth and shiny by much sitting and

reaching from side to side with the throw of the shuttle.

In the village was a house which seemed to have been converted from a farm, for though there was a big barn and some outbuildings, in place of the usual yard and immense muck-midden there was a well-kept garden. Jones and I were passing by the main gate and hailed the big, bearded man who was leaning over it farmer-fashion. We called, '*Bonjour, monsieur,*' and he answered 'Good morning, Royal Warwicks,' in perfect English. This was the first Frenchman we had heard pronounce the name of our regiment as 'Warricks' instead of 'Varr-ecks'. We must have looked surprised for he said, 'My English is hardly surprising, for I am English by birth and upbringing but I am now of French nationality.' He invited us into the house, introducing us to his French wife who spoke English in a very French way. He spoke to her all the time in French, by habit no doubt, but translated for us, with apologies, when he realised that our French was not very fast-moving.

Some good wine and cake was produced and cigarettes and cigars placed on the table. I am still ashamed that I do not remember our host's name, quite an ordinary English one. He noticed that I got up to look at the good original oil paintings on the walls, upon which Dennis told him that I was an artist. I assured him that I was an amateur, quite incapable of making a living out of it. He told us that he was a professional painter of animals and country scenes. I had my sketchbook with me and showed it. They liked the sketches and slight scribbles but I wanted to see my host's studio for I was sure he had one. He took us across to the great barn we had first noted. This was his studio. The big double doors at each side of it, each in its transept-like gable, were retained as the artist often had a farm wagon with its load driven in drawn by the splendid Percheron horses that were used in this country and of which there were many studies on the walls of the artist's house. His easels and painting gear were on a platform across one end and there was a big stove with its stovepipe soaring up and through the roof. There were canvases in various stages of completion against the walls, and stacks of finished ones. I hungrily turned them over to feast my eyes and to lift them up to sniff the fresh paint. The artist was delighted to see such appreciation of paint and turps, charcoal and canvas, and pots full of brushes and so on, letting me handle them. Had the Battalion stayed any longer, or had we found him sooner, I have no doubt he would have had me paint a picture. All too soon Dennis dragged me away. We said goodbye with, at least on my part, enormous regret, for we were to march away on the morrow up the line again 'where we belonged'.

Even before November 1916 it was obvious that the hoped-for breakthrough was a failure. We in the ranks could see that we had gained some ground, for we were condemned to walk over it. If we had gained only what we saw around us it was no imposing sight. Its importance *we* could not estimate. The weather had changed to almost continuous rain, fog and drizzle, and that made passage to and from the firing line increasingly difficult. From this point of view the gain in ground was no gain at all. We imagined too that Jerry made his way up to *his* firing line over ground comparatively undamaged. So, with added disadvantages we settled down gradually to the old War of Attrition.

Until after Christmas 1916 the 7th Royal Warwicks occupied trenches at places between Pys (in German hands) in the north and Flers in the south,[11] six kilometres of complete devastation with the notorious Butte de Warlencourt's little salient in the middle as the utter limit, we thought, of slimy misery, depressed to unimaginable depths of horror by German shelling and gas. Nevertheless we were lucky, for we did not have to make attacks at the Butte, whereas at Ypres[12] attacks never ceased whatever the weather or the state of the ground. In front of the Butte it was indeed a physical impossibility to advance.[13]

The Albert—Bapaume road ran in a straight north—east line through this area, cutting the front line at right angles at Le Sars. The villages had all been shelled to the ground and were now mere names given to roughly similar areas of heaped-up desolation, lying in an unvarying wilderness of shell-holes crossed by trenches in all stages of wreck. The connecting roads, with the exception of the Bapaume road, I do not remember and it is likely that they had been obliterated. The dykes and watercourse had been dammed and diverted by shellfire. Between the middle of June and 1 July some of this area must have suffered from our preliminary bombardment on roads, road junctions, bridges, railways and villages. Since then our very slow advance had been preceded, and then accompanied, by creeping barrages, box barrages, searching fire and fire on fixed objectives, always countered by German fire not much less in intensity at times. The fields, woods and remains of villages were criss-crossed by fire-trenches and communication trenches and gun pits, which became flooded as soon as abandoned. In some places shell craters were so numerous that only a tortuous and slippery path could be picked amongst them by day and not at all by night. In many places shell-holes were intersecting and quite impassable. In heavy rain they all filled with water and when a shell burst among them there was the sound of running water until the level was established again.

In such conditions there was only one way of getting about without loss of time and loss of life—the well-known duck-board track. Between Contalmaison and the forward area there must have been dozens of miles of them. Up to Contalmaison the Labour Battalions of over-age volunteers, whom we called Granddads,[14] were pushing on as fast as possible under difficulties, but this could not be done beyond the Pozières—Bazentin road, for there we came under direct enemy observation. Stores and ammunition, rations and water, the sick and wounded, all had to be carried on these wooden tracks by fatigue parties for at least five kilometres. I don't remember our gun positions exactly, but field artillery ammunition and other stores were carried by mule train for some distance to the forward batteries. Shelling, though apparently aimless and fitful, was endless, and the Germans must have thought it worthwhile. Tracks needed constant repair, and maintenance of them and of forward telephone lines employed Royal Engineers and Signallers day and night. The wires were hoisted aloft on sticks where they crossed the tracks, but the sticks never stayed upright for long and the lines caused many a tumble in the mud or a splashing scramble to avoid complete immersion in a shell-hole.

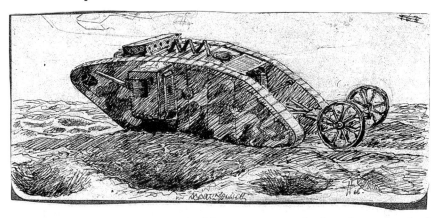

To this day if I hear the sound of footsteps on wooden boards or on a plank bridge, I see the awful landscape around Courcelette, Le Sars, Martinpuich, High Wood, Contalmaison and the Bazentins. Anyone who paused for a moment in this wasteland would hear the everlasting, *clump, clump, clump; clump, clumper, clumper-clump* of heavy boots on raised boards. The sounds would increase to become mingled with voices, or decrease but never wholly die away before another lot was heard on the way. There was no song and little conversation, indeed the most frequent vocal sounds were expletive, indicating where some sorely tried carrier was having words with a broken duck-board. The nights were often dark with mist so that concentration was necessary to keep the sandbagged bread out of the mire. There was enough steady going left for a good deal of thought if one was given that way. I found that most of my crowd just dreamed along, having learned instant reaction to duck-board trouble and the telephone wire nuisance. There was nothing else in this desolation, and as for shrapnel one had to ignore it, or appear to ignore it, for nothing whatever could be done about it.

Sixteen Platoon was on the way back from somewhere in this region one night when Dan Paragreen, who had been clumping along steadily without a word for maybe half an hour, delivered himself of the results of his thinking. 'Corp', he said, 'Napoo Big Push.'

In this unspeakable Butte de Warlencourt sector, late in 1916, a kindly but mistaken battalion commander sent his men into the morass equipped with rubber thigh-boots. So many lost them in the deep mud and spent several days without footgear at all that no commander ever tried it again. How the Germans fared in their jackboots I have not heard but for them conditions may not have been the same except immediately in front of the Butte. In the summer and autumn they had fallen back slowly until they came to a slight up-slope and there they stayed, with the British troops below them to receive the water they did not want and had the foresight to avoid.[15] This area was the gathering ground of the waters of the River Ancre. The terrific shelling it had received from both sides had made a chaos of water courses, dammed one day and undammed the next, of abandoned German trenches which, in front of the Butte, lay in a mazelike salient near the Bapaume road. The water came to rest (or would have done so had there been in that awful place such a state as rest for anything animate or inanimate) in no-man's-land and in our front and support lines. Not only that but we had to cross about five kilometres of devastation in little better conditions whereas the Germans had, close behind them, comparatively undevastated and dry land. It is quite possible that they could wear their jackboots in any weather—I never saw them in any other footgear. In any case they thought far more of their trench comfort than we did and were past masters of drainage systems.

Our ordinary leg wear consisted of long woollen pants and grey socks under the khaki long trousers,[16] and for footgear we had stout, heavily nailed boots. Over the top of the boots and reaching as far as the knees, we wore puttees. They were originally designed for service in India as a guard, it was said, against snake bite. They have received much adverse criticism which they did not deserve. The alternatives would have been leggings, long boots with legging tops, Wellingtons, rubber thigh-boots or jackboots. Thigh-boots were all right for water but not for deep mud and in static warfare, with permanent trenches kept in repair and duck-boarded, they were always worn. Jackboots must have been satisfactory in most conditions but the mud at the Butte, on our side of it, surely would have pulled them off.

The puttees kept out the mud, though not the water, assuming that the boots were properly laced up. Such boots should have had tongues extending sideways all in once piece and attached to the uppers but we had to make do with the ordinary kind. If a man in boots and puttees *could* be hauled out of deep mud, his leg and footwear came with him. The only trouble with puttees was that they were not easy to clean and the edges began to fray after much rubbing and brushing.

The soldiers who had to endure the extraordinary conditions soon found the answer to the problem, completely without the help—and, in fact, in spite of the frownings—of those who did not have to endure. We simply wrapped sandbags round our legs from ankle to knee to cover our puttees completely, having found that sandbags were much sooner divested of mud.

They did not keep legs and feet bone-dry and we had to put up with a state of continuous damp which varied a lot, being often clammy cold, sometimes steamy warm, sometimes dry in front but not behind. There was a report that some 'red-tabbed bloody walking advert for Nugget Boot Polish', as a soldier unkindly called him, had fulminated against the 'abuse and misuse of sandbags' but we continued to use them so it may be supposed that no battalion commander had the inhumanity to forbid their use as legwear. Blessed sandbags! I scrounged them whenever there was a chance. We carried rations in them, slung fore and aft over the shoulder; we used them as described on our legs; folded, they saved hips and ribs from extremes of cold and hardness or from temporary damp. I used one as a pillow inside my steel helmet in the line or on my boots out of it. I always carried a spare.

Ration and trench stores parties were made up from companies not in the front or support lines but lying in reserve a few kilometres behind them. Men on ration parties carried a rifle, a cotton drill bandolier (holding for this journey 25 rounds), two sandbags tied together for rations, a petrol tin full of chlorinated water and, of course, the ever-present and necessary gas-helmet bag slung by its tape over a shoulder. Over their tunics they wore a leather jerkin, and over all a rubber groundsheet, which by this time had been changed to a standard cape-cum-groundsheet, and above this the rain pattered with its forlorn music on steel helmets. In the open all went steadily forward on the tracks so long as they were there and not deposited elsewhere by shellfire, which occurred often enough to occasion no comment. But when the maze of front trenches was reached carriers were sure to get stuck somewhere. Sometimes, in spite of all reasonable care, ration bags were soaked and their contents reduced to a mass of wet bread well mixed with sandbag fibre, and from this were extracted tins of bully, 'meat and vegetable rations' (M & V for short), cigarettes and letters from home. But, though the ration party sometimes arrived late, sometimes exhausted, arrive it *did* to hand over what there was. Then, after a brief smoke and swapping of news and opinions in the comparative light and warmth of a dug-out, where there was at least neither wind nor rain, residents and visitors joined in a hearty general curse to include the weather, the General Staff and Jerry, and parted. Unimpeded, and once clear of the suck-and-plosh of the communication trenches, the party went 'home' at a good steady pace if the night were not too dark, an occasional stumble nothing to bother about since everyone was fairly well plastered with mud. 'Home' was nothing better than wrecked old German trenches, less muddy, less subject to shelling and gas, and therefore something to look forward to.

One day, in front of the Butte, when I was expecting the arrival of the ration party there was a burst of shelling where a communication trench

entered the front line. When it slackened I went out, for it was time to relieve
sentries on our platoon front. I heard voices and recognised that of the
corporal in charge of the ration carriers who were just arriving. The shelling
had occurred at the moment when they were leaving the communication

trench and were strung out along it and perhaps fifty yards of the front
trench. He told me that there were three new men in the party from a new
draft sent up to replace casualties. He thought all his men had escaped the
strafe and I sent him on to direct them down the dug-out steps to the
headquarters place while I went to shepherd the later arrivals, for it was
fatally easy to take a wrong turning. After a while two men struggled along
and to my enquiries answered that they brought up the rear. We went along
to where the ration NCO was counting his men and as we arrived he
exclaimed, 'Hey! three more yet and it must be them three.' The rear men
I had followed in swore that they had been at the rear all the journey therefore
the new men were in our trench. Fearing that the newcomers, unused to the
place and the circumstances, had been caught in the shelling or, in their
confusion, had taken refuge in the wrong turning, I hurried down the trench
with their corporal, looking carefully whenever a flare went up, into the gaps
the new explosions had made near the entrance to the communication trench.
There was an abandoned surface shelter there, roofless and no more than a
mere recess. I waited for another flare and then looked in. An inert figure
sprawled over the debris and, looking up, I saw against the dim sky another
on the very edge of the parados as if in the act of climbing out. He was
motionless. Now an enquiring German flare showed with painful clearness

a headless corpse at my feet as I stooped over it to find any sign of life. The
other was also dead. The shell had burst in the very shelter in which they
had sought refuge. The third man was making his way along the trench on
all fours, going in the right direction by sheer chance. He was in a pitiable
state, recognisable as human by general shape only for he was completely
encased in slime and was whimpering with shock and fright. We got him to

his feet and scraped him down as much as we could in the dark till he was fit to go in. I told him, 'Come on, chum, down here things ain't as bad as they look', and the ration corporal added, 'And only half as bad as they feel,' to which words of comfort his only reply was 'Christ!' We got him down the steps and when we stripped off his jerkin he wasn't *too* bad underneath. He was soon sipping a mug of hot tea and seemed none the worse physically though in a state of mind that needed rest. This was his introduction to the line.

At Eaucourt l'Abbaye, a kilometre east of Le Sars, one early morning, when light should have been making at least a promise, it was thick with mist. Some men of one of my sections were huddling together in a wretched surface shelter, the deep dug-out being flooded. They had found a plank and were sitting on it. In front of them was an empty fire bucket. I had come out with the idea of making a fire from something or other while the mist lasted. As I pulled aside their gas blanket, they raised their eyes in doleful chorus. 'No coal, no coke, no wood, no bloody nothing!' I replied, '*Something* came up in last night's rations.' ''Ow d'you mean "came up"? It bloody well *went* up in that shelling.' I made the obvious reply, 'What goes up must come down again.' 'Don't be funny, Corp, we ain't used to laughing.' 'It isn't meant to be funny. There's a thick fog on. Are you going to drink ration water neat?' The fog raised a faint interest in Private Marlowe's mind for he was usually more mentally alive than the others. Private Hamilton, big, lethargic, pathetic but not devoid of humour even here, said, 'Corp, I've dried the arse of my trousers by sitting on it. I'm all for keeping what I've gained.'

'Out of this hole, all of you! Scatter round where that lot went up and pick up every bit you can see. Jerry can't see us this morning.' We found enough bits of coal to start a fire. 'We've no kindling.' 'There's that plank, and your jack-knives and bayonets will make enough splinters off the edge for our job.' Splinters were cut and them somebody found bits of broken duck-boards to dry out and burn when the fire got going. Letters and envelopes were produced and someone rather grudgingly gave the piece of waxed paper in which he wrapped his match box, pathetically averting his face while he parted with it. It was an anxious business to get that fire started but it *was* lit, with dixies hanging over it to catch every tongue of the flame and, long before the mist had thinned, the section was drinking hot tea.

In civilian life Tom was a collier who worked at the coalface in a pit in the Bedworth district of Warwickshire. He was a man much older than most in D Company, heavily built though not tall, fair, ruddy, staid in demeanour and steady in action. He spoke but little, yet when his comment or advice

was asked for he spoke well, freely and much to the point. He liked his beer and carried it without trouble either to himself or to anybody else. I never saw him drunk. His blue eyes were slightly protuberant and choleric, belying his good nature. In billets he sat or squatted, quietly smoking his pipe, and he liked to take a stroll to see the countryside, looking as if he ought to be holding a leash or two with whippets at the end of them, or carrying a basket of pigeons. I had often heard of Tom from Jack Rainbow when I was with him in post-hospital days in 1915. Jack referred to him as Old Tom, though he was probably not much over forty. According to Jack, 'In a new place Old Tom would take a dekko at stand-to while he stood on the fire-step. He'd stamp on that, kick a revetment post on it with his heel and grunt "Humph!" and then turn round and glare at the parados for not being squared back proper. He'd be filling his pipe, quiet like, so's not to be in any hurry. He was never in a hurry wasn't Tom even when a 5.9 went over. He'd say, "That bugger's gone over so it's no use bein' in a hurry to get out of its way."'

The platoon moved one night into a slimy wreck of a support trench somewhere near Eaucourt L'Abbaye, carrying GS shovels with them though, according to Private Cooper, 'You don't want shovels, you wants bloody buckets.' However, if one dug far enough back one might come to earth and clay firm enough to stand up on its own, though this process resulted in an ever-widening trench with less and less cover. Roofing was a problem, for though there was wreckage in Martinpuich, that was three kilometres away with no duck-board track over heavy or impassable going according to weather and the darkness of the night.

As platoon corporals Jones and I had a lot to attend to, so we dumped our equipment in a broken-down affair which looked as if it might once have been a shelter and might again be made usable. Meanwhile this long-neglected bit of trench had to be repaired before our men could use it and there was no time for our private repair work.

At last we could see that the repairs were well forward so I left them and began on our own wreck. I was doing a hurried dig when Tom, having finished his portion, stopped alongside to light his pipe. I continued in a hurry when Tom said, 'Corp, you'm a schoo'master an' knows a thing or two that's no use in this bloody place but when it comes to pick an' shovel work, why, that's *my* job. I don't say you know nowt about it but you acts as if you don't, bein' in a 'urry, an' I'm goin' to schoo'master you. You come out o' that afore you've trodden it down hard. Give me that shovel while you colours your old corn cob wi' some proper baccy.' He puts his pipe in his pocket and hands me his pouch, seizing my shovel with the grip and balance acquired by daily use over long years. But he eyed it, and then me, with distaste. 'You want to keep her clean, lad. Make yourself one of these. Some call it a "minute killer" but a proper *mon* saves more minutes with it than he kills.' He produced a little piece of wood shaped like a spade from the top of his sandbagged right lower leg and scraped the muddy tool clean. 'Now then!' he growled and began at the edge of the funkhole or where he judged it ought to be. He shovelled out a hundredweight or two, placing it neatly behind the slurred edge of the trench to make room for roof spans, if any. While he worked he delivered his lesson, suiting the actions to the words or phrases and fixing me with that rather fierce gaze of his to make sure I was attending. 'Begin at back, an' keep your feet off till you've made a bottom to stand on. Always work from a clean bottom. Find your right level, then you slopes it up a bit towards the back unless you wants water there. There's the bottom!' (Slapping it with his shovel.) 'Now your shovel will slide, an' firm it down as you go sweet and easy like. Now find your side walls and *batter* them. Don't forget or else your edges'll be falling on your 'ead when you're trying to sleep. Clear your stuff as you go, don't *stand* on it.' (Looking at me severely.) 'Now, square your back corners, dead true and clean. No, you finish your smoke—you don't get baccy like that every day an' I'm not done schoo'masterin' yet! Get your right hand so's it backs agin the inside o' your right knee. Now you uses your knee to start your shove. That's usin' your weight. Easy! Throw o'er left shoulder workin' right-'anded, an' right shoulder left-'anded. No, a *proper mon* wi' pick an' shovel's as good wi' one as wi' t'other. Use body and legs to save your arms. An' *use your 'ead* on this job, same as you uses it on your own job.'

By this time Dennis Jones had returned and had been hugely enjoying the lesson. Tom came out with his eyes on him, saying, 'You'm another o' these book fellers (beggin' both your pardons) but you'll be a PROPER MON all round when you can dig an' delve as good as *them* lads.' Tom was pointing with the pipe he had just taken out to Privates Clerk, Grimes and Cooper, the inseparables, all young pitmen, who were grinning with delight in the corner of the trench. He grinned too when we thanked him. He asked for his baccy pouch and concluded, 'Don't forget, make a clean bottom to start on, then you won't get in a muck-puther o' sweat, tearin' your guts out like I seen you.'

The Warwicks were lucky to be out of the line at Christmas 1916 and spent it at Albert. There was a brigade of Australians there too and when, without considering the very probable consequences, I greeted them as fellow countrymen, they hauled me and two or three other corporals to an *estaminet* to celebrate. With such carefree and generous companions it was impossible to pay for anything. Warwicks could carry their beer but this was a severe test. Fortunately for us we got our hosts to talk of their experiences and life in Australia, at Gallipoli, and at Pozières, where we and they had gone over the top together. One of them, Charlie, knew Springwood where my father had a house at the edge of the tall bluegums, and where the family went from Brougham Street, Sydney, in hot weather. Time flew. More of our men came in. Songs were sung and it was a wonderful evening, ending with 'Auld Lang Syne', and never a fight or sharp word. At turning-out time we managed to find our own street and billet but I had two Australian corporals in tow, swearing eternal friendship and too drunk to care where they were provided they were not parted from their new friends. They were peaceable so we got them into our billet and let them sleep. At daybreak I roused them, got them out, not much the worse, and started them on their way to their own quarters. The affair was not at all popular with the platoon who said we'd be having the whole crowd of Diggers around for the rest of the time and we couldn't go their pace with our pay. Apart from this there wasn't much merrymaking in our part of Albert.

Not until more than six months of fighting in the big general engagement known as the Battle of the Somme, did the 7th Royal Warwicks *see* that river. It ran through the line at Curlu, about half-way along the twenty-mile battle front, and this marked roughly the southern end of the British and the northern end of the French lines. But now in 1917 the British lines were extended southwards to take in the Péronne sector.[17]

We reached the river by a devious route, for, although the distance from Albert to Méricourt-sur-Somme is only seven or eight miles as the crow flies and from Méricourt to Éclusier as much more, there were several halts at night when we billeted in barns or houses. Of course some of the halts would be to allow for troop movements, for the taking over of new territory by a division entails much staff work between French and British.

We arrived at Cappy, a village on the Somme Canal, with the Somme itself flowing about 500 yards west of it and parallel to the canal. By the time we reached this place we were familiar with the extensive swamps and

overflows of the river and with its windings. Sometimes river and canal seemed one and sometimes they were apart.

The weather had been frosty with slight falls of snow but a thaw was beginning so that the river looked leaden dark and sullen under a cold grey sky. Then the weather became bitterly cold with alternate snow and thaw. From Cappy we marched to Éclusier on the canal, which was bordered with tall poplars, and the water was beginning to appear in open patches among the ice when I made a watercolour sketch of the scene. On the far bank are French *poilus* so it is probable that we were the first to take over from the French. We were billeted here, as we had been at Curlu, in large wooden huts with wire beds in fair condition but with inadequate stoves, and our bread was frozen solid. The large windows were covered with cotton fabric,

torn in places, instead of glass and were rather more than adequate as ventilators.

The trenches occupied by 143 Brigade were in or near (I never knew *exactly* where) the village of Biaches which, never very big, seemed to have been blasted out of existence by combined French and German gunfire. Right in front was the Somme Canal and, running closely parallel, the Somme itself. On the far bank of the river or near it was the ruined village of Sainte-Radegonde and close behind that was Péronne in ruins. Canal, river and ruins all looked dark and dismally grey against the white of newly fallen snow.

Our support and reserve lines were in a wilderness of shell-holes recalling those of Martinpuich, and our headquarters was, at one time at least, in a deep quarry at Frise. In the devastated area were batteries of artillery thoroughly bogged-down and subject to much gas shelling among other kinds.

After a fine spell of dry, cold weather there came a sudden thaw with thick fog which worsened one night after the company had left Biaches trenches for the reserve lines near Frise. The usual landmarks, such as certain field telephone wires set up on poles, failed and platoons began to wander. There was no wind at all and no information could be gathered from distant sounds for they seemed to have been blanketed out. For once the 18-pounders were silent. Men began to string out in long lines, holding hands, when suddenly there was a shout, 'SMOKE!' A chorus of sniffing broke out in the chilly waste but this soon gave way to a happier chorus of heartfelt 'Aha!' and the men followed their noses till they led them, luckily for it might have been anyone's smoke, to their own quarters, such as they were, in that dreadful wasteland.

From these mudholes, from which they emerged nightly on ration and trench-stores parties, the men were relieved by another brigade and went back to Cappy. The weather changed again to dry and very cold, then snow and very severe frosts night and day. The marshes between canal and river, after long neglect, extended much beyond their normal bounds and were now frozen hard. At Cappy the ice was thick enough to bear the whole battalion and there was a day off for what sport could be devised without skates though a few pairs did appear, no doubt borrowed locally. There was ice hockey, ice football and sliding. There were a few Jocks in the battalion and they improvised bon-spiels with big stones, brushes made from reeds and twigs, and whatever else one needs for curling. For a brief but very happy day, trenches were forgotten.

It was on this day that company commanders announced that NCOs and men interested in the idea of applying for a commission were to parade at Battalion Headquarters for interview with the Commanding Officer. By this time I knew what I wanted and made my application. Many of us had discussed the pros and cons long before this. Officer's training would take a matter of months. That at least was something worth consideration on one side. On the other, no one with eyes or brains had any illusions about the life of a subaltern in this war. The fact that we were being asked told its own tale. It was a toss-up, and we decided that if the CO approved we would let our applications stand. If not we would put up with the ills we had learned to endure. The CO approved of mine at once without asking any questions though he said I might have to wait. I dismissed it all from my mind and rejoined the merry throng on the ice.

Sgt Charlie Davis of Biaches Feb 1917

When the Battalion returned to the front line at Biaches there had been a heavy fall of snow. The line was quiet and I was standing in a trench with Platoon Sergeant Charlie Davis, having one of our many long talks about men and things. While we talked he asked me to make a sketch of him as he stood in the trench with its covering of deep snow on parapet and parados. I did a head-and-shoulders and a full-length in my sketchbook, working very quickly because it was so cold. I always carried a miniature watercolour box and I gave both pencillings a wash of colour. Charlie chose the head, and I still have the full-length as a reminder of one of the best sergeants among the many good ones I have known and one of the best friends I had made in the Army. He was killed in action later in the war.

He carried a little white bone flageolet which could generally be seen in his tunic pocket. On this he would often play in private with me, though seldom in company. On the march it came out just when it was needed. In civilian life he was a locomotive fireman and was at this time considering an appeal for loco-men to work on our British front railway system. I do not think he applied.

A day or two after this trench portrait-painting the weather softened to a sudden thaw and the trenches began to splash again until in some places duck-boards were afloat. Rations had come up, and I had received a parcel from Muriel. At this period rum was sent up in half-size stoneware bottles in openwork wood cases and one of these with all its bottles had, with criminal carelessness, been stood on the top of the communication trench wall near the Company Headquarters dug-out. A string of sausage bombs came over and exploded in a line across the trench. NCOs and men who had been approaching HQ for rations and had flattened themselves against trench walls or duck-boards escaped injury, but even before we straightened up again our noses told us what had happened to our precious rum. Regardless of other strings of sausages we all dashed for the case which still stood there. By a strange freak only one jar had been hit by a fragment and it was this one that had been scattered over the trench and over us. While I stood sniffing Sergeant Davis came up the dug-out steps and handed me a chit from Battalion HQ dated 21 February 1917 and addressed to OC, D Company. It read:

Please hand the attached instructions to Corpl Ogle. This NCO must leave the trenches tonight and leave the QM Stores early tomorrow morning, viz. not later than 10 a.m. The QM will inform him how to get to Chuignes.

Charlie, as platoon sergeant, had read the chit and handed it to me without a word. When I read it his lips began to move and I expected the usual 'You lucky old devil!' but he just held out his hand and looked away down the trench. Then he said, 'Quick, as soon as you've seen the captain, get your stuff out and buzz off out of this before Jerry tries to say goodbye. And keep your pound down and don't stop till you're at the quarry.' He turned abruptly and went forward.

Quickly I gathered my equipment, parcel and a long mackintosh cape that I had found and thought might be useful, for a fog had begun to settle and threatened to turn to drizzle. In haste I set out, very soon stepping on the end of a floating duck-board in the dark. The other end came up to meet me but did nothing to prevent a wetting. At last I got out of the communication trench and began to cross the shell-holed open. Here some field telephone wires were down and I got well entangled in them and came down in the mud. When I got up again my cape refused to come so, remembering Charlie's injunction not to stop, I *ripped* out of it and went on. My guiding light to the Frise quarries were the gun flashes of an 18-pounder battery, which I knew I had to leave on my left when I reached it. As I passed close to the battery dug-outs I was hailed. A gunner was just about to enter and had seen the lone figure passing. I was invited to join in a drum-up of tea and accepted gladly. In the warmth of the shelter I was not the only one to be conscious of the smell of rum so I told my tale. They regarded the smashed rum jar as a tragedy to be mitigated only by a generous lacing of the precious spirit in my tea. I had hardly left these kind friends when a salvo of gas shells intended for the battery fell too far over, more or less in my path. The gunners had warned me to have my gas-bag ready and I quickly had it on, soon passing beyond the area. I kept it on for a minute or two and when I sniffed carefully to test the air what I did smell was a faint but unmistakable whiff of coal smoke. So I was near the end of my journey and nosed my way to the QM's store in the side of a quarry.

From this time until I was actually on the deck of the leave boat I remember nothing. On the boat I watched the attendant destroyers make foaming great circles about it under a sky that was leaden and on heaving water that was grey-green where it was undisturbed. We leave men stood on the deck wearing our life-jackets and there was very little talk. The water looked deadly cold and I for one forgot to be sick.

On board I made friends with a Birmingham man, a sergeant detailed, as I was, to the 19th Officer Cadet Battalion stationed at Pirbright, Surrey, though this we did not know at the time. We found that we could get to Birmingham that night so I travelled with my new friend and spent the night with him at his home. We had both done a bit of cleaning and delousing on our journey but could not have been particularly fresh. Next day I reached Snitterfield.

VI

COMMISSIONED

The nine months in 1917 during which Ogle was away from the war zone were, for the Western Allies, the most depressing of the whole war. The much-vaunted French offensive, which its architect, General Nivelle, promised would end the war in forty-eight hours, failed to produce any decisive results and led to a widespread breakdown of morale in the French Army, showing itself in indiscipline which, in many cases did not stop short of mutiny. For the rest of the year the British had to undertake the task of engaging the main strength of the enemy so as to prevent them striking fiercely at a French army which would be most unlikely to be able to offer effective resistance. Meanwhile the German Army, despite its heavy losses, was growing in strength. The onset of the Russian revolution meant that before the end of the year the Germans could start transferring large numbers of troops from their eastern front to the west. In November 1917 there were 150 divisions on the Western Front. By January 1918 the number had risen to 171; by March there were 192. Nor were events on the southern front encouraging. The Italians launched yet another offensive (11th Battle of the Isonzo) which resulted in heavy casualties (165,000) for little useful gain. In reply, the Austrian-Hungarians, reinforced by German formations, struck back at Caporetto and routed the Italians, driving them back almost to Venice. Italy suffered more than 600,000 casualties in 1917 and French and British divisions (among them the 48th, which Ogle had recently left) had to be dèspatched to stabilise the front. At sea the beginning of unrestricted submarine warfare brought Britain for a time to a situation where starvation was a real possibility.

On the credit side, the United States entered the war, giving promise that, eventually, overwhelming manpower would be available on the Western Front but, in the immediate future, there was no American army to put into the field—the first time a complete US division went into the line was in March 1918—and all the artillery for American formations had to come from Allied sources as did the vast majority of their aircraft and all their tanks.

The British could pride themselves on two magnificent (and relatively economical) feats of arms during the year—the seizure of Vimy Ridge, largely a Canadian victory, and the capture of the Messines–Wytschaete feature. They also captured the high ground from which for three years the Germans had dominated the Ypres Salient, but this victory, culminating in the muddy shambles at Passchendaele, had been a Pyrrhic triumph, costing 240,000 casualties even though it imposed on the enemy a loss in numbers and morale that they were progressively less able to bear.

One of the indirect effects of the heavy costs of the Third Battle of Ypres was an intensification of the war which had broken out between the Prime Minister, Lloyd George, and the military command, especially Field-Marshal Haig. To ensure that Haig did not undertake any more expensive offensives, Lloyd George refused to provide the reinforcements urgently required by the infantry of the BEF. He also sanctioned a further and considerable extension of the front held by the BEF while, as a measure of manpower economy, shearing off 141 battalions of infantry from its strength.

On 21 March 1918 thirty-two German divisions, with thirty-nine more in immediate reserve, struck at the right flank of the BEF, where fourteen divisions of Fifth Army held an overextended front which, since they had only recently taken it over from the French, was poorly fortified. The result was predictable. The Germans achieved the most spectacular gains seen on the Western Front since 1914. All the gains of the Somme fighting of 1916 were swallowed up, Albert, Noyon and Montdidier were lost and Amiens seriously threatened. In this fighting and in a second German stroke, which in April retook Messines and made the position of Ypres more difficult than at any time of the war, the BEF suffered more than 236,000 casualties, only 8,000 fewer than they had suffered in more than three months' offensive fighting to take Passchendaele.

Second-Lieutenant Ogle was, once more, extraordinarily fortunate in all this carnage. A trifling injury prevented him from joining a unit which would have been heavily involved in the last days of the Passchendaele fighting, and his battalion was not involved in either of the great German onslaughts of March and April 1918.

The 19th Officer Cadet Battalion was stationed at Pirbright, Surrey, in the Guards Depot. At the other side of the railway and canal was the town of Brookwood. Here the wives of several Officer Cadets lived during the training period. Cadets had to apply for sleeping-out passes which gave them Saturday night out and all Sunday until evening unless there was a heath fire; the camp was close to pinewoods, which covered a range of low, sandy hills, and as the summer was hot and dry Sunday fires were common. Everybody was expected to turn out and smother them.

The camp consisted of rows of long wooden huts raised on brick piles. At both ends of every hut was a door and steps. Beds were of the usual institutional type. A much larger wooden hut served as mess-room and smaller ones as classrooms, storerooms, guardroom and Headquarters. There were also some large huts to house the canteen and a reading room. The huts for the Women's Army Auxiliary Corps (WAAC)[1] stood at the far end of the camp beyond the mess and close to the woods. On arrival, all NCOs took down their stripes and all mounted a white cap-band labelled 19th OCB. This was the only thing to distinguish an OC from an ordinary soldier

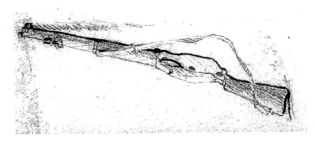

but it was very striking indeed. We were armed with the Short Lee-Enfield rifle and long bayonet, and our equipment, to my disgust, was of leather with its bad design of heavy flopping cartridge pouches slung on the belt in front.

The instructors were seasoned officers and NCOs who had been given these jobs as a respite and reward after arduous services. They were indeed very good. They did not try to make themselves popular but earned our respect and willing obedience. Many of us disliked the Commanding Officer. In his opening speech he told us that his job was to make us into Officers *and Gentlemen*. Why he thought we could not already be gentlemen I don't know. If that part of his job was really necessary, he made it no easier for himself by assuming that we were louts to begin with. There was a rota for cadets to dine at the officers' table, so many every day, so that he could note how we shaped at table talk and eating peas. Still, these table manners try-outs taught us that officers' messes were conducted in a certain way and the experience saved us from embarrassment later.

The food was good, well cooked and plentiful, and some of us wished that our wives could share it. We were served by WAACs, and some surreptitious friendships were begun, but did not end, in that mess-room. The penalty for being found out was being Returned to Unit (RTU). The canteen young ladies wore black and were distant in manner.

We had squad drills, platoon drills, company drills and battalions drills, firing on the nearby ranges, exercises in the open country with blank ammunition for realism, but they were most unrealistic, especially when the major's wife and children appeared in the woods with a picnic basket and the war was stopped for lunch. Drill under the NCOs was a pleasure but under our own orders the drills became battles of wits and very unexpected but logical things happened when orders were interpreted literally.

When examinations loomed they caused many fears and headaches. I was sorry for those who had no experience whatever of exams or how to make the best show of their knowledge. Fortunately for such, the exams were not entirely on paper.

After this came the excitement of trying on our officers' uniforms, supplied by Messrs Moss Brothers. They proved good in fit and subsequently good in wear under trying conditions. Finally we had a passing-out or farewell dinner in our officer's rig with our platoon commander, Captain Streatfield as guest. On the following morning we departed for a short leave before joining our various Regimental Depots. I had asked to be sent to a Lancashire regiment and was commissioned into 4th Bn The King's Own Royal Lancaster Regiment TF, a battalion with which I actually spent no time at all on active service.

I reported to the Battalion's depot near Oswestry for posting overseas and Muriel found lodgings in the town; the usual sleeping-out passes were granted without any fuss. The camp consisted of huts around barrack squares but I remember little of it but the Headquarters, the Officers' Mess, the men's mess hut and the football pitch covered with red gravel. Some King's Own men had contrived to stay in the camp for a long time, dodging the column. I can remember only one officer who may have been of this kind. He was there—had, it was said, been there a long time—when I joined and was still there when I left perhaps a fortnight later, and when I was sent back to the depot, then at Richmond Barracks, Dublin, a year later, he was still there. In a camp like this there was much coming and going so there could be no settling down to anything unless one was determined to stay, and knew how. The Commanding Officer realised this and had set up a YOTS, a Young Officers' Training School, although nobody seemed to take it seriously. We drilled each other in squads to practise words of command, voice-carrying and that sort of thing; if it did nothing useful it may have been a better way of spending time than merely hanging about camp.

We played football on the gravelled pitch, on which I received a nasty abrasion on the outer side of one knee just before I was posted to France. The MO's iodine did nothing to improve it but I did not think much about it, but on the boat to France the knee received another knock when a sling of officers' valises being swung on board caught it a glancing blow. Next morning at the reception camp at Étaples I could not get my breeches over the swelling and I was packed off at once to the Liverpool Merchants Hospital in Étaples where I spent at least two weeks with a very bad knee, amongst many genuine war-wounded men.

While I was recovering from a mere football scrape there was being fought the slimiest and bloodiest battle in the history of the British Army. I escaped it but, with first-hand knowledge of the Butte de Warlencourt, could form some picture in my mind of Passchendaele.[2] The state of the worst of the casualties in our hospital gave us some idea of the hell but those with lesser wounds or the effects of exposure were unwilling to talk about it. The 57th Division—to which I was on my way—had been in it and, in common with every unit engaged, had suffered heavily.[3] In those days of frightful wastage officers were afraid to be anything more than surface friends and many wore an air of bogus devil-may-care which deceived nobody but might be expressed in drinks at least. Some had plainly given up all hope of survival and just 'went with the pace' with visits to Paris Plage[4] and all the rest of it, sampling anything and everything as long as the money lasted or until they were posted up the line again. The average young officer brightened himself up by drinks and gay chatter to pass muster as a cheerful being. We had on our nursing staff some VADs who helped to keep us cheerful. It was a strange, unreal, unsatisfactory, even demoralising, life during the convalescent stage. There was an Officers' Club at Étaples and we spent much of our time there while we waited to be posted. Everyone knew what that meant but I am sure that it came as a relief. Anything would be better than this mere existence at the base.

The seaside resort of Paris Plage was only a tram ride away and one afternoon I thought of a possible sketch on the beach. The tide was out, far enough to be able to visit the wreck of a cargo steamer which had been torpedoed in 1916. It had been beached but was broken in two parts which became widely separated in a gale. I managed to get a very slight sketch of it before the tide made me leave the beach. At last I read my name on the posting list and left Étaples without regret.

I was one of a party of subalterns bound for the 57th Division, to be found somewhere about Estaires and, when in the line, in the Wez Macquart sector, just south of Armentières. Also in the party were Second-Lieutenants Grant and Turnbull, both King's Own men, and Second-Lieutenant Shaw of the Royals. We travelled by LGOC bus and were met at our destination by a staff officer. Without the least delay or hesitation he counted us four off the bus and told us to report to Battalion HQ of 2/5th Loyal North Lancashire Regiment TF. We three Royal Lancasters pointed out that we belonged to *that* regiment and not the Loyals and desired to be sent to it. He brushed our protests aside and said there could be no argument about where he decided to send us as the Loyal were in urgent need of officers. We were seconded and that was that.

The staff officer who could not be bothered to sort us out departed abruptly under the undisguised scowls and muttered imprecations of the three King's Own subalterns but we pulled ourselves together and told Shaw of the Loyals that we had nothing against his mob but objected to being treated like cattle. We hoped a swap could be arranged later.

In due course we reported to the Loyals and were received, not greeted, in a hut by the Commanding Officer, Lieutenant-Colonel Hitchins and his adjutant, Captain Hart. Hart was friendly looking and had a humorous eye, but the Colonel eyed our Lions[5] coldly. If he said one word of welcome, I don't remember it but I do remember sundry disapproving grunts and

L.M.M.H.

ETAPLES.

Canadian Bandsmen

Oct. 1917.

humphs as he told us, 'Anyway, you are now Loyal North Lancashire officers.' The protest which had already formed on our lips was noted with a heavy frown and he cut in with a peremptory order to report to companies as decided by the Adjutant. We saluted and went out, Shaw and I to Captain Evans of C Company, a trouble-free and friendly crowd.

I found my intimate knowledge of the East Lancashire dialect was much appreciated in my platoon. A remark in dialect or the share of yet another tackler's yarn helped to bring us into closer touch. My batman, Joe Pickering, was in civilian life a pitman. He spoke a hundred per cent Bolton dialect and could speak no other and on the few occasions when he took a turn as mess waiter he mystified even the company of Lancaster men and I had to translate. Though not a success as a waiter, he was a faithful friend to me all the time I spent with the Loyals. The RSM too was a good friend as he was to us all. He was perhaps the oldest man in the Battalion, an old Terrier from the very beginning of the Territorial Force and his fund of anecdote and 'buzz' was quite inexhaustible. He was a sort of institution in himself and to me and many others he was the Battalion.

Lieutenant-Colonel Charles Hitchins, the Commanding Officer, had a reputation as a formidable man. He was big, dark and powerful with the loud voice and confident manner of one accustomed to dominate any board meeting or assembly of men. I heard that he was managing director of a firm of agricultural implement manufacturers in Kent. With his battalion he had endured one of the heaviest attacks on Passchendaele late in 1917, when I would have been with them but was laid up in hospital at Étaples. 'Charlie' was a crack shot with a service revolver and I have seen him hit three bottles, each on a fence post, in succession. He was a great dog lover and breeder of Airedales. Of his two majors I remember Hesketh better than Eaves, who was second in command and whom I never got to know but I never saw him smile or look pleased. Major Hesketh, on the other hand, never looked anything else. A more good-natured and less *soldierly*-looking man I never met. He often paid us a visit and sat amongst us, showing his relief when he met us. How Captain and Adjutant Hart got on with his CO I don't know. He was youngish, tall and spare, ginger with blue eyes and, I should imagine, quick-tempered by nature but he had a sense of humour and the shiniest brown riding boots I ever saw.

We three King's Own men wore our Lions on caps and lapels as a matter of course, but that angered the CO. One day he had us all in before him as though we were delinquents. After a few preliminaries during which he cut short every attempt of ours to justify the wearing of our badges, his heavy brows met in a frightful glower as he growled, 'THOSE have got to come down! You will go *now* to the Quartermaster who has the necessary badges for you.' Perhaps we ought to have stuck out, but active service was a

157

"GUM-BOOTS"

difficult enough occupation without the addition of a private feud so we glared back with undisguised dislike, saluted His Majesty's Commission, *not* the bloke, as the old Provost-Sergeant said, and marched out.

When I first joined the Loyals the Battalion occupied part of the Wez Macquart sector just south of Armentières. It was a good, comfortable well-appointed rest-cure sector, wonderfully well sandbagged, duck-boarded throughout, revetted with sheets of 'expanded metal', had sumps and drains, pumps in working order, well-built dug-outs and shelters, and good communication trenches. The simple soul who pronounced that getting trench-feet was a crime must have imagined that all trenches were like these.

There was a gum-boot store, with whale oil, in a convenient shelter and there we anointed our feet and pulled on our long thigh-high boots, why I don't know. There may have been water and mud somewhere but I don't remember any. With sound gum-boots, whale-oiled feet and dry trenches, trench feet was *impossible*.

I was initiated into the mysteries of Company and Headquarters business in the line in Signallers' dug-outs with field telephones buzzing and squeaking, morse signalling, papers, chits and orders. In the trenches I found an established routine and little to do beyond it, but I wanted to see

THE WORKING PARTY   *The Loyal N. Lancs*

159

no-man's-land and learn about it from my new point of view as a subaltern in case of raids and being raided. I soon found plenty to do in setting out wiring, arranging covering parties and listening posts, and in leading patrols, but was not surprised at the general lack of enthusiasm for no-man's-land, for these men were survivors of Passchendaele. One night I saw a sort of will-o'-the-wisp in no-man's-land, which nobody could explain and I went out to investigate. I found, to my astonishment, an artillery officer, who had been trying the possibilities of a hideout somewhere and on his way back had dropped something. He was looking for the something with an electric torch covered with a handkerchief. He was peevish when I took charge of him as a non-resident and we were both lucky not to be hit by shots from Jerry during this display of lights and disregard for the trench-dwellers.

Christmas 1917 we spent somewhere between Sailly-sur-Lys and Estaires. Major Hesketh and all the Company enjoyed a Christmas dinner at a farm well known for good food, or at least for its preparation. Shortly after this Shaw and I were sent on a bombing course to a place near St-Florie, between Merville and St-Venant. There was deep snow on the grounds after a few days and one afternoon the 'school' picked sides to attack and defend a windmill on a canal near the river. Our ammunition consisted of snowballs. We also learned something about new types of grenades, British and German, and at the end of the course passed an examination on bombing and general military matters.

Lieutenant-Colonel Hitchins regarded our trench digging in the back areas with great pride and evidently considered soldiering in the line as secondary to it. We certainly had a lot of digging to do, such as burying telephone cables,[6] jobs which occupied much of our 'rest' periods. This point of view of his, together with my lack of appreciation of it, got me into the trouble which seemed bound to arise sooner or later. A combination of circumstances, Company Commander Evans being away on leave, put me in charge of the company which had gone sick rather heavily. The depleted company set out to dig a long trench and bury a cable in it. They failed to cover the allotted distance so that the job took far longer than the time allowed and of course a Brigade Staff officer happened to arrive and make a note of everything so that I knew I was in for a grilling. Shortly afterwards I was sent to report to the office of the Town Major of some place. There was no explanation. I had to pack and go. I arrived, and only then did I discover that I was to be Officer in Charge of Baths, the inference being that I was unfit to be in charge of troops. I noted the glumness and shabbiness of the Officers' Mess and its inhabitants and my spirits sank. Whatever these people's jobs were, they had no enthusiasm. I listened for a while to the grousing and general pessimism, asked to look at the baths and was told that I should not take over until tomorrow and, anyhow, why bother.

SAILLY SUR LYS

Early the following morning, however, I received a message from 2/5 Loyals ordering me to return to the Battalion forthwith. Again there was no explanation. I gave orders for my valise to be sent on as soon as transport was available and set off on foot. It was not long before I saw on the road ahead figures on horseback. These figures resolved themselves into the Brigade Staff and soon I recognised the formidable figure and face of Brigadier-General Guggisberg. He sent his staff on ahead and I had him all to myself. He looked grim but this was not unusual for brigadiers, especially this one. His very name was rather frightening but I looked him straight in the eye without a blink and waited for a broadside. Perhaps I did not look worth one for when he did speak his voice was calm and restrained. What he said I remember little of, perhaps because I was watching his fierce eyes for a sign of humour and rather admiring his face. The sign appeared at last and, after a growl or two, he said that he desired all his young officers to be given full scope for whatever talents they possessed and that probably I should find opportunities in my own regiment, seeing that the Loyals' future would no longer be trench duties, in which he gathered that I had a good record. In any case he did not think that OC Baths was a suitable job but I 'must learn, by God, that when a job had been ordered to be done, every available man who is well enough to be on his feet must be turned out to do it'.

His enquiries at first hand had had the effect of terminating what the CO meant to be my banishment. When I reported to the Loyals, the CO was not there but when he saw me later he looked at me with disfavour and said I was damned lucky. Hart, the Adjutant, gave me to understand that I had some good friends in the Company and in the Battalion, and that welcome information helped to hold my head up.

Of all my memories of the war, those of my time with the Loyals are the vaguest. During this time, about seven months, there was first a spell in the line as ordinary troops, repeated many times in the same sector, Wez Macquart. Then we became Pioneer Battalion to the 57th Division[7], not long before the German breakthrough in the early spring of 1918. All I can say of our pioneering is that we did a great deal of marching, still more digging. I don't remember where or why but we were always on the move, up, down and across the divisional front. Fairly early in these days we were in Sailly-sur-Lys. Enemy high-explosive shells were beginning to search these back areas and smash up the houses in what was, or had been, a very thickly populated countryside. Reed, Shaw and I once occupied an upper room in an empty house. It was a fine big room with very tall windows, shuttered but with a good deal of unbroken glass. There were two good beds, though without bedding, and though we did not fancy all that window glass, we took a chance on not being disturbed. In the small hours a great shell hit the roof, removing all the tiles, shattering all the windows, going clean through the unoccupied front-room wall of the house and bursting on the hard *pavé* of the street. We soon became all too familiar with the mighty rushing scream of these HE shells, the subsequent long-drawn out clatter of falling tiles, the rush and splintering of roofs as they fell in and the delayed crash of tottering walls.

I was sent on a fortnight's course at the Second Army School which was housed in a tall convent at Wisques, near St-Omer. The commandant at that time was Lord Claude Hamilton, Grenadier Guards. Many officers in those days said 'What-what?' occasionally, but Lord Claude said it all the time. But he was a very fine commandant with a very fine staff. By this time in the war the Army knew how schools should be run and this was a super-school. There was something of the Butlin Camp about it, so much was laid on that could minister to soldiers' needs and desires. The course was a general one and seemed to include a small concentration of everything. We were so busily engaged that I remember only one visit to the town of St-Omer. In an Officers' Club there we met United States Army officers for the first time. We gathered that they had a poor opinion of both French and British armies.

On the recreational side there was soccer, rugger, Australian rugger and boxing. The boxing instructors were no ordinary pugs. They were picked men led by ex-welterweight champion Johnny (or Harry) Basham and 'Gentleman Jim' Driscoll, lightweight champion, and they gave exhibition bouts. Many of us were afforded the privilege, and the pain, of trying to hit our instructors' faces or bodies. I for one failed completely to do so much as touch Johnny Basham except on his gloves and forearms.

The drill instructors were under the command of a quiet Scots Guards warrant officer whose voice, on occasions, easily cut through all other sounds. We thumped our rifles and *stamped* and when our platoon imagined it could compete with the Guards, our Scot produced a platoon of underage boys then being combed out from the Army and who had been in his charge for a few weeks. Under his quiet but incisive words of command these boys showed us how drill could be done. We were rather mystified. Mac smiled and said, 'After all, gentlemen, the lesson here is the Worrd of Command delivered to a split second. The reactions of a keen young laddie are quicker than those of a guardsman with all his training and discipline. So please don't imagine I am trrrying to show you up!'

There was quite a crowd of ANZACs, and the Diggers were a perpetual insurance against dullness or boredom. It says a great deal for the tact of our instructors, both officers and NCOs, that there were no incidents or any kind of ragging. One, an Australian lieutenant with the ribbon of the DSO,

WISQUES 2nd Army School 1918

was able to throw a little light on the fate of my younger brother Willie, posted missing believed killed, 9 August 1915, at Lone Pine in Gallipoli. He said that William Ogle was one of a Lewis-gun team in his company when it went over the top to attack a railway-sleeper covered Turkish trench. Many were killed in the withering rifle and machine-gun fire before they got there, many more in the hand-to-hand fighting in the covered trenches when at last they did enter them from behind, and the burning scrub in no-man's-land made recognition of the dead impossible.

We had a day at the rifle ranges at Lumbres as range instructors and organisers, but we also had some shooting. Every evening was taken up with instruction or entertainment. The WAACs who attended to our thirsts must have been chosen for their briskness, cheerfulness and glamour. Our courses were excellent, for our officer instructors not only 'knew their stuff' but knew how to present it and make it memorable.

A course like this was generally regarded as a reward or a respite but I had no illusions of that kind.

Having had seven days' leave I was on a station platform at Boulogne with other subalterns, all ex-rankers. The station was filling up with men of many different regiments, including Australian infantry. Most of us were glum but the Diggers were not. How many there were in their party I don't remember; there may have been fifty, with a sprinkling of NCOs but no officers. If they *had* been glum they had banished that mood with the aid of many bottles which protruded from haversacks or were being passed around. Our train was at last made up and rolled in, not all of it accessible from the platform. A harassed-looking Railway Transport Officer moved amongst us with a sheaf of papers as if looking for somebody. He was peering into every compartment and eventually arrived at ours. He glanced at us in turn, appearing to take note of our rank, which was second-lieutenant to a man, and seemed nonplussed; however, while we were wondering what he wanted, he shoved a paper or papers into my hand and barked, 'OC Train!' and vanished like a ghost between the trucks as if to avoid pursuit, leaving me holding a most unwelcome baby. To my grinning companions I said, 'Some of you blighters must be senior to me,' but they replied, 'We are mere babes. Hard luck, old man.' If the reader asks why I should have been worried, the answer is 'For the all-sufficient reason that there were Australians aboard.' I am an Australian myself but I must admit that an Australian in any circumstances other than a tight corner or a fight against odds is a heavy liability. To begin with, they got far too much pay and they possessed the high spirits and potential for mischief usually attributed only to schoolboys.

The train rolled out with several Diggers sprinting after it. I thought nothing much could happen so long as it kept rolling along but there was a good deal of noise where the Australians were and when the train began to round a big curve the subaltern opposite me exclaimed, 'Your friends are on the roof!' Thinking, 'Fellow-countrymen yes. Friends *no!*' I looked out. There were some half-dozen on the roofs of two or three of the carriages and vans but there was nothing to be done about it as it was not a corridor train. I just had to wait for an opportunity, and after a while we entered a station and the train stopped. I made my way back to the Diggers' carriages and called for their NCOs. Some did appear and I gave them orders to bring their men down and get them inside. This they did, with ill grace enough, and I thought the incident was closed, but once again a curve showed that the devils were up again. As I looked out I saw that we would shortly be entering another station and this one was my destination, so I sat down to wait. There was a shout of 'Man overboard!' and sure enough a figure lay still on the track some hundred yards behind the last carriage. I rushed out on to the station, found the RTO, thrust the papers into his hand, regardless of his rank, and reported the incidents and the accident. Meanwhile the other officers roused themselves and rounded up the Australian NCOs and got them to see reason, though naturally the accident had sobered some of them a little. My statement was taken down and I signed it. The man was carried in dead. As the Australians had further to go and I had arrived at my destination, there was nothing more I could do but carry on and wait for a summons to a Court of Enquiry. To this day I have heard nothing further of the affair.

About May 1918 Second-Lieutenant Turnbull and I were transferred to 1st Battalion, the King's Own Royal Lancaster Regiment in 4th Division. Why we were sent to a Regular battalion I do not know, but it was probably because they were short of officers after the capture of Riez-du-Vinage when they drove the Germans back and across the La Bassée Canal.[8]

I have no recollection of leaving the Loyals or of the journey, whether by train or bus, but we arrived at the Battalion Headquarters somehow, in bright, warm sunshine, which seemed to give me new life and spirit from that day and hour, and to shine on the King's Own all the brief but intense five months I served with them.

VII

THE TURN OF THE TIDE

By May 1918 when Henry Ogle joined 1st Battalion, the King's Own, the final climacteric of the war for the BEF had passed. The two great German offensives against them had cost them much ground and 236,000 casualties, to say nothing of 92,000 French casualties from those divisions which had moved to support the British; the Germans, however—whose casualty returns usually ignored the slightly injured—had lost 348,000 men, a loss they could no longer afford. Worse, their new practice of spearheading their attacks with picked men, stormtroopers, meant that these heavy casualties fell largely on their best surviving soldiers. The quality of the divisions not involved in the hammer blows was, in particular, reduced, since their best men were syphoned away to act as stormtroops, and in many areas they had been drawn from the defensive positions matured over months and years and consigned to occupy improvised defences in newly captured areas.

Frustrated astride the Somme and south of Ypres, the High Command, knowing that many French divisions had been sent north to assist their allies, launched three great offensives against the French in May, June and July. In the first of these they inflicted 28,700 casualties on a British corps which had been sent to recuperate in the supposedly quiet sector marked by the ridge of the Chemin des Dames. These three onslaughts cost the Germans more than half a million men and ended with a brisk and successful counter-offensive led by General Mangin's Tenth French Army. By the second week in August the Germans had had to yield the greater part of their gains from the French. It had been the German intention to bring their series of attacks to a climax by a final, clinching onslaught on the British in Flanders but they no longer had the strength for such an undertaking. Instead, the initiative swung to the Allies, a change signalled on 8 August when the Australian and Canadian corps, supported by more than four hundred tanks, scored a victory at Villers-Bretonneux, finally sweeping away the threat to Amiens. Then the British offensive spread northwards and, in a few days, swept over the old Somme battlefield that had been wrested from the enemy with so much blood in 1916 only to be recaptured when the Germans swept forward in March 1918.

In the sector north of Béthune, where 1st King's Own were stationed in 4th Division, there was no offensive to be undertaken in August, but there were signs that the enemy facing them was thinning out to provide reinforcements to oppose the British attacks. Meanwhile the Battalion, like the rest of the Army, was having to come to grips with a fresh conception of war—the moving battle. Since the end of 1914 all training had concentrated on trench warfare. With the high summer of 1918, new skills, dormant and largely lost since the first battle of the Aisne, would have to be learned if the advantages so hardly earned by years of attrition were not to be lost.

The 1st Battalion of the King's Own was doing a spell of duty in the trenches at Riez-du-Vinage but Turnbull and I found the details[1] at L'Eclème, a village a few miles north-east of Lillers. The Headquarters was in a house in the village street and not far away was the headquarters of either the 2nd Lancashire Fusiliers or the 2nd Seaforth Highlanders, according to their turn of duty in the line. Major Kennington was a reserved and rather severe man as a rule, but he met us with a welcoming smile and a handshake, calling an orderly at once for drinks. Then he called another to hand over our valises to our batmen, whom, of course, we had not yet seen, but they had already been detailed and set out at once to arrange things for us in our billet. All this was friendly and informal and heart-warming and not what we had expected from a famous Regular battalion.

Our billet was the top loft of a farmhouse under the pantiled roof and the sun streamed in warmly through a glass skylight tile or two to illumine the usual streamers of drying tobacco leaf. We found our valises had been unrolled, beds made with our blankets and, everything neat and tidy; at the foot of my bed, a smart, alert but somehow unsoldierlike man was waiting to speak or for me to speak to him. He was bronzed, moustached, dark-haired, wiry and of medium build, with a humorous eye and mouth and a very alert expression. This was my batman, Private Cecil Cockerill, in civilian life the manager of a department in a Plymouth store. He was a man of wide interests and knowledge and we soon became good friends. I am sure he did this job for the fun of it, taking a delight in being punctual, precise and thorough in all he did, with a wonderful eye for detail, a gift for improvisation and an imagination which produced many a pleasant little surprise. When I became Scouting Officer I gave him queer things to do in preparing my equipment and for training scouts, but he never failed and I can still hear him chuckle as he caught the idea. In the line he could never be sure when he would catch me, nor where, but he never failed to be there on time with food, drink or some oddment. Out of the line I soon ceased to *ask* for stationery, toilet gear, smokes and so forth. They simply appeared when wanted.

After a day or two the Battalion came out of the trenches and Turnbull and I were introduced to the Commanding Officer, to the Adjutant and, gradually, to all the officers, informally and genially. Lieutenant-Colonel Carter's first action was to offer us seats and say to the Adjutant, 'Gilbert, the occasion calls for drinks', and when the mess waiter had supplied Johnny Walker to the Headquarters Staff, he gave a toast: 'Gentlemen, our new friends, and may they find with the King's Own such happiness and friendship as this damned war can afford.' After that we had a talk with him and we were allotted to companies. I went to that of Captain A. R. Bosanquet.

The Battalion had been in France and Flanders since the beginning of the war in 1914 but there were not many of the Old Contemptibles left. It was a unit in the 12 Infantry Brigade in the 4th Division which, apart from the 8th, was the only all Regular division in the British Army. The brigade was holding the line which it had established through Pacaut Wood on the north side of the La Bassée Canal.[2] The sphere of operations extended roughly for five kilometres at this time from Robecq in the west to Hinges in the south-east.[3] Robecq, being just over the canal, was shelled regularly at certain times, such as reliefs, but the state of the line when I first saw it would be described as 'quiet'. In the middle of the sector the canal was in quite a hollow or at least at the foot of a hill called Mont Berenchon.[4] This hollow very frequently smelt of tear gas or phosgene or both and was a place to be crossed with both speed and caution in spite of the quietness of the line. The main part of Pacaut Wood was about a kilometre square, from which a long arm extended towards the north-east. Straight 'rides' divided the main block into roughly equal parts. We held the two southern quarters. Our front line was along the southern edge of the [east–west] ride and this was the road to and through the ruined village of Riez-du-Vinage recently captured. The line straggled through this village and its surrounding cornfields which were soon to ripen in the summer sun.[5] The German line was no line at all but consisted of holes improvised here and there and held now and then with a few very strongly fortified points with machine-guns. They held nooks and corners amongst the ruined buildings and farms and surrounding farms, and no one knew until we began to probe just where wily Jerry might be, but he could be relied upon to produce a machine-gun almost anywhere and to leave snipers about in a puzzling way. Maps produced by Brigade showed a trench line in the long arm of the wood but I never saw it and there was nothing near Malo Street at the north of this arm, where one was marked, when I reconnoitred there later on. He managed much better with an indeterminate line, for we never knew where to shell him.

Junior subalterns in Battalion Headquarters at rest did many odd jobs and errands. While the 1st King's Own was out at Cense-la-Vallée I was sent to fetch the money for pay day. My destination was the small town or large village of Burbure, some four kilometres as the crow flies but considerably further by road. The weather was hot and windless, the roads dusty, and I was no horseman though I wore a pair of riding breeches of lovely cut and with buckskin strappings. I went to the Signallers and borrowed a bicycle after studying a map. The bike was the usual creaking heavyweight and, by the map, the way seemed long. Rather more than half-way there was a hill. The proper road skirted this at its base but at night transport made a short cut over the hill, making thereon an ever-widening track which on wet days soon turned a muddy trail into a greasy slide to be avoided. Now it was all too dry and deep in dust. By day it was under enemy balloon observation, but that I was not to know until later. I looked at my map again and chose the hill, walking it with my heavy bike and only then realising how dusty it was. I arrived very hot and grimy. However, drinks as well as pay were available and I set off on my return journey refreshed.

When I came to the hill track again I let the bike go as fast as it would and raised a cloud of dust which, no doubt, hung in the air behind me. I did not look round to see it because my attention was engaged, less than half-way down the long slope, by a familiar rushing whine overhead in front. The whine became a roar, then with a mighty crash a shell exploded behind me as I pedalled furiously, probably raising more dust, which proclaimed my continued existence. Before I reached the flat another shell exploded about the same distance behind me as the first. Back on the road I pedalled harder than I had ever pedalled in my life but there were no more shells. Away in the distance I could see the enemy sausage balloon which until now I had not thought of. I arrived at Battalion Headquarters almost unrecognisable from the dust which had stuck to my sweating face, to the quiet amusement of the Adjutant but he got me a long drink before even asking for the pay packet. I began to explain my condition but he cut my story short, telling me that he had guessed and that the Staff Sergeant should have warned me. There were several junior subalterns in the room as it was close to lunchtime and Captain Lupton, the Transport Officer, said very firmly, 'Anyone who goes to Burbure on any errand whatever, goes round by the *road*.'

After a spell in the line as a platoon commander I went to Battalion Headquarters, first as Intelligence Officer, that duty being combined with scouting, and then as Scouting Officer only as the need for a proper organisation for reconnaissance work became apparent. The German line was not fixed at this time and there was a lot of ground to cover, including Pacaut Wood. I was given two or three men from each company to train and return, but retained a nucleus as specialists. A smart Lance-Corporal A. Zelly was made Scout Corporal and attached to Headquarters. Later he was awarded the Military Medal, and it was well earned.

Training was carried on both in and out of the line. What we learned in peaceful training we put into practice 'over the top' next time 'in', and the minor mistakes we made then we rectified by practice when 'out'. Apparently no major mistakes were made or our job would have come to a sudden end. In training at our rest quarters we simulated conditions as they were in the line by day and by night as far as it was possible to do so. Of course we could have worked by night but for many reasons day work was the better plan and did not interfere with the men's sleep. We obtained a few yards of fine black net and made eyeshades like bandages round the head. They were folded double or triple or worn single according to the degree of darkness we wished to simulate. The idea worked well and we practised crossing the areas of overgrown herbage, with or without sticks and branches, or we crossed barbed wire, got through hedges and over ditches and other likely obstacles. We practised various formations and swapped positions, simulating casualties and getting them out. The practices were enlivened by the throwing of a stick or stone with a shout of 'Bullet!' 'Stick bomb!' or 'Gas!' We finished the period with a few minutes' arms drill.

The dictionary says of reconnaissance: 'Examination of tract by detachment to locate enemy or ascertain strategic features.' In ordinary trench warfare the location of the enemy was known but not his strength at any particular point or time. At Riez-du-Vinage and Pacaut Wood neither his location nor his strength was known except in very general terms. Normally a reconnaissance (which we called a 'recce') was an examination for a particular purpose, whereas a patrol was a routine check of forward defences such as shell-holes, ditches or saps not permanently occupied. There were patrols acting as visiting rounds to detached posts in no-man's-land, occupied at night only. A fighting patrol was one which went out looking for trouble or expecting it, and therefore prepared for it but was not meant to attack enemy trench systems. It might break up an enemy working party engaged in consolidating a disputed shell-hole or ditch. It was not usual to molest enemy wiring parties, nor did they molest ours, for that was a game that paid nobody and pleased only the fire-eating sort of commander who insisted that there was no such place as no-man's-land.

A reconnoitring party went out to gather information and had nothing to do with routine patrols except mutual warning with passwords. When the line became more fluid in 1918, never having really settled down after the German breakthrough and our recovery of some of the lost ground, reconnaissance became all-important and never-ending. In addition there were constant raids made on enemy posts for identification of troops, which could lead to knowledge of their movements, and success in this might have far-reaching effects. In these the idea was to locate an enemy post first of all, then surprise it, take a prisoner, beat the others back and decamp before

— Rifle Bombers — 1918

the enemy could send out superior forces. To effect a capture like this
without undue loss, reconnaissance was necessary to establish the best way
there and back and to get some idea of the enemy strength likely to be
encountered.[6]

As plans matured for an advance, or at least for continuous pressure if the
Germans fell back on our 12 Infantry Brigade front, scouts had to locate the
enemy at as many points opposite our line as possible, for he had no line as
such. His few strongpoints were formidable and very well sited to command
many approaches and had good getaway routes. Almost any of his temporary
lurking places could be turned into strongpoints by means of a machine-gun
and a few picked riflemen, but these had no escape routes by day, being in
the open, and ran the risk of attack from any direction, even the rear. This
difficulty he surmounted by means of innumerable snipers and by cunningly
contrived crossfire from machine-guns in the strongpoints proper.

My scouts were fully occupied night after night in the business of location,
and I began to carry out daylight solo recces to facilitate and relieve the night
work. Later on we all worked as much by day as by night. It was an

enormous advantage to be able to see far and wide and to move rapidly in places whereas at night every step had to be considered. Day work, of course, meant a lot of crawling and had its disadvantages.

On our left flank there was a square enclosure consisting of an orchard, with a building at the far side and within it. Its near corner was some two hundred yards from our trench. Behind it and down the far side of it ran the little river Hennebecq towards and then under our line, where it was plank-bridged and the tunnel well wired. We did not know how or when the Germans held this place, which we called the Hun Farm, and I had to find out. We tackled it as soon as it was dark. As the obvious way to reach it unobserved was by way of the Hennebecq river-bed we avoided that as being a possible trap and entered the orchard near the jutting-out corner by crawling. As we fully expected, the orchard ground was covered with dry crackling twigs and some undergrowth. We did very well, the five of us, to get into the orchard at all without discovery, for there was a hedge with some barbed wire behind it, quite invisible until we touched it. We prepared an escape gap and then went diagonally towards the buildings which looked so dark and mysterious in the far corner or near it. We went without a sound until perhaps twenty yards from it, in a sort of loose diamond formation, as well as we could with the obstructions. Then the inevitable happened and a twig broke with a malicious crack. Before we could move there was a flash from the barn and a rifle bullet plugged into a tree somewhere near. Other shots followed rather aimlessly and obviously from more than one rifle, for we were noting the flashes. Then up went a Very light, one of the lingering kind, slowly floating and descending, at first illuminating the front for our inspection and then silhouetting the group of buildings and putting our party in shadow. The bright glare showed an opening in the near building, probably one from which the Germans had fired. I saw movement across it and then came the sudden hard rattle of a machine-gun, but it was firing in the wrong direction. They had expected us to come up the stream-bed. By this time we had turned back, taking advantage of the deep shadow, for I found one of my men had a slight bullet wound, or so he described it, but he was not out of action, fortunately for us all. I had gathered a fair amount of information or enough to go on with and with a man wounded it was time to get back.

We got through our escape gap and filled it in again while the machine-gun racket absorbed our noise, if we made any, and got into an outer ditch as arranged beforehand. The ditch ran outside the orchard hedge, its direction being at right angles to our trench line and ending in the orchard corner where we went in. The Germans could be relied upon to shoot along it towards our trenches so, the moment we were in it, I pushed the men out towards a parallel ditch which led eventually to our trench. We had barely reached the second ditch, a very shallow one, when a burst of machine-gun fire was directed down the first one. Jerry was evidently quick to guess at our probable movements and quick to realise a mistake, but we were lucky and kept a move ahead of him. We had to wait until his parachute flares ceased to illuminate our way back, but reached our trench without further incident. The information gathered, some of it obvious, was that Hun Farm was occupied at night by riflemen, machine-gun crew and NCO, or possibly officer, with Very lights. Either there were two machine-guns, which was unlikely, or there was an easily traversed track to an alternative position. In that case there were enough men to carry gun and ammunition quickly. The inadequate wiring indicated that the place was not regarded as a strongpoint of great strategic value and its position behind so much orchard growth made it fairly safe from surprise. Whether the place was occupied by day was for us to find out.

We thought the Germans in the Riez-du-Vinage and Pacaut Wood area did not quite live up to their reputation. Recently Second-Lieutenant Marsden had been given the job of finding out whether a German post in a cornfield was occupied by day. Since identification of the troops opposing us was also 'urgently required', it was decided to surprise the post and extract a man as prisoner. As a diversion and to cut off reinforcements, our field artillery shelled the area behind this post while Marsden and his men were on their way out, crawling through the corn which was now fairly high. They found the post occupied, but all eleven men were asleep. They secured a prisoner but as they were leaving the others heard movement and our men had to fight their way out. All eventually got away, including the prisoner, but Marsden and one of his men were wounded. For this raid Marsden was awarded the Military Cross and for him it was the end of active service as his shoulder was badly damaged.

We had the initiative and maintained the pressure on the enemy at all points. Certainly the scouts gave them no rest. Our job was to probe, prod and generally stir them up, to make them give away their positions and strength, and we never failed to find any enemy post and form a tolerably good estimate of how and when it was held. It was not entirely due to our skill as scouts that we succeeded, but to quite an extent to the enemy's nervousness. Jerry almost invariably gave away his position by sending up flares, of which he had a wonderful assortment both for signalling to his artillery and for illuminating no-man's-land. We were practised in dropping instantly and noiselessly to the ground at the first pop or flash of an enemy flare or any suspicious sound, and we were never caught standing. He also gave away his strength by aimless rifle fire, by traversing with machine-guns, by throwing hand grenades and, on at least one occasion, using them all together. What we did was to lie still and observe rifle and machine-gun flashes, how many and how far apart, and at what intervals of time and in what direction they fired. Every man did this for himself and we compared observations afterwards. Naturally this was a ticklish business. Under the brilliant illumination of Very lights we dared not move a finger. Sometimes the parachute flares seemed to float interminably but they were far more valuable to us than to Jerry even though ours was often merely a worm's-eye view.

At first I was afraid that when their machine-gun traversed backwards and forwards there would be little chance of escaping casualties but I found that by passing *beyond* the calculated position of the German post we were outside their traverse, for they stopped at the point where they would be firing into their own positions. Rifle bullets whined and ricocheted uncomfortably close sometimes but were evidently not *aimed*, and grenades were also thrown aimlessly, though on one occasion one fell amongst us. We were well spaced out and were lucky. Indeed we had a great deal of luck, and after the first Hun Farm reconnaissance our luck held. Retirement was the biggest trial. Everybody admitted to a great temptation to get up and run and to getting careless when within easy distance of our own trench. All this had to be resisted, for our aim was that of all good scouts, 'To see without being seen and to hear without being heard', so that Jerry would not know exactly where we lay or how we had come. Yet we had to rouse him to give his position and strength away.

After the first Hun Farm reconnaissance we wanted to find out whether the eastern edge of the orchard, some 300 yards from our trench line, was held and in what strength. The night was dark but we reached a spot nearly opposite and slightly to the rear of our objective without trouble, following the line of a shallow ditch into which we could drop if necessary. The enemy ditch I thought was beyond bombing range. We spread out along our own ditch which was no more than eighteen inches deep, then the five of us crawled forward inch by inch, covering distance enough to be within hearing of definite movement from the German trench or ditch, when either something gave us away or Jerry got nervous. Up soared a Very light but we were already lying flat. We were rather closer in than I had calculated, for the flare went right away over our heads to burn out about the ditch by which we had come or rather beyond it. I had noticed that it had been directed at an angle from their position towards our lines, and we concluded that they thought somebody was coming from that direction whereas we had not only arrived but had in fact almost passed them. Just as the flare burned out a machine-gun opened at the place, no doubt with the intention of catching us as we stood up again to come or go. At the same time two or three stick grenades were thrown towards the same place. We could hear them fall, with their familiar tinny rattle so unlike the solid bump of ours, and they went off almost together, as we could see by the flashes. Obviously they did not know where we were, and as I had all the information I wanted I had to get back before they sent out a party. Getting away was far more difficult than approaching, for I had to warn the others to withdraw, each man communicating with the next on his left. That done I stayed behind for a minute or two to cover their retreat, then followed, and we were lucky again for no further flares went up. We crept back to our 'safety' ditch by several low breastworks rather like the things put up by grouse-shooting folk on the moors but much lower. By the time I reached these the last man was just leaving one of them and lugging a German cow-hide pack. There were four or more German dead there, all with the complete marching equipment of troops on the move, including pack and *pickelhaube*, and one of them was a bugler. Our men could never resist such loot and did not mind the sickening job of removing it. When we got into our trench I got our men to search for anything likely to be of use to our Intelligence Officer but there was nothing to add to what was already known from bodies nearer the canal and in Riez-du-Vinage. In one pack was a little coffee mill and in others were tins of coffee beans and *lederfet* (dubbin). It is strange that all this equipment was left there. The rifles and ammunition had been taken by the Germans but strangely enough they left the bugle behind.

One night the King's Own were being relieved from the Pacaut Wood area. My men had been crossing the La Bassée Canal. I had seen them all across the plank bridge under Mont Berenchon and they were climbing up the bank while I was still on the bridge. There came a salvo of shells, amongst which sneaked one or two phosgene shells. The men yelled 'Gas!' and kept going upwards and therefore out of the dangerous hollow. Just as I stepped off the planks there was a flash and a bang and I felt a sudden wrench across my chest. Down I went and had I been on the bridge I would have been knocked into the canal. Gasmask and satchel, straps and all, had been wrecked and were hanging loose but I was up again immediately and pressed a handkerchief over mouth and nose. How I managed to scramble up the bank I don't know but I got out of the hollow probably without drawing another breath. The men were waiting with gasmasks on, having seen what happened. A stretcher bearer put a white-covered tablet against my mouth, at the same time pinching my nose and I inferred that I had to breathe through the tablet only. We were soon out of the gassy area. The men said they saw the smoke blow away along the canal and therefore from our track. It must have been accompanied by most of the gas otherwise I would have breathed some of it in while going up the bank. What the white tablet was I don't know. My only damage was a bruised neck and shoulder where the gasmask satchel strap had pulled round. So I escaped drowning, gassing and wounding by shellfire all in one go. The men were delighted with my luck for they liked a lucky 'bloke' to command them.

In August the Battalion held a line close to the main ride of the wood, running parallel with the canal and some five hundred yards from it. This ride was also the road, ditched on both sides, to the village of Riez-du-Vinage. The trench line was irregular and sketchy here, dodging about to avoid tree roots, and was not continuous. Between trench and ride was a wide, rather deep ditch, quite dry at this season. We had a little barbed wire in it and amongst the undergrowth. It was an unpleasant place, though cool and shady, for, as in all this sector, there were many unburied German bodies about and tear-gas seemed to hang about long after it had cleared elsewhere. Where the ride emerged from the wood on our left, or west, was a spot where two other rides from the German side met at a fine angle. There was a ruined brick building in no-man's-land on the left of this junction, standing almost on the roadside and fairly close to our trench. On the right of the junction and perhaps fifty yards within the wood was a German strongpoint, guessed at as such because of the enormous amount of barbed wire protecting the corner and by the frequency and volume of machine-gun fire which proceeded from the place at any time both by night and by day. The Battalion lost many men here. On the wire the Germans had hung little iron bells which tinkled musically but balefully when their strands of wire were touched. Just at this time it was becoming increasingly plain that Jerry was in some way altering his dispositions. On our side it had been proposed to attack the lone building opposite the strongpoint. Fortunately for the attacking party, the scheme was held over while reconnaissance was made elsewhere. Meanwhile I carried out a solo daylight reconnaissance of the strongpoint corner for if that were manned now, as it had been, by day and by night, the house attackers would be caught in their right flank by machine-gun fire and wiped out within seconds.

At the spot where I intended to enter the wood I had roughly a hundred yards between me and the junction of these rides at the corner of the wood where the strongpoint lay. From our lines nothing could be seen of it but the wide belts of barbed wire, and I did not know whether to expect it fifty yards or more or less from their side of the main ride, and though I had had their machine-gun flashes to go by, there appeared to be some variation. I had to make a guess at twenty-five yards within the wood and be prepared for more. I wanted to approach it from the flank. This meant entering the wood at my chosen spot, going into it for twenty-five yards by guess, then turning left and keeping parallel with the ride, judging the distance by the sunshine on it as seen through the trees and bushes. Before I started I had a good look through my binoculars for movement but saw nothing to give suspicion. The only way to cross that ride unseen by day was to cross it when the German sentries were not looking. That was the gamble. Our own sentries were warned all along the line in the wood and then, trying to make no noise with my heavy boots, I walked carefully across that excessively broad and sunlit road. On the far side was a ditch exactly like ours and wired in exactly the same way, the wiring being more in the nature of a deterrent than a defence. As I lay there in the cool shade I could see more wire amongst the bushes, just a few strands arranged to be troublesome in the dark and a check to anyone in a hurry. I continued to lie low and listen. Very considerately for me what little breeze there was came from the north and was innocent of smoke of any kind or of coffee aroma or of any signs of human activity, even sleep. The only sounds came from our side. I crept under some strands of wire and over others which were lying loose and, finding a thick bush, emerged from the ditch and raised myself enough to look round.

Immediately I found a worn track which saved me the trouble of making a way through the undergrowth, giving easy passage along the edge of the wood at perhaps ten yards but beginning soon to diverge inwards. As far as I could see into the wood there was no sign of earthworks or any more wire and with my field-glasses I could see very clearly into those cool shady depths. Turning the glasses left towards the strongpoint, there it was showing between the trees, very strongly illuminated by the morning sunlight which came through a gap in the foliage above it. I wanted to get near enough to make as sure as I could by listening whether it was occupied or not at the moment. I felt the sun on my cheek so pulled my cap-comforter over it, then got down and crawled. I had not far to go. There was piled earth round a rather wide excavation of about ordinary trench depth probably, though I could not see the bottom. At the back of it was a sloping entrance from a well-worn track which led back and into the wood. There was more than enough taut wire round it to prevent any possible entry from my position. The amount of piled earth at my side of the excavation indicated a dug-out under it, but I could not see the entrance as that would be facing away from me. There was a trip-wire with bells and some strands higher up, easy to negotiate in broad daylight but no doubt invisible at night. On the wide elbow rest of a machine-gun emplacement were hundreds of cartridge cases, including a few Very light cases. There was no sound from within the dug-out and no sentry at any of the possible observation posts.

I spent a seemingly interminable five minutes listening with an ear to the ground. I began to pick up the innumerable little sounds that indicate human occupation but they were all from our side of the road. Marsden's raid was fresh in my memory but I simply dared not make any attempt to enter this little fortress from the rear which afforded the only possible entry. This was so far back and defended by a lane of wire that I could imagine myself being caught like a rat in a trap if there was any shooting, with the certainty of the post being reinforced from some probable source not far away. I felt sure that this post had been abandoned for good but, remembering that Jerry was fond of setting traps, decided to make a careful retreat. This was uneventful. I made my report and the raid on the lone house opposite to the strongpoint was called off. We had more important things to do. Jerry was on the move.

Immediately after my solo recce in Pacaut Wood the scouts were told to be in readiness for a general advance but to be under Battalion Headquarters command until further notice, while scouts already trained and now with their own companies would act under their company commanders' orders. The little group I had chosen for special jobs were to go out with me when required as soon as the advance had brought our lines to the next objective.

Patrols had been out in succession all night, roaming far and wide but not deep and meeting with no opposition. There were no enemy shots fired and as soon as it was light enough, platoons had advanced from three hundred yards to a quarter of a mile all along the line except in the wood itself. By 10 o'clock all the wood except the northern arm was cleared. Possession was taken of a row of houses at the far edge of the main part of the wood, the chief building being called Wood House on the 12 Brigade sketch map. These buildings were entirely exposed to view from the north-east and at the time our forward troops little knew the risks they were running so light-heartedly. In fact Battalion Headquarters was set up in Wood House with enemy field guns pointing at it at 1,000 yards.

I was now given permission to reconnoitre forward. I called Scout Corporal Zelly to choose three scouts to form, with him and me, a party of five to penetrate the north-eastern edge of the arm of the wood. We set off

in the afternoon, keeping just within the edge of the wood in order to be visible to Battalion HQ. This course brought us behind some excavations marked as enemy posts, but they were unoccupied and we pushed on, still keeping near the edge and following a southward projection until we came to a ride. My map showed that this was crossed two hundred yards higher up, that is northwards, by a trenchline. Of that trench I saw nothing at the time but the ride had to be crossed and if the trench was occupied, a sentry would be posted to watch the ride and was bound to see us. We all crossed together in line, very quickly. Nothing happened. We pushed on again north-eastward towards the outermost corner. There was no trench here, though some sort of work was marked on the map but there was the end of another ride which continued as a road to the right, or east, along the end of an orchard, and seemed to end at a farm on the Hinges road.[7]

We were now 1,000 yards ahead of our battalion line. In front of us at about 150 yards was a street of houses, Malo Street we called it from the name of the locality, Le Cornet Malo. Most of the houses were on the far side of the road but there were some on this side, in or near the orchard. It was not easy to see everything because of the orchard trees, especially from our crouching position at the foot of bushes, and a fence. We were at the corner of a fenced enclosure like an allotment and, as we saw later, it was the first of a series of a dozen or so. At the far end of the allotment was a house, probably one of the row at the other side of the road.

There was no time for further observation of the locality. We could hear German voices. The only German I could think of at the moment was *Hände hoch!* — 'Hands up!' That might or might not have been effective had the emergency arisen but, very fortunately for us, it did not. The German that we heard was evidently a lot or orders spoken rapidly and forcibly and there was a reply. Raising myself near a bush I saw, not in the near plot but in the next one, a group of German artillerymen around a field gun and, approaching them from the direction of the house, an officer who seemed to be in a hurry. Corporal Zelly and the other three were having a peep through the palings of the fence. Safety catches were off and every man was in a position to fire in an instant through the gaps in the fence. My finger was crooked round the ring of a Mills bomb, for the range was just right. Never had we seen such sitting targets but this was no time for a shooting match as we were a thousand yards from home with the certainty of trouble for us from the village. Moreover, I wanted to make sure of what the Germans were about to do. I scribbled a message: 'Enemy field gun Q 28 d 3 4[8] and probably rest of battery extending NW. Think about to pull out.'

Private Brain was immediately sent back with this and we began to extricate ourselves from what at any moment might become a tight corner. If the battery were pulling out there was no time to lose if our artillery were to catch them. Nor was there any time to lose if they were *not* pulling out, for 1,000 yards was as good as point-blank with open sights for the gun nearest us. We got away from the immediate neighbourhood of the gun, inch by inch at first, but we were soon going quickly with the uncomfortable feeling that a parting shot might suddenly blow one or more of us to pieces.

We found later that our guess was correct. The German officer was giving urgent orders to pull out. Brain had delivered his message and our artillery was opening up on Malo Street before I reported in person to our CO. Later on, when Le Cornet Malo was captured, a gun team was found in a state of smash at the Malo Street and Hinges Road junction. This caused a horrible stench as the horses lay across the road in the hot sunshine but the place was exposed to enemy machine-gun fire so we had to put up with it.

When we got back to Headquarters at Wood House orders came through to attack Malo Street at dawn the next day. That was the objective assigned to the King's Own, ours being the centre sector of the brigade. The advance would take us over three-quarters of a mile from our present line through Wood House.

Again my party of scouts was kept with Headquarters. At dawn our guns gave us a barrage to follow and placed another to catch the departing Germans. They replied with only moderate shelling and a little mustard gas. Jerry's main body had gone but, as usual, machine-guns opened fire and a fairly strong rearguard was encountered amongst the houses. The Commanding Officer and HQ staff brought up the rear so I was no more than a spectator of what went on in front. We followed our own flashes and smoke into the orchard, at the corner of which I had crouched less than twelve hours ago. Colonel Carter fixed his monocle and we sampled a few apples which we hoped would freshen our smoke-filled mouths. Finding them unripe, the Colonel switched them away with his swagger cane. I have no recollection of where our new HQ was set up because I began to plan a reconnaissance beyond our new front as soon as there was such a thing. It was, of course, somewhat indefinite and could only be described as in front of and about the houses of Malo Street. Ahead were the villages of Bohème, Paradis, Pacaut, and others, not easily distinguished because the houses and farms straggled and seldom grouped. The nearest houses to our front were about half a mile away, and those of Pacaut village about five hundred yards on our left, not strictly in our sector. A little stream, the Courant de Turbeauté, ran right across our front at a distance of five hundred yards and flowed through Pacaut village. The ground between our position and this stream was entirely covered with growing corn, but beyond was open pasture and fallow without any cover. For the next few days this area of cornland was the scene of many reconnaissances. It was almost dead flat. The watercourses were marked by pollard willows, somewhat overgrown, especially along the Turbeauté, and these occurred at irregular intervals all the way to Pacaut village. The ground did not look as if it could hide many snipers and machine-gun crews but it did, making reconnaissance a laborious and painful crawl.

We found a nice big, dry shell-hole behind the Malo Street houses in or near the orchard, and there we set up Scout Headquarters so that we might be found when wanted. We now had a roving commission to bring in information about enemy positions and movements, location of snipers and machine-guns, as quickly as possible direct to Battalion HQ to save time.

Our first recce took us past the dead artillery horses, through the edge of the cornfield, along the continuation of Malo Street road eastward to the Courant de Turbeauté. Forward of this there was no more cover. The moment we arrived at the stream a message was sent back, for a line established along it would mean a further gain of at least a quarter of a mile. So far there had been no sign of the enemy. Now we turned northwards along the near side of the stream, keeping within cover of the corn, which was growing about two and a half foot high at the highest, and about two foot in places. I paused to spy with field-glasses from the base of any pollard willow which gave the necessary cover. There were two possible machine-gun positions along this quarter-mile stretch, less than a hundred yards from the stream. The place had evidently been prepared, for there were narrow plank bridges across the stream in two places and they were loosely coiled with barbed wire. We could see no sense at all in these, for who would bother about wet feet? The siting of the machine-gun posts, if that was what they were, did not seem good but at night the case would be altered so we reported them as possibilities. There was no movement in them, but as we approached the corner of this big cornfield, where a cart track ran alongside for about fifty yards towards us southwards, and then crossed the stream to the east, there were sniper shots and then a short burst of machine-gun fire. We were sure the latter came from an orchard about a quarter of a mile due north of us near Pacaut but the snipers were rather close. All this area was intersected by shallow ditches, which could, and did, give sniper cover. We had had enough of crawling, and returned to our line by the cart track aforesaid, or rather, along its ditch, keeping well down and, as there were no more shots, we assumed we were out of sight.

Though Pacaut was not on our battalion front, any fire from it enfiladed our advance on that front, so the following day the scouts carried on from where we had turned at the cart track, the companies having advanced to new positions during the night. Again we crawled through cornfields and observed from behind pollard willows on the course of the Turbeauté. Sniper shots continued but not at our party, and there were occasional short bursts of machine-gun fire from Pacaut. We reached a spot equidistant from Bohème on our left, Pacaut in front, and the orchard on Glebe Street on our right, the distance being about one hundred yards. My field-glasses gave me a good view right into the village of Pacaut and considerable movement was going on. It settled and I saw German steel helmets. Another movement and there was the unmistakable shape of their machine-gun shield and barrel, swinging slowly as if expecting a target. That was not surprising because there was far too much movement in our lines in front of Malo Street and the range was, at most, about six hundred yards for the machine-gun. It may have been mounted in such a position as would command three approaches, the centre one being our approach along the Turbeauté. But we had finished with approaching and had to consider how to get back without being seen. From my position against a willow I could see that we might make use of some of the many ditches or even deep plough lines, as I did not fancy a return along the way we had come. At one time the German gunner was drawing a perfect bead on me but obviously did not see me. We managed to find a way out by ditches which brought us to the Hinges–Bohème road, but it was a painful journey and a close call indeed. We had almost reached our cart track, crawling all the way, when a German sniper must have wondered why the corn moved and waved about without any breeze to stir it, and a few shots ripped viciously through it. The machine-gun fired along the stream-bed but by that time we were quite a hundred yards away from its line of fire. I made my report without delay, hoping that our artillery would soon clear Pacaut and let us get forward to somewhere clear of corn. We had all had more than enough of it. Corporal Zelly's knees were so badly swollen with crawling that he was sent to hospital with what the MO said was housemaid's knee.

I was approaching our shell-hole when a scout came to meet me. He said that Brigadier-General Fagan was there talking to the men. When I appeared he came forward and gripped my arm above the elbow. He asked many questions, shaking my arm at every one and saying 'Hah!' at the answers. Finally he released his grip, turned to the scouts in the hole, said, 'Good show!' and went to our Battalion Headquarters.

Scout Riley took Zelly's place and did very well. For his work over the whole Pacaut period Zelly was awarded the Military Medal and for mine I was awarded the Military Cross. It took many men to earn that, all but Zelly and I without tangible reward.

VIII

BREAKTHROUGH

With the end of the fighting around Pacaut about 18 August 1918, 1st King's Own, with the rest of 4th Division, was pulled out of the line for a rest and, a week later, was transferred from XIII Corps in Fifth Army to the Canadian Corps in First Army. The Corps's objective was to break through the main German defensive system, aiming for Cambrai from the north-west to coincide with a drive on the same city by Fourth Army from the south-west. This defensive system, perfected well out of reach of the enemy in 1916–17, was known to the British, who had misinterpreted something said by a prisoner, as the Hindenburg Line. The Germans designated the various stretches of it by names from Norse mythology and the sector to be attacked by the Canadian Corps was known as Wotan. The British referred to it as the Drocourt–Quéant Line or Switch since the original Hindenburg Line at this point had been outflanked in the spring of 1917, almost before it was completed, in the First Battle of the Scarpe and the fighting that included the storming of Vimy Ridge, thus making it necessary to build a switch line to cover the gap. The objective of 4th Division was a stretch including the large village of Dury, to the south of which another switch line had been built leading south-west, and the little town of Étaing which was protected on its northern and western sides by rivers which had been encouraged to flood and form marshy, impenetrable areas.

In the advance to the Drocourt–Quéant defences 12 Brigade was in reserve but it was brought forward for the main attack on 2 September when it attacked on a front of 1,500 yards with two battalions forward—2nd Essex on the right and 1st King's Own on the left. They were completely successful in breaking the main line, powerful as it was, but were checked south of Étaing itself and the town was occupied by another brigade on the following day. When the King's Own returned to the line their task was to try to find a way northwards through the tangle of marshes and waterways north of Étaing and it was on a reconnaissance to this end that Ogle sustained a wound that kept him out of the fighting until after Armistice Day in November.

The next big engagement in which the 1st King's Own took part after the minor one of Pacaut Wood was the [second] Battle of the Scarpe. Our approach was through Arras, along the Arras–Cambrai road to Monchy-le-Preux, the scene of grim fighting in April,[1] and Boiry-Notre-Dame. Then came the crossing of the Cojeul river between

Remy and Éterpigny. This brought us to the road between Éterpigny and Étaing on the Sensée river, our 'jumping-off line' for a big attack on the Drocourt–Queánt Line or 'switch'. My memories of events leading up to this attack on 2 September 1918 are hazy. I have a sketch of a house at Siracourt, a few miles west of St-Pol, and one of our Battalion Headquarters at La Thieuloye, a few miles [north-] east of the same town. While at La Thieuloye we took part in a mock battle centred on Monchy Breton but I have only some pencilled lines on a map to assure me that such a thing took place.[2] There was a train journey at some time in horse vans, possibly from Lillers or Choques to St-Pol. All I can remember of it is that Chaplain McGowan and I had a friendly bout of flat-handed fisticuffs in the truck and that I nearly went out of the open sliding door.

The Arras–Cambrai road, the old Route Nationale No. 39, was dead straight all the way, and looked it, with its bordering trees, but the country was not all flat. This was chalk-hill country. Between Monchy-le-Preux and Guémappe the road went down to the valley of the Cojeul river, climbing again from the St-Rohart factory, then down again to Vis-en-Artois on the Sensée. Away due east from Monchy was Boiry-Notre-Dame, three kilometres away, like Monchy looking down on the Cojeul. Still further east

from Boiry was Étaing but this was on the Sensée river, the Cojeul having joined it just above the little town. The village of Éterpigny, near which some of our stiffest fighting took place, was two kilometres from Étaing, up-river and overlooking the Sensée. These two valleys, converging at a fine angle, made rather complicated terrain for a fighting advance. The river crossings below Éterpigny were over a complex of watercourses curious at any time but now made more so by bridges, broken and unbroken, temporary and alternative crossings of various kinds, under a fair amount of shellfire and surrounded by woods, which were very dark at night. Below Éterpigny the Cojeul and the Sensée joined but there were also watercourses and ditches running parallel with them, one of them being a big sluice from a mill. In places they had overflowed through neglect and formed swamps. The Sensée, with its attendant watercourses, ditches and marshes, ran past the northern end of the town of Étaing but one at least of the watercourses, very much like a continuation or artificial 'escape' from the Cojeul, bore away northwards from the Sensée to join the Trinquis river. The Trinquis in turn flowed north-westwards to join the Scarpe, and all the low-lying ground about all these rivers was flooded. It was all *very* complicated and watery, so much so that the Drocourt–Quéant Line itself was interrupted by water as no real line was possible because of these combined rivers between Étaing and Sailly-en-Ostrevent on the north bank of the Trinquis. At the latter town it began again and this was to be one of our later objectives. In the meantime Étaing formed the northerly pivot of the attack and was on our battalion's open left flank.

The first part of the advance was finished when our battalion arrived at Monchy-le-Preux, about seven kilometres from Arras. I was in the Headquarters group following in the rear of the companies. We were in the old German front line and I have never seen such a maze of trenches. From Monchy there were four lanes or sunken roads leading into and along the Cojeul valley. Crossing these were trenches innumerable, front, support, reserve and communication, for a depth of quite a mile east of Monchy and crossing the Cambrai road. We had been given maps dated August 1918 and somebody had industriously named every trench or bit of trench, and perhaps somebody knew why. There were lanes called Infantry, Carbine, Saddle and Stirrup; trenches called Shovel, Spade, Fork, Pick, Sod, Tape and Trowel. There were Pommel, Saddle and Bridle, Spur, String, Lanyard and Brace; Badger, Beetle, Bat and Frog. Further north were Foal, Fox, Hen, Gander and Swan. There were German names in places. All of these may have had their uses. Most visitors to these parts had no idea that the beastly holes had names at all. To memorise them was hopeless and useless.

Down in Long Valley, that is the valley of the Cojeul, our artillery was massing for the big attack, and there was cavalry somewhere near. There were some scares about booby traps in some of the deep dug-outs. I was asked to inspect a dug-out and a Signaller risked disconnecting something which was wired but I don't know what. After a good deal of circumspection and hesitation I picked up a neat little grey steel box labelled 'Nadeln', presumably for gramophone needles, though it was empty. I put it in my pocket and still have it in use—one of my very few souvenirs.

Our progress was rapid at first but slowed down at the Éterpigny woods and at the crossings of the river where there had been some rearguard opposition. For days afterwards there were corpses of our men bobbing about in the swirling water by one of the temporary bridges. We came to a halt at about the Éterpigny–Étaing road where the German outposts had been driven back to their first trench system of the Drocourt–Quéant Line.

Battalion HQ was set up in a deep dug-out between this partly sunken road and the Éterpigny woods. During the evening of 1 September we received orders and the plan of attack for dawn on 2 September. Officers gathered in the HQ dug-out to hear about it and to gaze in awed silence on the maps of the trench system which lay opposite to our battalion front. These were copied from [aerial] photographs. Many of these photographs we saw also. By that stage of the war most of us knew something about barbed wire but the wiring of the Drocourt–Quéant Line beat all that any of us had ever seen or heard of. The battalion front extended southwards from a switch defending Étaing for about 1,300 yards. If we took all our objectives, the advance would amount to well over a mile. There were five lines of trenches, all wired. The first had a double row or belt of wire. About three hundred yards behind this line was another with a zig-zag belt of wire. Eight hundred yards behind this came the main line, a double one, the second or supporting line being about two hundred and fifty yards behind the first. The wiring of this first main line was a double belt. Behind all was the Drocourt−Quéant Support Line, about 250 to 400 yards further back. What its wiring was like I forget.

The main wiring was probably the most fantastic ever devised by a desperate enemy. It was arranged in a series of salients, some obtuse-, some acute-angled. It was said to be about forty yards wide but I think that is measured from the apex of a salient to the base line. When I reached it later it seemed to me quite as wide as, say, a cricket pitch plus the average fast bowler's run up to it. The second belt was less wide and not angled. Machine-guns were sited to enfilade the outside edges of the salients from emplacements in the main trenches, giving a maximum range of from 120 to 200 yards. I think the wiring posts were of timber mostly, all so close and so high that a leg could not be lifted over their wire if they were taut, or a foot placed on the ground between them. That was my impression though I did not make the attempt. I chose ready-made passages, as did everybody else, made either by our shellfire or by two tanks that led our attack. They crushed it down in a few places but it lay there in leg-catching profusion, except where our shells had blown it away. These shells exploded on impact, making scarcely any crater.[3] The preliminary belts of wire defending the first and second were fairly well shot away, or perhaps I was too excited or preoccupied to notice them. Of the main belt one of our runners said, 'Looks like Jerry's afraid of us.'

Close behind the main trench line ran a light railway, with a little 'railway triangle' leading to a branch line to the village of Dury, about five hundred yards further south.

Colonel Carter looked calmly at the aerial photographs and at our faces, then he reminded us of the array of massed guns in Long Valley[4] and told us that our assault would be preceded by a couple of tanks. We hoped that there would not be many 'shorts', for the destruction of the wire was to be by those terrible shells which exploded on surface contact and which were causing many German casualties and as near as a German can get to demoralisation. Another hazard was that of 'hugging' the tanks as they advanced, for they would be the main targets for the enemy artillery although they could not know beforehand how many we would use or their routes forward. There would be a lot of smoke, some of it a protective screen, and platoon commanders would have to be ready to seize opportunities for crossing the wire where shellfire had made gaps or where the tanks had

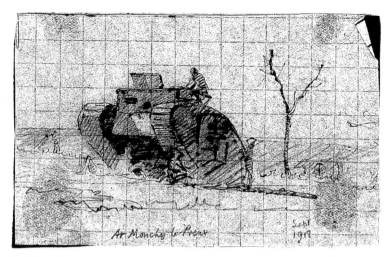

At Monchy-le-Preux   Sept 1918

crushed it. 'Give the tanks a wide berth but follow their lead and don't group anywhere.' I remembered that later.

My job was going to be to get in touch with all our companies and with the Battalion on our right flank,[5] who would attack from Éterpigny to Dury. Signallers would lay field telephone wires to whatever forward HQ could be established, all of us following on the heels of the attack. Meanwhile, I was to put the scouts in readiness for a reconnaissance on our left, open, flank when the main event was over. The MO had set up a first-aid post in a dug-out in the sunken road on our right flank.

It was barely light on 2 September when from the Long Valley of the Cojeul came an unnervingly sudden eight-mile *bang* of artillery, while overhead, and very close indeed, whined the first shells of our barrage. The enemy wire and first trench line seemed, all of a sudden, to spout fire, earth and debris, and the smoke wavered and then began to drift slowly further while again and again our shells descended. Presently the flashing, spouting, smoking line, which seemed strangely alive and as if dancing up and down, backwards and forwards, as the shells exploded, appeared as if doubled behind the first objective, from which the smoke lifted and rolled forward to disclose a single line again, flashing and smoking in exactly the same way. Then our men could be seen on the far side of the wire, having jumped into the trench and out again, going forward with barely a pause, there being practically no opposition from the stunned Germans. Meanwhile, the drifting smoke and apparent confusions had obscured the dramatic entry onto the scene of our pair of tanks. They were steering a course nearer our right flank than our left[6] and were equidistant from that right flank and from each other, slowly advancing in line abreast. What was happening on our left flank, where a switch line ran forward to cover Étaing, could only be guessed at, but as there was no enfilade fire on our advance, it may be assumed that our artillery had dealt with it.

So far men and tanks moved without either hurry or hesitation behind an accurately timed creeping barrage, which only halted at an enemy trench line. The second line offered little more resistance than the first and our line went forward under perfect control, every advance being timed to fit in with the creeping barrage until the tremendous obstacle of the main line was reached. Until the passing—it could hardly be called taking—of the second objective, I stood with our Medical Officer, Lieutenant Low, near the first-aid dug-out entrance which commanded a wonderful view, watching this thrilling and terrible spectacle with feelings I cannot describe. I might myself have been in that first wave of men, crouching low, watch in hand, ready to signal my platoon forward while the barrage lifted to fall crashing a hundred yards ahead at the exact second when we rose to resume our steady plod. I felt out of it but knew that my job was to begin in a few moments more, and my two runners were waiting with an apparent unconcern and calmness that would have been remarkable were it not so common.

The three of us reported to Battalion HQ and with them I set out up the middle of our front. Almost the first thing we saw as we approached the first line of enemy wire some two hundred yards ahead was a group of five of our men, all dead. One red-haired boy lay on his back, legless, and the others were more or less dismembered. In their midst the crater made by the exploding shell that had killed them was no more than sod-deep. Our shell or a German? We could not tell but I remembered the warning 'Don't group'. Ahead was the first line. We entered it to find several German under-age boys and over-age men, too scared to emerge into the open from this almost unharmed shelter. One of my runners gave a cigarette and a light to a trembling bald-head and we went on into the now thinning smoke and into the second line.

There was very little enemy shelling. Here again were some unguarded German prisoners who seemed unwilling to go towards our lines without escort but began to trickle back when we pointed. Here then were two lines of German trenches not much damaged but we had hardly noticed the wire. We went on again, beginning to find dead bodies of our men and passing many walking wounded on their way back to our first-aid post, some in charge of Germans. Now we were within sight of the main belt of wire. Over it the smoke had thinned and in places it was clear. The hammering of machine-guns had ceased and there were only odd rifle shots and an occasional outburst from our own Lewis guns. The whole northern part of the Drocourt–Quéant Line was in our possession.[7] There were no moving figures to be seen on our side of the wire, and not many forward but we knew that they would be 'consolidating' the trenches taken. As we came up

to the main belt, where a tank had crushed through, we saw many dead, caught by machine-gun fire at the wire's edge. There were wounded also but we could do nothing for them at that moment. We found ourselves at the apex of an enormous salient of wire, and as we were approaching the tank's tracks a shell burst in the wire somewhere at its far base, perhaps forty or fifty yards away. Bits of barbed wire and picket-posts flew, mostly over our heads but a fragment of something bent up the end of the D buckle of my webbing equipment shoulder strap (we all wore webbing now). My two runners also escaped.

We began to pick our way through a tangled forest of barbed wire and pickets, shell-holes and scattered chalk debris, amongst which our dead lay, but it became increasingly evident that our casualties were not heavy. We three could do nothing for the badly wounded but ease their positions, extricate some from the tangled wire and assure them of approaching help, for stretcher bearers were already coming up behind us or were busy in and about the line. We crossed the main belt where it had been crushed and, looking up forward, I saw a tank apparently stranded on or near the German support line, broadside on to us. The main defence line was enormously strong and well-appointed. Behind it ran a narrow-gauge railway line which had served the line from Étaing to the Buissy Switch and the Cambrai road. Near our left flank was a first-aid or dressing station very clearly marked with a big Red Cross; it was very full of both British and German wounded, but far more German than British, as if they had been saving them up for us.[8]

After collecting what reports I could get from a lot of very busy and preoccupied people I got in touch with the battalion on our right flank and heard that our Major Kennington was in command of them, having been sent for when their headquarters was reduced by casualties. He was awarded the DSO.

On our way back after a second visit to the captured line in the afternoon,[9] we saw many horse-drawn limbers on the battlefield, and our dead were being loaded into them, wrapped in their groundsheets for removal to a cemetery. By nightfall they had all been gathered in. I thought of the Somme and the thousands of unburied dead.

On the night of 2 September I was given the order to lay a tape line. This was to mark the starting line or 'jumping-off line' as we called it, for an attack which, if successful, would bring the British line up to Étaing, though this was not a job for our battalion.

I gathered some scouts and was given a white tape. We began a line near the captured trenches in front of the first-aid post and began to work along in front of the Étaing Switch, carefully observing and listening for enemy occupation. We found the white tape much too short, of course, but continued with pieces of white chalk, which was plentiful in this district. We moved as a fighting patrol, quickly but with care. There was no sound from the Switch but it could not for a moment be imagined that Jerry would leave it unguarded except by belts of wire and an empty trench. We soon had our line laid out and returned to Headquarters. I believe that this attack was never delivered, but much later the place was bypassed when it was abandoned by the Germans.[10] We were relieved and went back to La Thieuloye that night.

At La Thieuloye Headquarters Staff had a dinner which was obviously very much better than the usual, with wine even, and towards the end of it I was told that I had been recommended for the award of the Military Cross and that it had gone through but would not appear in orders yet as it was

unofficial. This was 6 September 1918. The citation appeared in Routine Orders for Immediate Awards to Officers and Men of the Fifth Army, dated 18 September. On 19 September, being still at La Thieuloye, we had a Battalion dinner, crowding everybody in at several tables in the largest room. This was to celebrate the award to Captain Carr MC, DCM, of a bar to his Military Cross and the award of the Military Cross to me. I think Major Kennington's DSO was to have been celebrated had he been able to be present but he was still seconded.

While the Commanding Officer and Assistant Adjutant were both on leave, the Adjutant, Captain Gilbert, was acting CO and I was acting Adjutant. I told Gilbert that I knew nothing of the Orderly Room side of soldiering, with all its forms, chits and returns. I said, 'I've just put my signature to a thing called "Administrative Instructions to Operations Order No. 70". Staff Sergeant simply pushed it over for me to sign. I didn't compose it or think of any of the things on it. He did all that.' Gil answered, 'Oh, no, he didn't. That's routine. Officers' kits, stores, mess stores and all that. Company quartermaster-sergeants know all about that and the items are merely filled in in the usual long-established routine order. Staff's business is to see that the thing is typed out and he gets the information from the various people concerned and checks with them.' I said, 'He seems to have thoughtfully pinpointed a couple of cemeteries for our use on our 51B map!'[11] Gil laughed and said, 'Remember that a lot of this stuff comes from Brigade. *We* don't arrange it. Anyhow, Bogy, the Orderly Room didn't get the Battalion through Pacaut Wood, nor break the Drocourt–Quéant Line.'

My last reconnaissance was not the artistic triumph it ought to have been. It was ill-conceived and worse planned. In technique it was wretched, it achieved little at great expenditure of effort and travail of mind, its personnel survived by sheer good luck, and its ending was most undignified. As you ought to have guessed it was not of my contriving!

The 1st Battalion, The King's Own had arrived at its appointed lines east of Boiry-Notre-Dame about 21 September 1918. I had made reconnaissances from Galley Wood[12] down towards the town of Étaing. Below the wood, the rivers Cojeul and Sensée join and there are also overflows from sluices at the mills higher up the Cojeul. All this water, coming together in front of Étaing, made an impassable barrier, for it had been allowed to overflow to form wide, brimming marshes. Likewise in front of the neighbouring town of Sailly-en-Ostrevent the river Trinquis overflowed to form marshes which extended to the river Scarpe, which it joined a mile or so north of Sailly. The Scarpe in its turn was more like a succession of marshy-bordered lakes than a river, all the way to the old front line at Fampoux. This indeterminate maze of river, lake and marsh formed a watery crescent round the foot of our Boiry-Notre-Dame spur.[13] As if this natural barrier were not enough, the Germans had run a defensive switch from the Drocourt–Quéant Line to join Étaing with Sailly. This was shown on our maps as defended with a double row of wire. It ran along the roadside, a few feet above the floodwaters, and there seemed to be water on both sides of it. The map showed also a bridge over the Trinquis to Sailly at the end of the switch and near it, but on our side, in no-man's-land (though this expression was falling into disuse), a German dump of Engineers' stores. This bridge seemed the obvious and indeed the only dry way to reach the Drocourt–Quéant Line behind Sailly.

Information about the German defences at this bridge and its vicinity was wanted, and I had assumed, naturally enough, that it would fall to the Battalion scouts to obtain it. But *They* (I don't know who), because of its importance, made the required reconnaissance a captain's command. I was up against the seniority evil. I was in high dudgeon. A small party of trained and experienced scouts under my leadership, who had trained and led them on many a reconnaissance, could have done the job safely and well. But *They* must give it to a captain who was no scout, not that he could be blamed for that. He was no better pleased than I was. Who chose the party I don't know but there were only two scouts in it. It was too big for a quick reconnaissance, far too small for a fighting patrol and, worst of all, it was timed to set out far too late. Then, when all was arranged, the captain asked me to join. There could be no refusal, of course.

I remember saying to myself as I led the way out, 'The pitcher goes often to the well...', a phrase I had often used to our Medical Officer, Lieutenant Low. I was puffed up with indignation and wounded pride and no doubt looked very severe but my looks, however impressive, were lost on the party in the darkness of the night. I expected things to go badly or even wrong and might even have been disappointed if they had not. The men had been wakened after a short sleep. They had therefore lost their first enthusiasm and were cold, clumsy and noisy. We made a living illustration of the army expression which describes an enterprise as 'setting off on the wrong foot.' On this occasion initial speed at the start was essential, and should have been possible because the way at first was downhill and part of it had already been reconnoitred, but I soon found my speed being reduced to the stumbling slowness of the party. At point after point I waited, chafing sorely at this divided command which in effect placed the burden of a figurehead on my hands. I could hear the men's clumsy progress by the unmistakable sounds of steel helmets in collision with rifles and wished that I had at least insisted on proper scouting order. But our luck was in. Mist arose and thickened.

The captain was in a twitter of impatience because it was perilously near dawn and nothing found, so now, when they should have crawled like snails, the movements of the party became almost recklessly precipitate. Finally I had to make them understand that we were very close to the bridge for I had heard the sound of running water and other sounds that made me pause. We had entered a patch of dense mist but it was irregular and in a sudden clear passage I more than suspected movement ahead. We had paused by a mound of grass-grown debris which gave a certain amount of cover. At the far end of it stretched what looked like a raised breastwork but the shifting mist made it indefinite. I expected wire and, leaving the party in the charge of the captain, I crept forward, my Webley cocked ready for action. Ten yards or so brought me to the foot of what was without doubt a defensive work of some kind but unwired. I debated whether to move left or right to find out how far the thing extended and whether it was manned. Fortunately I looked to the right. The mist was drifting in swathes of varying thickness as if about to break up and I was conscious of dawn. As I looked up from my crouching position close to the breastwork I saw that well-known squarish shape, the German steel helmet, begin to rise above the parapet and very quickly indeed its owner rose to lean over, the early dawn light silhouetting him and projecting a long gleam which I knew was his rifle barrel. That gleam, pointing directly at me, shortened as I watched and told me that he was coming up to a careful aim. That care was to be his undoing. In a vision which came as quickly and clearly as light I saw crackshot Colonel Hitchins of the Loyals, whom up to this second I had hated, firing as one points a forefinger, and I did likewise, taking no other sight. The two reports were almost simultaneous with the difference in my favour. I heard the metallic clatter of helmet on rifle barrel and I felt a burning pain in my disengaged left hand.

Almost immediately came the deafening clamour of a machine-gun at very close range but the mound and the drifting, patchy mist had saved us. Our luck was still in and I felt better. But I had to locate that gun and was lucky to spot its familiar shape, with its shield and low squatting figures, before another shred of mist covered them. I had seen the gun but not its *exact* location and I wanted to see where that bridge was. Meanwhile the captain had ordered the party to make for the German dump, remaining at the mound to cover their retreat and give me help if required. The mist parted again and there was gun and crew against what was without doubt the parapet and there were, behind them, running figures advancing. Then everything disappeared. It was indeed time to go home! I turned, to see a strange sight as I stood upright for a moment before my sprint. The tops of innumerable stacks of narrow-gauge railway metals stood above a level sea of mist like rafts, and in full daylight. A moment too late the disappointed machine-gunners and I don't know how many riflemen had a clear view of our disappearing backs. Then the mist must have hidden us.

The stacks were piled in squares about seven feet high, in rows parallel in width and depth, leaving lanes for access, covering perhaps nine acres of ground which rose gently towards our trench lines on the Boiry Spur.[14]

We had rushed gladly into what we thought was cover, and so it was but *what* cover. The German defences at the bridge were so arranged that they could fire into the dump up the long lanes. And fire they did, venomously and blindly into the mist. The hail of bullets which now swept the stacks made a deafening and dreadfully confusing clangour, impossible to describe except in mad-musical terms. Those bullets which hit a rail at a fine angle shrieked with a vibratory note along a groove or flange until they shot out at its far end to whang into another stack. I suppose if they met a nut *en route* they probably fragmented. Bullets ricocheted and re-ricocheted like jumping fire crackers in movement but with varying sonority. Many hit the rails head-on with sonorous long *zongs* if high on the stack, or flatter notes if lower down, and may have hit every note in all the major and minor scales, but in a mad confusion which was excruciating. To add to both clamour and confusion there was at first a decided echo which doubled the noise and made it impossible to be sure exactly where it came from, though its general source we knew only too well. My hair must have stood on end and for once I wished that I was wearing a steel helmet instead of a cap-comforter. My high-horse had fled and all hatred had gone out of me. Nothing remained but the desperate desire to get out of this ridiculous situation without losing a man. At one point, two of us nearly met head-on, having dodged respectively left and right behind a stack. At the sudden sight of each other's sweating faces, eyes and mouth wide open, we both burst into hysterical laughter and then one of us turned and we ran giggling side by side until we parted for lack of room. The dump seemed limitless but at last we realised that the machine-gun had given up and only an occasional vicious crack and splash of lead warned us to keep going. We were all wearied to exhaustion. The mist thinned rapidly as we began to climb the spur and we stepped out into sunshine before the last row of stacks. I realised that I had been carrying my heavy revolver raised in case of pursuit and thankfully put the thing away. It was a very slow procession of tired men that at last fell into the trench.

MO Low's greeting was 'So the pitcher's been to the well again, Bogy!' I was off my guard and replied, 'But I'm not broken, only *cracked*.' Brother Low took full advantage and remarked, 'Yes, and from his own lips! Bogy, I've thought so for a long time. No, your antics in no-man's-land have come to an end, I hope. Let's have a look at your hand.' He gave me a cigarette and a light but my discomfiture was not yet complete. I puffed too quickly and too hard, and passed out.

Before I left for the Casualty Clearing Station I was told to call at Brigade

HQ to say goodbye. As I sipped Brigade's generous whisky (my third that morning), I answered questions to their evident satisfaction, but I must have warmed up when I described our flight through the dump for they showed great amusement. I wondered how it all compared with Captain B's correct and probably unenthusiastic report. Possibly that had reached them first and explains why they were so tickled.

My faithful Cockerill arrived to carry my traps and see me off. It was goodbye to the 1st King's Own, to the 4th Division, to active service and, very soon, to France and Flanders, for my wound was a Blighty.

I arrived at a Base Hospital late at night with other officers. All in the ward seemed to be asleep. I slept soundly and in great comfort and woke in daylight to a pleasant surprise. In the bed next to mine a man was looking at me with considerable interest. I looked back at him and immediately recognised Harold Crook. We called each other's names at the same instant. We had both left Silcoate School, Wakefield, the Northern Methodist School, in 1904 when the school was burnt down. We had hardly met when we had to part, as I was sent away after breakfast and surgical attention to join a party for the boat that carried me to England. All I remember of that journey is the very end. When the train stopped at Marylebone Station there were cheering crowds at the barriers, to our great surprise, for we had been used to coming and going without demonstration. Marylebone Station Hotel had been turned into a reception hospital and we went straight in from the platform.

Muriel came down from Colwyn Bay immediately and found lodgings in a third-floor back bedroom in Marylebone Road. She had entered a London rapidly becoming overwhelmed by a great influenza epidemic that was worldwide, claiming victims comparable in numbers with those of the war.[15] Doctors were working day and night and were themselves being struck down. Many of that trainload of wounded men died of it within a few days. Muriel caught it after about a week but an overworked and really heroic doctor helped to save her, though I think she survived mainly by her own will and courage. I do not remember much of what happened at that time, which now seems dreadful to look back upon but which we then took calmly enough, for we had become accustomed to the risks of war and all it brought in its train.

After a fortnight or less I was ordered out of the hospital, which was badly overcrowded, and was sent to the Savoy Hydro at Blackpool which was then used as an Officers' Convalescence Centre. I went with the intention of finding Muriel lodgings in Blackpool and then returning to fetch her but, because of the risks of spreading infection, I was not allowed to return. Meanwhile she sent a telegram to say she was coming. She paid her landlady and took a taxi to the station, having no strength to walk. This left her only

The Gynn Inn *Blackpool*

enough money to get as far as Manchester, where she arrived weak and with no money. But Uncle Harry and Aunt Alice had come to Blackpool to be near me and Uncle had the foresight to decide on meeting her at Manchester and was there just in time. I met them both at Blackpool with a Bath chair.

We spent the cold and windy winter of 1918 at Blackpool, Muriel in convalescence and I at first receiving treatment for the wound in my hand. The Savoy Hydro was then at the extreme northern end of the long promenade, not actually on the prom itself but a few hundred yards from it towards Bispham, being in fact the last building in Blackpool. From nearby, officers took a tram right down the prom to the camp at Squire's Gate at the extreme southern end of the South Shore. At this famous and detestable camp (I must admit that I considered *all* army camps and their personnel detestable), officers received treatment for their injuries, and remedial exercises, after which subalterns had to attend courses of lectures in various army huts. The subjects included such things as trench sanitation, care of feet, construction of trenches and shelters, and construction and maintenance of barbed-wire entanglements. This last, after about four years' intimate experience of the stuff, culminating in that of the Drocourt–Quéant Line, was more than could be endured but we did not like to insult the lecturer by openly going to sleep so we just sat with glazing eyes directed inwards to our memories of the real thing or, more likely, to pleasanter things we promised ourselves.

It was during a lecture on the attack and defence of strongpoints that, on the morning of 11 November 1918, we brightened when we heard distant cheering. In those days there was only one thing that could be worth a cheer. The lecturer faltered. Running footsteps were heard and after a very cursory knock an NCO burst in with a note for the lecturer. We knew it! We did not wait to hear what the note said but I believe the officer said, 'That of course will be all this morning, gentlemen.' We gave one yell and dashed out to join the others, and a surging throng of all ranks mingled with civilians to converge on the Town Hall Square just when the Mayor of Blackpool announced the Armistice. The town went wild with relief and joy. Processions of all sorts were hastily improvised and celebrations continued all night long.

At the end of April 1919 I was discharged from Blackpool and sent, after a short leave, to the King's Own depot, then at Richmond Barracks, Dublin. Muriel did not go with me, for my stay there was not expected to be long and in those days Ireland was not the place for any kind of holiday since there was Trouble, as ever, and our sentries loaded with ball. I was waiting for my discharge, or disembodiment as it was called, from the Territorial Force. Almost immediately on my arrival I was detailed as escort to an officer under arrest, thus I saw very little of the Officers' Mess or the barracks in general.

After about a fortnight I was sent to Fovant in Wiltshire to be disembodied. I was interested to find there rounded greyish-green chalk hills which, though bigger, reminded me of those of the Somme and the Scarpe. Then, after a short leave, I went back to Bridge Street Boys' Council School, Redditch, but had not been at work long when I received a Command to attend an Investiture at Buckingham Palace. There was a crowd of people outside the gates and on the Queen Victoria Statue steps, and this seemed to be the normal thing for these functions. After leaving our Service caps and canes in a cloakroom we waited in an enormous room decorated in blue and gold and with great chandeliers. There seemed to be a big crowd of officers,

Dublin
Richmond ₂/₅ 9

203

for it filled the room. We were marshalled in the correct order for the ceremony and slowly moved along the corridors which led directly to the top, or dais, end of the big room. As we moved forward we could see King George V and Queen Mary on the dais, I think under a canopy but I was too scared to observe closely. We had to march in turn to the steps in the middle front of the dais, turn left, ascend the steps and bow. Then His Majesty pinned the decorations to our tunics, said a few words and shook hands. Then, after another bow, we backed down the steps, turned right and marched off. While we marched to the dais there was just time for an officer of the Royal Household to read the citation. Upon this the King had to base his few words. Mine read as follows:

Second-Lieutenant Henry Ogle, Royal Lancaster Regiment.[16]
He carried out numerous patrols with his party of Scouts, bringing back most valuable information. It was mainly due to his daring and able reconnaissance in a locality infested with enemy snipers and machine-guns that it was possible to establish a line on the left centre of the brigade.

The King said, 'You have worked hard for us under dangerous conditions. Well done.'

After leaving the Throne Room, in which we were acutely conscious of a seated assembly of distinguished-looking people, we turned right to a room where liveried attendants stood at a long table covered with little leather cases of different kinds. One of these men *snatched* my Military Cross, *clapped* it into a purple case which he *thrust* into my hand, and then immediately turned to snatch the next. How I got out I don't remember except that the crowd seemed denser, for it was not easy to make a way through it. Afterwards I found that the Cross was not engraved as I had expected it to be, with name, rank and regiment. There was nothing on it to show that I had any right to it. All my other medals are engraved.

And so, like a proper soldier, I end this narrative with a grouse.

APPENDIX

Two of Henry Ogle's War Poems

Very Lights*

Young and untried, we watch from the hill-top
Behind the barn—our billet for the night—
In twilight, silent and with shining eyes,
Though careful to avoid a mutual glance.

With hearts too full for common talk or jest,
We watch, absorbed almost to breathlessness,
The distant flares beyond the Salient
That random rise and fall incessantly.

Those far-off tiny points of wavering light,
Appearing suddenly and hovering,
to fall extinguished in the mists of night,
Reveal to us the fateful battle line
That loops the ghost of Ypres, a name
By sacrifice of youth immortal made.

* In billets near Winnezeele, March-April 1915 (see p. 27)

J.T.*

So here you lie, so still and quiet now
White-faced with the dim whiteness
Of the shovelled chalk that no one reached
In that brave dash through leaden hail.

Old Ugly Mug, you were no ornament,
Your speech unguarded, raucous and obscene.
You lied—to save me trouble, cheated, doubtless
And pilfered—so that I might have a treat.

I am not guiltless of your cheerful crimes,
But never unashamed and unafraid
Like you, having a poor and secret self
That even you seemed not to know.

You were my friend; unsought you came.
I blush when I recall your praise of me,
Not knowing I was near enough to hear
Your rasping voice, emphatic and cocksure.

In danger, in discomfort, in the petty joys
That soldiering affords, so fleetingly,
You were my friend, keeping a place for me,
Sharing your spoils, cheering with ready jest.
Your Number's Up, 'Top of the Whack', old pal.
You've handed in your card. Lie now and rest.

* Jack Taylor (see pp. 64,68,71-5) was killed in an attack near Ovillers in 1916.

NOTES

Introduction

1 The first Territorial unit to land in France was 14th London Regiment (London Scottish), who arrived on 16 September, followed four days later by 1st Bn, the Honourable Artillery Company. In the same month 42nd Division (TF) (East Lancs) sailed for the Mediterranean to relieve Regular troops. The first Territorial unit in action was the Oxfordshire Hussars (Queen's Own), which fought a skirmish south-west of Ypres on 5 October.

2 In the First World War all British staff officers wore the red gorget patches now worn only by colonels, brigadiers and general officers.

I England 1914: Your King and Country

1 The Austrian Archduke Franz Ferdinand had been assassinated at Sarajevo on 28 June.

2 Under the 'Pals' Scheme, groups of friends who enlisted together were permitted to train and serve together.

3 Retitled 48th (South Midland) Division on 12 May 1915, it comprised 143 Brigade (5th, 6th, 7th & 8th R. Warwicks), 144 Brigade (4th & 6th Gloucesters, 7th and 8th Worcesters), 145 Brigade (5th Gloucesters, 4th Ox & Bucks LI, Bucks Battalion, OBLI, 4th R. Berkshires).

4 The Long Lee-Enfield had a barrel length of $30^3/_{16}$th inches and a 12-inch bayonet while the SMLE had a 25.19-inch barrel and a 17-inch bayonet. It was some eight ounces lighter and was sighted to 2,000 yards compared to the 2,800 yards of the longer model.

5 In the early days of the war any recruit bringing his own overcoat, boots and a suit of clothes was paid half a sovereign to wear them until a uniform became available.

6 The practice of forming square to receive cavalry had been abandoned towards the end of the nineteenth century except 'in savage warfare'. Thereafter the instruction was 'It will usually be sufficient in open ground to throw back the threatened flank of a firing line, and the unmolested flank may, if desirable, be advanced.'

II Holding the Line in Flanders

1 48th Division had been allocated to III Corps (Lt-Gen. Sir William Pulteney), where it served alongside 6th Division, to which 2nd Bn Durham Light Infantry belonged. Strictly speaking, DLI had not been 'out since Mons', as they reached France only in mid-September 1914, in time for the Battle of the Aisne.

2 Armentières had briefly been occupied by the Germans in the autumn of 1914 but had been reoccupied by 6th Division on 17 October. Since then that division had had hard fighting, in which the DLI had been conspicuously engaged, to maintain the line in front of the town.

3 H. H. Asquith, the Prime Minister, paid a short visit to the BEF in May-June 1915.

4 When the first gas attacks were made the troops were advised to press wetted handkerchiefs

over their mouths or to use pads of lint, soaked for preference in bicarbonate of soda, and held in place by tapes. By July 1915 the whole army was equipped with a 'smoke helmet' consisting of a bag of flannel, soaked in some suitable liquid, and having a celluloid window.

5 Pozzy = jam.

6 In February 1915 Sir John French limited the expenditure of 18-pounder shells (only shrapnel being available) to 10 rounds per gun per day. This was reduced to 3 rounds daily in April. By that time production in Britain was running at a quarter of a million rounds a month but in May the BEF had to part with 20,000 18-pounder shells for the Gallipoli expedition. On 17 May the total reserve for the Army in France was 3,014.

7 The large missiles fired by the German 21cm mortars looked so black and menacing as they soared apparently slowly through the air that they were known as Jack Johnsons after the American boxer (1878–1946) who was heavyweight champion of the world between 1907 and 1915.

8 While the supply of .303 ammunition for rifles and machine-guns was never in as parlous a state as that of artillery ammunition, the whole British Army's reserve had fallen from 400 million rounds in August 1914 to 2 million rounds at the end of March 1915, despite severe restrictions on musketry practice by troops under training in the United Kingdom. The rate of production rose from 26 million rounds a month in September 1914 to 93 million in May 1915. Thereafter, with the help of supplies from the USA, the provision of .303 ammunition was never a serious problem.

9 Harry Ogle frequently uses the name Flanders as being co-terminous with western Belgium although it is usually held to include the old French province of Artois with its capital at Arras.

10 this was the Château de la Hutte on Point 63, 206 feet above sea level. It is one of the features of the northern battlefields on the Western Front that quite small rises in the ground assumed great tactical significance. The Ypres ridge, for example, is barely visible from a distance.

III Holding the Line in Artois

1 Houchin (Houchain) is 3½ miles south of Béthune.

2 These, the *territoriaux*, were elderly soldiers who had completed their reserve liability after their full-time service under conscription.

3 Between 7 and 13 June XI French Corps had erased a German salient south of Hébuterne and held their gains against a number of counter-attacks.

4 Warsaw fell to the Germans on 5 August 1915.

5 The steel helmet cannot have been worn at the time indicated (August 1915). At the end of July a few French models had been tried by the BEF and found unsatisfactory, and the first British-made helmets, a sample batch, did not reach France until September. By the end of October, when 3,500 had been issued, they had been rejected as inadequate, and production of the model finally adopted did not start until November. By March 1916 140,000 of this final type were with the BEF, the figure rising to a million by early July. It was observed, apparently with surprise, that their issue reduced the number of head wounds by 75 per cent. Ogle must have been combining with this memory a later one of a similar occasion. There is nothing to say, however, that he did *not* hear the raindrops falling—dripping onto hats or whatever served as shelter. One gloomy rainy day is much like another whatever the circumstances.

6 *Minenwerfer* were trench mortars, of which the Germans had three types, the largest being of 240mm (10in) calibre. Captured models were tested at Woolwich where the type of ammunition was reported to be dangerous (to the user).

7 The rifle grenade is a normal fragmentation grenade which is fired from a discharger cup fixed to the muzzle of a standard service rifle which is loaded with a balastite cartridge thus making an improvised small mortar though one that is extremely difficult to fire with any accuracy. In the British Army its use had to await the development of an adequate grenade (see pp21-21).

8 It was not until late in 1915 that the British produced anything more than unsafe, inaccurate, improvised trench mortars. Then, in time for a few to be used at Loos in September, the Stokes light (3in.) mortar was made available, medium and heavy models following later. They were used in companies under brigade control, a section being allocated on occasions to infantry units for special tasks.

9 The 'coming push' was the attack at Loos starting on 25 September.

10 When the BEF was mobilised in August 1914 Lord Kitchener, as Secretary of State for War, ruled that canteens should not accompany it overseas as 'This war is not going to be a picnic.' The early canteens were, therefore, established privately by organisations (YMCA, Salvation Army, etc.) or by patriotic individuals. It was not until the early months of 1915 that Expeditionary Force Canteens started to appear. To assist in their establishment a loan was made from the accumulated balances left over from the Field Force Canteens run during the South African War. The Expeditionary Forces Canteen Organisation eventually evolved into NAAFI.

11 At this time in 1915 Elverdinghe was three miles from the nearest point in the German trenches.

12 Brielen is midway between Elverdinghe and Ypres, and the Château des Trois Tours is 500 yards to the west of the village. During the 1915 Battle of Ypres the château was Headquarters to 1st Canadian Division and continued to house headquarters throughout the war, miraculously surviving almost unscathed.

13 Company sergeant-majors wear a wreathed crown as a badge of rank.

14 The meat and vegetable stew tinned by Maconachies was an only too frequent part of British Army rations between 1914 and 1918. Through mere relentless reappearance it earned a measure of opprobrium that it did not wholly deserve.

15 On 1 October 1915 the meat ration was reduced from 1¼lb (fresh or frozen) or 1lb (preserved) daily to 1lb (fresh or frozen) or ¾lb (preserved). Three weeks later the mustard ration came down from $\frac{1}{20}$ oz. to $\frac{1}{50}$ oz.
The remainder of the ration in the period 1914-17 comprised: Bread 1¼lb; bacon 4oz.; cheese 3oz.; vegetables 8oz. (fresh) or 2oz. (dried); tea $\frac{5}{8}$ oz.; jam 4oz. (reduced to 3oz. on 4 April 1916); sugar 3oz.; salt ½oz.; pepper $\frac{1}{36}$oz.; condensed milk $\frac{1}{16}$ tin (increased to $\frac{1}{12}$ tin on 4 April 1916); pickles 1oz weekly; butter as an extra.

16 GS = General Service. The GS wagon was the standard transport vehicle of the British Army until the nineteen-thirties and examples could still be seen around Aldershot at least as late as 1941. Drawn by two horses, it had an authorised load of 30 cwt.

17 Trench flu was spread by lice.

18 Mailly-Maillot is five miles south of Foncquevillers and opposite Beaumont Hamel, a German strongpoint.

19 The fact that the soldier was secured to a wheel suggests that he had been awarded Field Punishment No.1 rather than 2. According to the Field Service Pocket Book:

No.1 The offender may, unless the court-martial or CO otherwise directs —
(a) Be kept in irons
(b) Be attached by straps, irons or ropes for not more than 2 hours in 1 day to a fixed object. Must not be attached for more than 3 out of 4 consecutive days or for more than 21 days in all.
(c) Be made to labour as if he were undergoing imprisonment with hard labour.
No. 2 Same as No. 1. except that he may not be treated as above in (b).

20 Snitterfield is a village four miles north of Stratford-on-Avon.

21 From 20 November 1914 to November 1915 home leave of seven days (including travelling time) was granted to troops in France; the two following years the period was increased to ten days; to be further increased to fourteen days in November 1917.

22 Hoddlesdon is some five miles south of Blackburn.

IV The Big Push

1 VIII Corps (Lt-Gen. Sir Aylmer Hunter Weston) had fought at Gallipoli and was reconstituted in France in March 1916; it consisted of 4th, 29th (both Regular) 31st and 48th Divisions. 48th Division was transferred to X Corps (Lt-Gen. Sir Thomas Morland) on 15 July.

2 The American-designed Lewis gun, a light machine-gun which could be operated by one man, fired the standard .303 rifle ammunition from a drum holding 47 rounds. Its rate of fire was in excess of 500 rpm. The weight of the weapon was 25 lb (cf. the Bren gun of 1939−45 which weighed 23 lb). Four Lewis guns were issued to each battalion in June 1915, a number increased to eight in September and to sixteen (one per platoon) in the early months of 1916. (For the Stokes mortar, see Chapter 3, Note 8.)

3 During 1915 each brigade had formed a grenade company (later called bombing company) of 120 trained men. A platoon of 20 men normally accompanied each battalion.

4 The Mills bomb had a cast-iron body which, being grooved, fragmented when it exploded. The German stick grenade had a body of sheet iron. It could be thrown further than the Mills but was less lethal.

5 Many of the misfortunes of the First World War can be attributed to the inadequacy of the communications between the forward troops and their commanders and, in particular, their supporting artillery. The wireless sets of the day were too cumbersome to be usable further forward than Brigade Headquarters (more usually Divisional HQ). Field telephone cables, except on the rare occasions when they could be deeply buried, were usually cut by shellfire or by the iron-shod wheels of artillery or transport vehicles. Flag or lamp signals exposed the operator to every kind of hazard since he necessarily had to remain stationary and exposed while signalling. Thus the solitary runner, using what cover was available and moving as fast as was possible, bore most of the burden of reporting back or of bringing forward new orders. In consequence, senior commanders could gain only the most inadequate impression of what was happening in the fighting and there was no way in which artillery fire could be brought to bear on unexpected centres of enemy resistance.

6 The bombardment preceding the Battle of the Somme had to be prolonged by two days because of bad weather—the original date of attack had been 29 June. Ammunition shortages meant that the scale was somewhat reduced on the two final days.

7 The original 31st Division (formed in November 1914) had been broken up to find drafts in the following April. It was later re-formed from 38th Division and consisted of battalions of the East and West Yorkshire Regiments, the York and Lancasters, a single battalion of Durham Light Infantry and, as Pioneers, a KOYLI unit.

8 In July 1916 the Royal Flying Corps had almost complete command of the air over the battlefield and low-flying aircraft were used in an attempt, not always successful, to establish the positions of the advancing troops. The problem was, of course, to distinguish one side from the other. Following a practice evolved at Gallipoli, all infantrymen in VIII Corps wore a triangle cut from a biscuit tin on the haversack (which was worn on the back) in the hope that it would glint in the sun. It was also hoped that the artillery would also see the flashing of the tin. The practice was unpopular with the infantry, who claimed that the flashes gave their position away to the enemy, and it was never used again.

9 Beaumont Hamel was a natural fortress which had been strongly fortified by the Germans, while the efforts of the artillery to cut the barbed wire were notably unsuccessful. The attack on 1 July by 4th, 29th and 31st Divisions cost 14,349 casualties and achieved nothing. The place was not finally taken until 13 November.

10 The reason why Ogle had no recollection of this day is almost certainly that 7th Royal Warwicks had a static role on 1 July. Their task was to secure the flank of VIII Corps by holding their trenches and there seems to be no evidence that they did more than that.

11 48th Division had been in reserve throughout the day but apart from 5th and 7th Royal Warwicks holding the left flank, the regiment's 6th and 8th Battalions had been attached to 4th Division and suffered heavily.

12 General Hunter Weston had used the phrase 'brilliant success' in his message to the troops which Ogle heard on 4 July. It did little to improve his credibility.

13 Since the British Army had no troop-carrying vehicles the LGOC sent 330 buses with volunteer drivers to the BEF in October 1914. The number was gradually increased to 773.

14 This was the famous Lochnager mine consisting of two charges comprising 60,000 lb laid sixty feet apart beside the La Boisselle–Contalmaison road, which destroyed the German strongpoint known as Schwaben Höhe. The crater, which is still visible, measured ninety yards across, was seventy feet deep and had a lip fifteen feet high above the surface of the ground. The occupation of the crater was one of the few British successes on this part of the front on 1 July.

15 The assault on La Boisselle was initially made by the Tyneside Scottish and Tyneside Irish of 34th Division. The village was finally taken by 19th (Western) Division on 5 July.

16 7th Battalion, Loyal North Lancashires had been among the troops of 19th Division which had completed the capture of the village.

17 Bomb-stops were barricades placed across trenches to obstruct the enemy troops, especially bombers, fighting their way along trenches.

18 In the war of 1914–18 platoons consisted of four sections each commanded by a lance-corporal. The two platoon corporals each commanded two sections.

19 This light railway ran round the northern and north-western outskirts of Pozières to the quarry north of the main road about 1,000 yards north east of La Boisselle.

20 Ovillers was captured on 16/17 July by 25th Division (which had 5th Royal Warwicks under command) and 144 Brigade of 48th Division.

21 Known to the British as Mash Valley in contrast to the re-entrant to the south of the main road which was named Sausage Valley.

22 Not unnaturally Ogle somewhat exaggerates the part played by 7th Royal Warwicks. 1st Australian Division (which had fought at Gallipoli) captured much of Pozières on the night of 22/23 July. 144 and 145 Brigades of 48th Division were on their left and made some small gains at heavy cost. The Australian attack was renewed on the night of 24/25 July and extended the earlier gains. By this time 143 Brigade had come into the line with 7th Royal Warwicks on their right next to but not in contact with the Australians. This is the attack here described, although the Official History wrongly ascribes it to 8th Royal Warwicks. The battalion, by means of Corporal Ogle, first got in touch with the Australians early on the morning of 26 July.

23 The idea of a major night attack was a very new concept, the first such offensive having taken place as recently of 14 July when XIII and XV undertook one on the villages of Bazentin-le-Grand and Le-Petit. The idea was received with forebodings by GHQ BEF and with incredulity from the French, but proved highly successful.

24 The ground throughout the Somme battlefield is chalky, making it all but impossible to conceal trenchworks.

25 It is hard to see how these Germans fled towards Pozières (then almost wholly in Australian hands) since the Royal Warwicks would have been between them and the village. It seems probable that they would have retreated towards either Courcelette or Mouquet Farm.

26 Mouquet Farm was eventually taken by 11th Division on 26 September.

27 *Malz* was a coffee substitute made of roasted malt.

28 In fact, 48th Division was relieved by 12th Division, 31st being further north, near the Aubers Ridge.

29 This was the Slade Wallace equipment originally issued in 1888. It was superseded by web equipment in the decade following the Boer War but served out to Kitchener's Army since there was nothing else to give them.

V 'Napoo Big Push'

1 Mesnil Domquer is ten miles east of Abbeville on the road to Doullens.

2 The statue fell on 16 April 1918 after being hit by a shell while Albert was in German hands.

3 The road comes from Albert, passing about a mile from Aveluy where it crosses the Aveluy–La Boisselle track.

4 Leipzig Redoubt was the culminating strongpoint at the south-west tip of a system known as Leipzig Salient which crowned the spur east of Authuille.

5 The redoubt itself had been seized on 1 July by 17th Battalion, Highland Light Infantry. It was subsequently held against repeated counter-attacks. On 21 August a concentric attack by 4th and 6th Gloucesters (48th Division) and 1st Wiltshires (25th Division) cleared the Leipzig Salient down to its base.

6 7th Warwicks went into brigade reserve. The division did not leave the line until 28 August.

7 Gunners were always anxious to shell a stretch of trenches while a relief was taking place since there would be twice as many infantry present and, almost certainly, insufficient shelters for all of them.

8 Bazentin-le-Petit and its wood were taken on 14 July.

9 15in howitzers were railway-mounted and it seems improbable that a battery of them—there were only seven of them on the Somme front—could have been in the shell-torn morass between Bazentin and Mametz Woods. The weapons described were almost certainly 9.2in howitzers, throwing a 290lb shell to a range of 10,000 yards.

10 Allery is a hamlet two miles west of Airanes, south of the Somme and eight miles south east of Abbeville.

11 After the mid-October fighting (Battle of the Transloy Ridges) the British line ran roughly east from north of Thiepval to a point north-east of Gueudencourt where it turned to a southerly direction.

12 The mention of Ypres refers to the 1917 fighting which culminated in the mud of Passchendaele.

13 The Butte de Warlencourt is an artificial chalk mound some sixty foot high (though now somewhat lower) which gave invaluable observation over the flattish countryside. In January 1871 it played a part in the small northern campaign of the Franco-Prussian war. In 1916 it was honeycombed with tunnels and resisted all attempts to capture it. It was relinquished by the Germans in their retreat to the Hindenburg Line in February 1917.

14 At the outbreak of war it had been assumed that French civilian labour would be available for such tasks as the unshipping of stores, constructing camps and depots and building roads. This assumption proved to be false (which did not prevent it being repeated in 1939), and labourers were brought over and formed into companies (each more than 500 strong) of the Army Service Corps. By the middle of 1916 there were thirty such companies (and three under naval command) in France. In addition there were eleven Royal Engineer Labour battalions formed of navvies and tradesmen commanded by civil engineers, and twelve infantry labour battalions made up of men of reserve units who were overage or otherwise unfit for active service. In addition there were eight non-combatant companies formed of conscientious objectors.

15 Much of the misery endured by the BEF was due to the fact that in 1914 the Germans had been able to establish themselves on the available high ground between Ypres and the Somme, thus gaining observation over the country held by the British. It also gave them much drier ground in which to dig their defences—it would have been physically impossible on most of the front for the British to provide themselves with deep dug-outs on the German model since they would have filled with water. The result was that from 1915 until the late summer of 1918 the British had to attack uphill against defences far better than they had been able to construct for themselves.

16 They were scarcely long trousers since, like knickerbockers, they reached only to just below the knee where they met the puttee.

17 In December 1916 and January 1917 the British extended their southern flank from north of the Somme near Maricourt to a point west of Roye, adding more than twenty miles to their front. This was to enable the French, who had suffered half a million casualties in 1916, to concentrate troops for an offensive which their new Commander-in-Chief, General Robert Nivelle, convinced both the French and British governments would win the war at a blow.

VI Commissioned

1 The Women's Army Auxiliary Corps was established in 1917.

2 Although 'Passchendaele' is frequently used to mean the whole of the Third Battle of Ypres (1917) there were, in the official nomenclature, two battles of Passchendaele, the first on 12 October, and the second lasting from 26 October to 10 November.

3 57th (2nd West Lancashire) Division, a second-line Territorial Division, had been heavily involved in an unsuccessful attack on 26 October. The division reached France in February 1917.

4 Paris Plage is a seaside resort at Le Touquet.

5 The cap badge of the King's Own was the Lion of England, a lion *passant regardant*. The Loyals wore the Rose of Lancaster surmounted by the Royal Crest.

6 It had been found that, to be proof against all but the heaviest shells, telephone cables had to be buried to a depth of six feet.

7 When infantry brigades were reduced from four to three battalions in February-March 1918, 141 battalions were left surplus to establishment. To achieve this reduction 115 battalions were broken up for reinforcements, thirty-eight were amalgamated in pairs to form nineteen units, and seven battalions were made into Pioneer units. Each division had one Pioneer battalion whose function was the digging of trenches, the building and repair of roads, and the construction of forward field depots. Such battalions were armed and on occasions fought as infantry.

8 The second great German offensive of 1918, codenamed *Georgette*, opened near Armentières on 9 April and, thanks largely to a breakthrough on the part of the front held by the Portuguese corps, achieved substantial gains. On 18 April they attempted to swing south across the La Bassée Canal. They were frustrated, but their initial advance exposed the right of 1st Bn King's Own, whose two companies on that flank were driven back leaving the enemy with a tenuous hold on the scattered hamlet of Riez-du-Vinage. That evening two subalterns and one hundred men of the King's Own counter-attacked and retook the hamlet.

VII The Turn of the Tide

1 The 'details' of the battalion would comprise not only the non-fighting personnel, clerks, storemen and drivers together with the quartermaster, but a number of officers and men from each company who were left out of battle so as to form a cadre on which the company or the whole battalion could be reconstructed should the unit suffer very heavy casualties.

2 See Chapter 6, Note 8.

3 This was the sector of the whole of 4th Division rather than that of 12 Brigade alone.

4 Mont Berenchon rises only about fifty feet above the level of the canal. On the north side of the waterway the ground is very flat and intersected with drainage ditches except in Pacaut Wood.

5 Riez-du-Vinage would have been about four miles behind the front line at sowing time.

6 A revealing insight into the kind of training thought to be required during the period of trench warfare. It is clear that the front-line troops had plenty of experience of fighting patrols but the idea of a reconnaissance patrol was strange to them. The 1914 (revised 1915) edition of the *Field Service Pocket Book*, the most widespread general training pamphlet available, gives advice on reconnaissance patrols but does not mention fighting patrols; actual experience had, however, for the time being, made this obsolete.

7 On the contemporary trench map (1/20,000) the name Hinges Road is given to the road

running northward from the canal at Pont d'Hinges, past the eastern side of Pacaut Wood and through Bohème and Pacaut village before going on towards Merville. The 1/100,000 map shows most of it as a first-class metalled road but only second-class on either side of Pacaut village.

8 During the First World War the method of giving grid or map references was totally different from that used later. The area was divided into squares with sides of six kilometres which were each designated by a capital letter (in this case 'Q'). These six-kilometre squares were subdivided into thirty-six squares of one kilometre, each of which was numbered in the centre ('28') and divided themselves into four squares which were lettered a, b, c, d, in a clockwise direction starting at the top left-hand corner. The lines marking the kilometre squares were, on large-scale maps, marked with graticules at fifty-metre distances so that each of the subsidiary squares had ten of them on two sides. From these a closer reference could be given, the easting being given before the northing.

VIII Breakthrough

1 There had been no fighting at Monchy-le-Preux in April 1918, as the start line for the German attack on Arras (Operation Mars) was to the east of the village. In April 1917 it had been the scene of bitter fighting when Monchy was taken by British troops and held until 22 March 1918 when it was relinquished voluntarily since there were not enough troops to ensure its security.

2 The map survives but the pencilled lines give no idea of what the 'mock battle' was intended to practise. It can be assumed that it was a rehearsal for the assault on the Drocourt–Quéant Line. Such rehearsals were becoming standard practice before major British attacks.

3 The Fuse 106, which exploded on impact with the ground, had been devised specifically to cut wire entanglements. It had first been used on a large scale in the successful Canadian assault on Vimy Ridge in April 1917. Earlier attempts to nullify wire defences with shrapnel had been markedly ineffective, notably that on 1 July 1916 on the Somme.

4 The support available to the leading two battalions of 12 Brigade comprised five brigades of field guns, three batteries of 6-inch and one of 8-inch howitzers with forty-eight machine-guns.

5 2nd Battalion, the Essex Regiment.

6 The Official History states that 'The tanks found it impossible to come from behind the 12th Brigade owing to marshy ground; they therefore went round by the north [left] and caught up with the infantry in the D–Q front system.' Ogle writes that they came up towards the right, and it seems likely that he is correct, not only because he was an eye-witness but because a study of the map suggests that the tanks were much more likely to meet marshy ground if they approached from the north.

7 A pardonable exaggeration. The D–Q Line continued beyond the break caused by the water obstacle around Étaing and Sailly for a further seventeen miles northward to a point where it joined the Lille defences near the village of Drocourt, south-east of Lens.

8 This seems to have been Prospect Farm, some two hundred yards south of the southernmost point of the Étaing Switch Line. On the trench map dated 20 August 1918 the farm is marked as a hospital. The Official History, however, describes it as a German strongpoint which held out until late on 2 September when it was taken by a company of the King's Own.

9 As soon as the King's Own and Essex had consolidated the D–Q Support Line, 11 Brigade passed through them in an attempt to pursue the enemy. They were unable to make much progress thanks largely to enfilade fire from Étaing.

10 The attack on Étaing was delivered at 5 a.m. on 3 September and found the enemy evacuating the place.

11 Sheet 51B of the 1/40,000 map covered the area east of Arras to beyond the Canal du Nord.

12 Galley Wood is a small narrow wood on the west bank of the Sensée, some 1,200 yards from Étaing.

13 At this time the division was forming a defensive flank facing north across the flooded Trinquis river while trying to devise a method of outflanking the northern part of the D–Q Line which was all but unapproachable from the west.

14 The dump served a German narrow-gauge single railway line which supplied the old front line facing Arras. From the bridge at Sailly it climbed the Boiry Spur and, at that village, turned northward to cross the Scarpe at Biache-St-Vaast. It rejoined the light railway system of the D–Q Line at Vintry-en-Artois.

15 The so-called 'Spanish' flu epidemic of 1918–19 apparently started in the Near East and spread worldwide. It reached Central Europe in August 1918 and killed 400,000 German civilians and 186,000 soldiers, thus doing much to hasten the deterioration of German morale. It reached Britain in October, killing some 150,000 before the following spring. Its ravages were at their worst in India, where 16 million are estimated to have died. By contrast the four years of war cost only 7¼ million deaths.

16 The title was The King's Own (Royal Lancaster Regiment) until 1921 when it was changed to The King's Own Royal Regiment (Lancaster).